glob

3 DAY LOAN
THE UNIVERSITY OF LIVERPOOL
SYDNEY JONES LIBRARY
RESTRICTED LOAN

ed by | 70

Please return or renew, on or before the latest date stamped below. A fine is payable on late returned items.

Items may be renewed by telephone 0151 794 2678.

For conditions of borrowing, see Library Regulations

70 | globalization

contents

70 | editorial globalization

The late 1990s saw an explosion of protest against global capitalism. Women and men around the world took to the streets to resist the ill effects of globalization, while many of the world's most powerful political/financial institutions declared the processes of globalization to be unstoppable. Some commentators have argued that these processes constitute a major historical transition, from industrial capitalism to informational capitalism, and that this transition demands a paradigm shift in social and cultural analysis. This paradigm shift includes a new emphasis on global networks and flows (of people, objects, wealth, information, dangers); on 'time—space compression', in which new technologies allow such flows to occur across vast physical distances in seconds; on the reconfiguring of relations between the local, the national and the global; and on the new politics of (dis)enfranchisement in which inequality and exploitation are deployed as global strategies — and meet global resistances.

It has not always been clear, however, what role feminisms are playing in the politics of globalization. Political and sociological macro-analyses of globalization seem to have been left to male intellectuals who pay, at best, limited attention to feminist social and political thought. Thousands of women around the world, however, participate in anti-globalization movements. This issue of *Feminist Review* seeks to consider both the macro- and the micro-processes of globalization as they affect women's lives, and to make a distinctively feminist contribution to current debates over globalization.

If the term globalization has become omnipresent, it is both contested and controversial. In this issue all of the contributors bring new perspectives to the understanding of the processes invoked under the rubric 'globalization' including problematizing the term itself. Central to these interventions has been a restating of feminist analyses of postcolonial identities and positionalities, the question of gendered time, the refigurings of both public and private domains and their intersections with immigration and global citizenship, and the gendered and racialized economics of global privatization. If feminist insights have been eclipsed by the mainstream debate on the character of globalization, the events of 11 September have even further marginalized the issue of the positions occupied by women in the new global order. The immediate political realities of globalization illustrate how powerfully stereotypes can be mobilized by Western powers and how important feminist analyses and imaginations are in the political assaults on those hegemonies.

(1–2) © 2002 Feminist Review. 0141-7789/02 $15 www.feminist-review.com

It is our hope that this issue will begin the process of locating feminist analyses at the centre of debates attempting to understand the new global order. The lives of women throughout the world are being refigured, often in the harshest ways, to sustain globalized capitalism: a deeper understanding of these processes is essential to all strategic resistances.

Avtar Brah, Helen Crowley, Lyn Thomas, Merl Storr

70 | the gendered time politics of globalization: of shadowlands and elusive justice

Barbara Adam

abstract

This paper seeks to bring a time perspective to the discourses of globalization and development. It first connects prominent recent gender-neutral discourses of globalization with highly gendered analyses of development, bringing together institutional—structural analyses with contextual and experiential data. It places alongside each other 'First World' perspectives and analyses of the changing conditions of people in the 'developing' world who are at the receiving end of globalized markets, and the international politics of aid. To date, neither of these fields of expertise has made explicit the underpinning time politics of globalization. Naturalized as *status quo* and global norm these temporal relations form the deep structure of globalization and its neo-colonialist agenda. The paper uses feminist epistemology to explicate the taken-for-granted time politics of globalization and time-based ontology to render visible the gender politics of globalization. The combined conceptual force makes connections where few exist at present, maps complex processes and traces naturalized relations. It offers not a new or better theory of... but an approach to globalization that makes transparent hitherto opaque relations of power and it identifies openings for change, resistance and alternative political practice.

keywords

globalization; gender; time politics and time creation; commodification; control and colonization

(3–29) © 2002 Feminist Review. 0141-7789/02 $15 www.feminist-review.com

introduction

Globalization is a predominantly male discourse. Whether the emphasis is on economic and political processes,[1] social relations,[2] the role of technology[3] or environmental impacts,[4] gender is rarely the focus of attention. Yet, it is clear that globalization impacts differently on men and women as workers, consumers, service providers, re/producers and loan/aid recipients. Viewing globalization almost exclusively through a male lens creates blind spots in the analysis and 'shadowlands' of practice in which women dwell and toil in unequal numbers. Only in the field of work and global labour markets has the gender blindness in the globalization literature been largely transcended. In this research the feminist focus has been extended from national to international and global labour markets.[5] Moreover, in the field of work time-blindness has been extensively reduced.[6] Given that the task for my contribution to this Special Issue is to theorise the connection between globalization, time, and gender, the challenge is not to summarise this existing work but rather to use the triple focus for gaining new insights and a novel perspective on established ways of seeing. In this paper I therefore want to bring together three discourses that thus far have developed along parallel lines and have pursued their respective research agendas with little reference to each other.[7]

Towards this end I first establish a connection between 'Globalization' and 'Development' so that we may see together what the current literature tends to keep apart, that is, Western grand theories of the First World's socio-economic and technological creation and analyses from those at the receiving end of its imperialism. Development studies are important for a gender perspective on globalization for a number of reasons. Development is the field of expertise that primarily documents the impact of contemporary globalization on the daily lives and experiences of Third World communities in general and women in particular. It presents analyses from the perspective of the afflicted, and the recipients of loans, aid and accompanying structural adjustment policies. It provides a view of globalization from below, as lived experience. In contrast to globalization, the development field has a strong feminist tradition that takes account of the gendered nature of Western capitalism and its imperialist incursions into the Third World.[8] It thus complements the dominant globalization literature, where gender tends to feature in a rather limited way at the level of structure and institutions.

To date, studies in *both* these fields of expertise have tended to be largely time blind; the globalization theories of Bauman (1998, 2000) and Castells (1996) being notable exceptions. Focus has been primarily on space and matter: territory and resources of a material and monetary kind are the dimensional substances of the respective analyses. What tends to be left unaddressed in the above are the time politics that underpin the neo-colonialist agenda. It is these, as I seek to show below, that make explicit what are naturalised power politics that penetrate the very fabric of everyday

1 Beck (2000a), Chossudovsky (1997), Hutten and Giddens (2000), Giddens (2000), Korten (1995), Madeley (2000), Martin and Schumann (1997), Sassen (1996) and Singh (2000).

2 Albrow (1996), Bauman (2000), Beck (1996, 1998, 2000a,b), Guyatt (2000), Held *et al.* (1999), Lechner and Boli (2000), Sassen (1996) and Starr (2000).

3 Castells (1996, 2000), Urry (2000) and Virilio (1991, 1995).

4 Beck (1992, 1999), Goldsmith *et al.* (1995) and Sachs (1993).

5 For example, Anderson (2000), Elson and Pearson (1981, 1997), Hochschild (2000), Leacock and Safa (1986), Nash and Fernández-Kelly (1983), and Tzannatos (1995).

6 See, for example, Adam (1993 and 1995, Chapter 4 for time and work and Adam 1998/2001 for time, work, globalization, and gender), Blyton *et al.* (1989), Davies (1990), Hareven (1982, 1991), Thompson (1967) and the numerous articles on time and work, as well as time, work and gender that have appeared since 1992 in *Time & Society*.

7 Examples of exceptions with respect to globalization and development are notably Shiva (1989, 1991a,b, 1992, 1993a,b, 1995, 2000a,b), Shiva and Moser (1995), who writes extensively within and across both fields, the economist Korten (1995) whose analyses accompany global economic policies from their origins to their destinations, as well as George (1984, 1989, 1992) and Chossudovsky (1997) who have charted the link between economic globalization and the systematic creation of poverty. Exceptions with respect to time and globalization are Adam (1993, 1995, 1998), Castells (1996), Cwerner (2000) and Virilio (1991, 1995).

8 Publications in the field are extensive. For the purposes of this paper, however, I have drawn mainly on work that makes the gender link explicit, for example, Boserup (1970), Elson (1991), Elson and Pearson (1981), Enloe (1989), Escobar (1995), Mies (1986), Mitter (1986), Rajput and Swarup (1994), Robertson (1992), Rogers (1981), Scott (1995), Sen (1994), Swantz (1985), Swarup and Rajput (1994), Tinker (1990, 1997), Visvanathan *et al.* (1997) and Young (1992).

life. Brought to the forefront of our attention, the time politics provide a coherent rationale for the associated gendering relations. I therefore want to show the relevance of time for understanding globalization in this expanded sense, consider whether and to what extent the spatial and male bias in the politics of globalization are related, examine what a shift in bias towards the temporal and female might look like and explore the desirability of such re-vision.

Cwerner (2000) developed the concept of chronopolitanism as an alternative to the excessively spatial conceptualisations of globalization and cosmopolitanism.

> [C]hronopolitanism... is developed as a theoretical as well as an ethical opening that reconfigures the search for a world political community in time and history. It is a move that has the explicit aim of extending social and political responsibilities to past, present and future generations, as well as to the diversity of histories and rhythms of life that co-exist in the global present.
>
> (Cwerner, 2000: 331)

In this paper I seek to begin to do justice to this noble aim. The threads of argument I want to pull together here tell a tentative story of blatant oppression and the subtle creation of invisible inter/dependencies, on the one hand, and of alternative visions and practices on the other. In the second half of the paper I attempt to show how the social relations of time are background, precondition and context for the econo-political drama that is played out on the global stage with such penetrating social and environmental effects.

The structure of the paper is as follows: in the first part I briefly set out some of the key features of the parallel discourses of globalization and development. Placing them next to each other provides an opportunity for social structure, institutions, and everyday gendered practice and experience to touch. In a short section on transnational institutions, the one focus where the globalization and development literatures overlap, we can see most clearly the gendered impact of globalization. This joining of literatures for the purpose of foregrounding the gendered and context-specific effects of globalization is followed by a feminist analysis on the time politics of globalization. Here, I sketch out the temporality of being before theorising the distinctiveness of the time politics of industrialisation, its globalization and associated creations of socio-environmental inequity and gendered relations of power. In this part of the analysis the politics of time becomes the connecting thread between the critical perspectives of the North and the view from the afflicted, between structure and gendered experience. In the final section of the paper I begin to open out the debates to consider some of the temporal issues involved in gender politics of global justice.

globalization and development: a question of gender

In the Collins Dictionary of Sociology 'globalization' is defined as

> A multifaceted process in which the world is becoming more and more connected and communication is becoming instantaneous. Aspects of this process include: (a) the transformation of the spatial arrangements and organisation of relations... (b) the increasing extensity, intensity, velocity and impact of global social relations and transactions... (c) the creation of new networks and nodes... (d) a dialect between the global and the local...
>
> (2000: 249)

This non-gendered definition puts globalization firmly into the 20th and 21st centuries and ties its material expression to information and communication technologies. Among social scientists concerned with understanding its development, however, there is much debate as to whether or not globalization is a new phenomenon and to what extent it is to be seen as discontinuous with the global expansion of religion, trade and colonialism of previous centuries. Thus, while there is agreement that globalization is a characteristic of contemporary existence, there is little agreement about its motive force and its proper analysis. This becomes apparent from even the most cursory glance at the dominant globalization literature. The most recent work, for example, focuses on the global processes of economic production (Martin and Schumann, 1997; Korten, 1995), electronic communication (Castells, 1996; Virilio, 1991, 1995), finance capital (Chossudovsky, 1997; Korten, 1995; Singh, 2000; Soros, 2000; Volcker, 2000), labour markets (Beck, 2000d; Martin and Schumann, 1997), mobility (Urry, 2000), risk production (Beck, 1992, 1999) and trade (Madeley, 2000), offering social analyses from technological, economic, political, institutional and environmental perspectives.[9] In most of these analyses globalization seems genderless and atemporal, a purely econo-technological and institutional process with a pervasive, if uneven, impact.

Work in the field of development, in contrast, is highly tuned to gender and in its own development seems to parallel the (Western) history of feminist thought. In her introduction to *The Women, Gender and Development Reader,* Visvanathan (1997: 17–19) charts the approaches as 'Women in Development', 'Women and Development' and 'Gender and Development'. 'Women in Development', she suggests, marks the first phase where equality was sought from within the Western modernist perspective. 'Women and Development' is characterized by a broadly Marxist approach that focuses on work as a source of status and autonomy and emphasises exploitation by transnational corporations (TNCs) through low wages and production policies. This perspective locates Third World women's inequality in the wider global capitalist economy. 'Gender and Development', the third approach, is rooted in feminist activism and draws most explicitly on the socialist feminist tradition. Here, the emphasis shifts from

9 A breadth of perspectives and foci is covered, albeit with different emphases, Castells' *The Rise of the Network Society*; Giddens' *Runaway World: How Globalization is Reshaping our Lives*; Lechner and Boli's edited *The Globalization Reader*; the edited collection *On the Edge* by Hutton and Giddens; and the co-authored *Global Transformations* by Held, McGrew, Goldblatt and Perraton.

women to gender relations in the labour market and the reproductive sphere, and stress is placed on empowerment for Third World women on the one hand and responsibility for male-dominated corporations and political institutions on the other. In order to identify some of the globalization literature's differences from and connections with these gendered perspectives on development, I will first need to outline some of the most prominent recent social theory approaches to the subject of globalization.

For Castells (1996), one of the most notable of current globalization theorists, the root of contemporary globalization is primarily to be sought in the technological achievements of the 20th century. To him the revolution in communication technology has brought about the 'network society', an information-based economy and globally connected socio-economic relations that extend to the furthest reaches of the globe. While this is undoubtedly the case at the level of the economy and political process, the argument applies less well for the social networks and daily practices of peoples across the world. From a development perspective it is the socio-economic relations based on artisan food production, small-scale rural economies and work in the home that retain primary importance at the level of everyday existence. Since this kind of work is mostly done by women in the Third World, a significant number of people fall outside the charmed circle of this electronic net of socio-economic relations (Madeley, 2000; Shiva, 2000a; Tinker, 1990; Visvanathan et al., 1997, esp. Parts I and II).

The associated networking logic, Castells suggests further, is one that allows for increasing complexity and flexibility in its structuring, which in turn facilitates creativity accompanied by a high degree of unpredictability. It has the capacity to reconfigure ever new permutations and facilitate the 'convergence of specific technologies into a highly integrated system, within which old, separate technological trajectories become literally indistinguishable' (Castells, 1996: 62). From the vantage point of Third World development we find that the 'network society' is in need of connecting to the base of everyday practice and lived experience. With its strong focus on information technology, Castells' perspective applies primarily to Western TNCs located in developing countries and operating in economic bubbles that touch people's lives only to the extent that they act as employers for a select few. Where women are employed by TNCs, they tend to make up the largest proportion of workers at the lowest end of the pay scale (Elson and Pearson, 1981, 1997; Leacock and Safa, 1986; Visvanathan et al., 1997). Female global assembly workers are, in Seager's words (1993: 135), the equivalent of the 'English mill girl'. On the one hand, their cheap labour makes women more employable than their male partners and thus raises their status and their families' prosperity. On the other hand, it also makes them the most expendable and thus vulnerable group of workers in the global job market. Given women's position in this employment market, the globally constituted technological net is clearly not theirs for appropriation. It does not permeate the lives of those who provide the cheap labour to the privileged globally networked minority (Baker, 1994; Boserup, 1970; Chossudovsky, 1997; Elson and Pearson, 1981, 1997; Escobar, 1995; Rajput and Swarup, 1994; Rowbotham and Mitter, 1994). According to Castells, the power of globally networked financial flows takes precedence over the flows of power (1996). However, when the torrent of networked financial flows rushes past you in a parallel universe, you may be thrown off balance by the accompanying waves, but for the rest of your life the established flows of power continue to reign supreme.

Networked capital, in Castells' analysis is irreducibly global while labour, as a rule, is local and is becoming ever more so in the context of increasingly strict immigration laws, which seem to accompany the deregulation of markets and the dismantling of national borders in aid of global trade. This means that the relations of production have become disconnected from labour. From a gendered development perspective this relation, however, is a highly complex one. There is no question that labour at the lowest end of the global pay scale is local, that financial resources are a precondition to global mobility, and that Western nations are increasingly tightening their immigration laws. And yet, there is one area of migration that is flourishing under these conditions: the global care chains of domestic labour (Anderson, 2000; Hochschild, 2000). Here the network is one not of technology and money, but of women locked in seamless webs of care where domestic workers from the Third World, looking after families in Europe and North America, have carers employed to tend to their own families, and these in turn have other women to care for their dependents and so on. These global care networks of (predominantly) women are tied to each other by a series of personal dependencies of paid and unpaid services. They are clearly not the networks Castells has in mind when he argues that the effects of the 'network society' are pervasive, that they permeate collective and individual existence, including the gendered world of work. Overly heavy reliance on the technological sources of the 'network society' gives Castells' globalization an air of inevitability and, despite the very detailed historical analysis of some of the processes, projects a sense of 'technological agency'. As a result, human agency, motives and interests tend to disappear from the analysis and experiences are moved outside his frame of reference, which, in turn, weakens Castells' grip on associated gendered relations of power.

Bauman's (1998) analysis of globalization, though much less gender sensitive than Castells', nevertheless can be mapped much more easily onto the gendered perspective of development analyses when he suggests that globalization divides as it unites and argues that what constitutes globalization for one means localisation for the other and what are gains for one group are losses for another. The same applies when Bauman argues that mobility, in both physical and virtual space, is not evenly distributed and, for the majority of the world's people, immobility is not a choice but an enforced condition. Thus, he sees new hierarchies developing around the freedom to move and new powers emerging with the freedom from territory. Like Castells (1996), Bauman (1998) understands the history of capitalism to be a war of independence from space, a war that, if won, will free TNCs from responsibility to a locality and its immobile citizens. He too understands this liberation from space to be predicated on the access to information technology and goes on to argue that for those excluded from this source of liberation new enclosures of an 'information commons' are being erected that divide the world into hierarchical categories of owners and non-owners of the means and forces of information. While the development literature would broadly confirm Bauman's analysis, it brings to it the particulars of contextual difference. Furthermore, contextual differences need not just take account of gender but, more importantly, the contextual differences between women living in particular cultures and socio-economic situations. As Mohanty (1993: 211) stresses, we must not lose sight of 'the complex and mobile relationships' between women's specific historical materiality and the discourses around the gendered nature of Third World development.

The defining features of Beck's theory of globalization are the globalization of risks (1992, 1999), reflexive modernization (1997, 1994 with Giddens and Lash) and cosmopolitanization (1996, 1998). In his early work on the 'risk society', Beck talks of the global distribution of 'bads' (as opposed to goods) that know no boundaries and permeate the globe irrespective of their place of origin. However, he is very clear in his insistence that the globalization of risk does not mean a global equality of risk. On the contrary, low-level producers of risk (the world's poor) tend to be the recipients of the highest level of associated disasters, ecological crises and pollution. Beck acknowledges that the prominence of globalized risk is inextricably tied to

> ... a *systematic violation of basic rights,* a crisis of basic rights whose long-term effect in weakening society can scarcely be underestimated. For dangers are being produced by industry, externalised by economics, individualised by the legal system, legitimized by the natural sciences and made to appear harmless by politics.
>
> (Beck, 1999: 39)

The development literature leaves us in no doubt that these institutional issues have a strong gender component. Moreover, if this gender dimension is not addressed, or left implicit, the analysis automatically assumes male as standard and norm. Responses to the dangers produced and legitimized by Western institutions will take a different form when they are cognisant of women's legal and institutional needs and rights.

Similar to Bauman's argument, Beck (1999, 2000c) understands power relations as closely tied to 'relations of definition', to the legitimated capacity to define truth and falsity, safety and danger, to what counts as valid knowledge and proof, what constitutes socially valued activity and what does not. Analogous to Marx's relations of production, Beck's relations of definition permeate the social fabric.

> Risk society's relations of definition include the specific rules, institutions and capacities that structure the identification and assessment of risk in a specific cultural context. They are the legal, epistemological and cultural power-matrix in which risk politics is conducted.
>
> (Beck, 2000c: 224)

And thus, we might continue, to erase the gender/power dimension from debates around the globalization of risk renders it invisible, non-existent and with it, vulnerable to exploitation.

The modernity of the 'risk society', Beck argues further, has lost its clearly defined edges and boundaries and is marked by uncertainty and reflexivity. Reflexivity here is a structural term that operates at the level of institutional and global processes. It refers to the boomerang effect of the modernist industrial logic that produces paradoxes and unintended consequences, out-of-control effects and disorder from control and the relentless imposition of order, 'a kind of collective return of the oppressed' (Beck, 1999: 47). Reflexivity creates an opening for power relations to be newly negotiated, for the relations of definition to be repositioned, and for established institutional power to be usurped. In the gendered development literature this opening for a renegotiation of established power relations is detailed in work on women's movements that have utilised global networking to their advantage (Visvanathan et al., 1997, esp. Part V). Responding to the globally distributed 'bads', to what Seager (1993: 73) calls 'designer tragedies', women have organised to implement their own solutions. Operating in the paradox spaces that are part and parcel of the industrial logic of risk, women the world over are implementing moral codes and practices that expose the 'pious globalism' (Seager, 1993: 147) as a neo-colonialism from which the rich countries reap the bulk of the benefits and impose their own agendas.[10]

gender politics of the triad of intergovernmental institutions

The neo-colonialist exploitation is nowhere more visible than in the history of the global institutions associated with the 1944 Bretton Woods Agreement, namely, the World Bank, the International Monetary Fund (IMF) and the World Trade Organisation (WTO).[11] The three intergovernmental institutions were created initially to establish a new stable framework for a post-war global economy. This

[10] See the extensive work of Shiva and, for example, Escobar (1995), Mitter (1986), Rajput and Swarup (1994), Rowbotham and Mitter (1994), Scott (1995), Tinker (1990), Visvanathan et al. (1997) and Young (1992).

[11] The WTO replaced the General Agreement on Tariffs and Trade (GATT).

was to involve them in the control and regulation of capital funds, maintenance of currency stability and the development of world trade. Since their inception, however, the three institutions have changed their original mandate beyond recognition (Chossudovsky, 1997; Korten, 1995; Martin and Schumann, 1997; Ransom, 2001). It is important to understand the history of these institutions since they are central to global post-war 'development' and the gendered impact on its recipients.

The World Bank was set up to revive war-damaged European economies by making loans at below-normal bank rates and to help them adjust their economies to globalization. Its mandate was later extended to developing countries. The IMF was created to maintain currency stability. This was achieved by members pegging their exchange rate to the gold standard and worked reasonably well until 1971 when the US allowed the dollar to float and currency *instability* became a major source of financial speculation and profit creation. Today, IMF loans to developing Third World and Eastern European countries are attached to stringent economic measures that effectively allow this institution to run the economy of sovereign states. Seven rounds of tariffs were negotiated under the General Agreement on Tariffs and Trade (GATT). When GATT was replaced by the WTO the mandate was expanded into new directions to cover agreements on trade in services (GATS), trade-related investment measures (TRIMS) and trade-related intellectual property rights (TRIPS), each with their own globally binding rules, each a variation on colonization by post-colonial means.

Irrespective of whether authors of this institutional globalization are concentrating on the globalization poverty (Chossudovsky, 1997), charting the corporate take-over of the world (Korten, 1995) or detailing the global socio-economic race to the bottom (Martin and Schumann, 1997), they are equally damning in their analyses of the impact of these institutions on nations that are forced to call on the triad's services: loans and aid are given with punitive strings attached. And once enmeshed, recipients of the coercive carrot-and-stick cycles find it impossible to extricate themselves from the unrelenting downward spiral of debt.[12] Without exception, these writers on globalization have given some attention to the gendered impact of globalization. Their analyses, however, tend to be conducted primarily at the level of institutions and organizations and are thus de-contextualized with respect to the effects of the measures implemented by the triad of intergovernmental institutions. Given their general applicability, they necessarily leave the depth of gendered experiences largely untouched.

When we turn to the development literature on gendered relations, in contrast, we find that the de-contextualized, de-personalized workings of intergovernmental institutions become contextualized as real components of people's lives and experiences (Enloe, 1989; Escobar, 1995; Mitter, 1986; Rajput and Swarup, 1994; Scott, 1995; Sen, 1994; Shiva, 1989, 1992; Swantz, 1985; Tinker, 1990, 1997;

12 For details on the debt cycle see specifically the work by George (1984, 1989, 1992) who has been tireless in her exposure of the processes by which the richest countries are getting richer on the backs of the world's poorest nations which invariably implicate the triad of World Bank, IMF and WTO.

Visvanathan *et al.*, 1997; Young, 1992). Analyses are predominantly from Third World perspectives, more people and policy oriented, and less focused on information and communication technologies. Their emphasis is on power politics and the capacity of a small minority to impose their will and interests on the majority. The majority of the studies offer insider accounts of *living with the effects* of having been 'helped' by the Bretton Woods institutions, of what it means to be at the receiving end of 'structural adjustment', the 'medicine' that comes as a compulsory part of the loan, and aid packages associated with 'development'. Their subjects have accusing faces and voices. They feel the pain, are helpless with rage and indignation, struggle for survival and dignity in the face of insurmountable economic oppression, corporate colonialism and socio-political injustice.

Concerned with the politics of aid and economic colonialism, this literature details the creation, maintenance and deepening of inequality associated with 'development'. It shows how structural adjustment tends to be tied to a number of conditions. Authors writing about these conditions are too numerous to list here. The following, therefore, is a summary of the key points extracted from a wide range of articles. First, aid and loans are tied to trade conditions: mono-cultural export of cash crops on the one hand and import of goods from industrial donor countries on the other. Second, it involves abolishing import quotas and reducing import tariffs to a minimum. A third requirement is tied to the value of the recipient country's currency, which needs to be lowered so that exports become more attractive to the lender country, and has the unpleasant side-effect of making Western imports more expensive. Tight requirements about reduction of the recipient country's internal spending on welfare services and subsidies for food and agricultural production are the fourth set of conditions associated with 'structural adjustment'. The mechanisation of food production and the adoption of western unsustainable, high input and yield, mechanized agriculture makes up the rear of this Draconian package of 'structural adjustment' measures. Promoted by industrialised nations as the 'green revolution', it creates markets for seed and fertilizer companies. The effect of such conditionality is, as Seager points out, that

> economists, financiers, and government officials from leading industrial democracies are now key players in the reconstruction of the Commonwealth of Independent States' political and economic systems.
>
> (Seager, 1993: 132)

It gives lenders the right to run the economies and social policies of sovereign states that are in receipt of their loans and aid packages and to stack the decks in their own favour.

Development scholars agree that irrespective of where it is happening, women are disproportionately affected by this economic colonialism. Women tend to be

13 Swarup and Rajput (1994: 104) provide the following figures: women own less than 1% of the world's resources and less than 10% per cent of the world's income. The situation is aggravated further by the growing privatisation of traditional commons such as grazing pastures and forests to which women had rights of access and use.

among the poorest members of countries in receipt of aid and loans.[13] The reduction in welfare provisions and food subsidies that accompanies the 'rescue packages', therefore, hits women hardest given that they tend to be responsible for the family's health, safety, security and well-being. Since much of Third World subsistence agriculture is carried out by women, moreover, any cheap food imports and the introduction of mechanised agro-chemical agriculture deprive them of their primary bases of existence. On the one hand, the policy of export–import-oriented industries displaces women artisans and renders their 'un'productive labour in the household and food production invisible in a system that calculates productivity exclusively on the basis of profit (Baker, 1994; Norberg-Hodge, 1995; Seager, 1993). On the other hand, the greater participation of women in cash crop production increases their earning capacity while devaluing the traditional spheres of women's work and expertise, thus hastening their further marginalization (Baker, 1994).

With few exceptions (Adam, 1993, 1995, 1998; Bauman, 1998, 2000; Castells, 1996; Urry, 2000), the analyses discussed so far tend to be oriented towards space and matter and conducted on a basis where time features primarily as the historical calendar and clock time frame within which changes take place. Yet, the politics and relations of time are inseparable from their multi-layered socio-economic impacts. They are the missing link between the two discourses that allows us to connect institutional processes to recipients' experiences, underlying assumptions to their material expressions, and hidden agendas to gendering relations. In order for these complex relations to become apparent it is important to outline the historical distinctiveness of the time politics of industrialization and render visible the associated systematic construction of inequality between groups of people and cultures. This involves us in a conceptual journey very different from the one travelled by the globalization and development literatures. The apparent disjuncture between the discourses begins to dissolve, however, as the temporal perspective is built up, component by component, into a coherent whole.

The intention is to utilise feminist epistemology to explicate the taken-for-granted time politics of globalization and to use time-based ontology to render visible the hidden gender politics of globalization. The combined conceptual force enables us to focus on the disattended, make connections where few exist at present, map complex processes and trace naturalized relations. The attempt to triangulate globalization, time and gender is thus extremely experimental, not only because it has not been done before but also because the systematic institutional structuration of inequality involved is not in any straightforward or exclusive way one of gender. It is a search for a conceptual framework that connects experience with institutional analysis, context with pattern, process with event, present with past and future, and power with wealth, knowledge, opportunity and political praxis.

With its impeccable track record of uncovering hidden oppression and masked gender biases, feminist theory is ideally placed to investigate globalization processes and associated structuring relations of power. Showing what is silenced and rendered invisible is the established strength of feminist theory just as it is a central aspect of theorizing temporal relations. It is a transferable conceptual skill that is eminently suitable to debates around globalization. Applied to globalization, such decoding, however, will not provide 'a better theory of'. Instead, it offers an *approach* to globalization that renders the invisible visible, makes implicit assumptions and conceptual tools explicit, and opaque relations of power transparent. It shows the role of time in the legitimation of corporate imperialism, economic colonialism and the global creation of local inequalities and glocal[14] socio-environmental destruction.

14 'Glocal' is a concept developed by Robertson (1992) to denote the inseparable interdependence of global and local processes.

globalization from a temporal perspective

Birth, death and transcendence—the shared temporal context

To understand the role of time for globalization requires that we first know some of the backcloth against which the time economy of contemporary globalization has developed. Since the beginning of life and human existence, time, space and matter formed an inseparable unity. Since their pre-history, societies have embodied the temporal relations of their past and present members and institutions. This is so because all cultures, ancient and modern, have established collective ways of relating to the past and future, of synchronising their activities, of coming to terms with finitude. *How* we extend ourselves into the past and future, *how* we pursue immortality and *how* we temporally manage, organise and regulate our social affairs, however, has been culturally, historically and contextually distinct. Each historical epoch with its new forms of socio-economic expression is simultaneously restructuring its social relations of time. The industrial mode of life and the attendant globalization are no exception.[15]

Death is an inescapable condition of human life and as such it forms a central if implicate feature of our existence. In their encounter with death humans have not only differentiated themselves from fellow species but have established their uniqueness as cultures. Burial chambers and megaliths, pyramids and temples, catacombs and cathedrals are physical records of predecessors' relations to finitude; burial of the dead, religion and the construction of artefacts embodied practices of that temporal relation. Without knowing the time and place of death, as suggested by Heidegger (1927/1980), our lives are lived with reference to it. *Dasein's* (contextualised being/existence) total penetration by death is our ontological condition, our basis of existence. With it comes the encoded fear of non-existence, of nothingness after the end, and the desire for mastery and control over the inevitable. Feminist theorists have made important contributions

15 There are numerous fascinating books on the subject of time and culture. Reference to a small selection of these is therefore inevitably arbitrary. The following, nevertheless, are reasonably representative examples: Bourdieu (1979), Dunne (1973), Eliade (1954/1989), Kern (1983) and LeGoff (1980).

16 See Brodribb (1992) for an extended discussion on this particular feminist corrective.

to this body of knowledge and offered pertinent correctives to Heidegger's masculine perspectives on the subject matter. Irigaray (1983, 1989) and O'Brien (1989), in particular, have balanced the death-oriented theory with a celebration of birth.[16] To reintegrate birth as central to human temporality is to re-appropriate an ancient relationship to continuity (Forman, 1989). It is to foreground life and reproduction in a context where the orientation towards death predominates and the quest for permanence, certainty and control defines the temporal relations (Adam, 1990, 1995, 1998).

The steady distancing from the times of the cosmos and mortal life on earth brought enormous gains in control and mastery over the earthly conditions and, for societies that have followed this path, a whole raft of consequences for their relationship with nature and the environment. It has lessened some of the human dependence on, but not overcome our rootedness, in the rhythmicity of the cosmos, the seasons and the times of the body. Irrespective of calendars, clocks and standardised world time, our lives continue to be bounded by birth and death, growth and decay, night and day. This embodied time is lived and experienced alongside, in spite of, in conflict with, and filtered through the culturally constituted social relations of time. As the balance shifts between the pre-given and socially created rhythms, so does our relationship with finitude and transcendence, life and reproduction.

17 It has received particular attention in the field of gender, work and employment. For example, *Time & Society*, now in its 10th year, rarely published an issue without the gender dimension of time and work.

As part of the deep structure of taken-for-granted assumptions, time shapes not only everyday understanding but also the theories that social scientists develop to explain their world. Until the early 1990s, the explication of social time was considered to be a fringe activity of social science and feminist theory. Today, this is no longer so. Interest in social time is burgeoning and work on its gendered dimension gathering pace.[17] In the following sections of the paper I want to locate the gendering of globalization in the time politics of the industrial way of life and explore some feminist time-literate re-vision. I structure my discussion on the temporality of globalization with reference to four C's: the creation of time to human design, the commodification of time, the control of time, and the colonization with and of time.

C1 — the creation of time to human design

Our first task is to consider the change from social life predominantly embedded in the earth's rhythmicity to social organization chiefly anchored in clock time, the time created to human design. We can think of this shift in primary temporal location as a move from time in things and processes to a decontextualized time where one hour is the same irrespective of whether it is day or night, summer or winter in New Delhi, New York, Nairobi or Nicosia. This means focusing on abstraction, decontextualization and rationalization as processes that underpin globalization.

Clock time has a number of features that are fundamentally different from the temporal processes of nature: where nature's rhythmic cycles are marked by variance, the hourly cycle of the clock is invariable and precise. Where each rhythmic return in and of nature is simultaneously a context-dependent renewal, the return of the same hour of clock time is independent of context and content. Where animals and plants have time encoded in their being/becoming, clock time is external to and abstracted from the processes it measures.

Clock time had been gradually adopted worldwide, but not until the end of the 19th century was it imposed across the globe as standard time, when it brought to an end the myriad of local times and dates used by the peoples across the world (Bartky, 2000; Kern, 1983; Luhmann, 1982). Standard time, time zones and world time became essential material preconditions for the global network of trade, finance, transport and communication. Today, they underpin the daily operations, cooperations and transactions of local businesses, global institutions and TNCs. Difficulties and conflicts arise when the invariable measure is imposed *as norm* on highly context-dependent, rhythmic and variable social and environmental situations and processes. This applies regardless of whether the industrial norm is foisted upon cultures that do not organise their social activities to the clock, on work practices dominated by temporal variability, or on livestock and plants tended under an industrial agricultural regime. Therefore, it is not just information technology that changes information, as Castells (1996) suggests. Long before this, the adoption of clock technology as the primary temporal marker and organising frame had altered (and still does alter) socio-economic and socio-environmental temporal relations and practices.

Work practices that are particularly difficult to subsume under the clock-time regime are all those loosely classified as care work and caring activities. Feeding an infant or a person with dementia, for example, takes the time it takes in the particular situation at the time. Equally, the time involved in growing and caring for livestock and crops varies greatly with context. Across the world, work that is not easily fitted into the clock-time structuring is considered 'women's work', irrespective of whether or not it is carried out by women. Unless, as in industrial farming, the work is done with machines, in which case it becomes 'men's work'. Notably, one of the central tasks associated with this shift to mechanization is the transcendence of the limits imposed by the seasons and the context-dependent times of growth and reproduction.[18]

18 Creative work too resists incorporation. Here, however, the ascription does not separate so neatly along gender lines.

The global structuring with the aid of a time created to human design has to be differentiated from the globalization of industrial time and its associated economic values as unquestioned norm. In the latter case it is the time values and the social relations of industrial time that are being *imposed* as well as *adopted* on a worldwide basis. To be 'modern' and 'progressive' means to embrace the industrial approach to time. Therefore, it was not only ruthlessly prescribed as the norm for colonial subjects but also self-imposed by a number of societies who saw it as a precondition to becoming fully fledged industrial nations. Towards the latter part of the 19th century, for example, Japan (Nishimoto, 1997) and Russia (Castells, 1996) proceeded to 'Westernize' their social relations of time. The political leaders of these societies realised that there is a heavy economic and political price to be paid for any deviance from the industrial temporal norm. For carers in the home and subsistence farmers the world over, the shift to clock time is not an option. Such resistance to incorporation into the logic of decontextualized time means that their work, and similarly placed activities that badly fit the machine-based clock-time regime, are consistently accorded low value on the global labour market.

The fact that clock time, world time, standard time and time zones have become naturalized as the norm vastly increases the difficulty of recognising the role this created time plays in everyday life. Other temporal principles fade into the background. They become invisible. The clock time norm acts as a filter through which everything is sieved and as a lens through which social relations and structures are refracted. It affects how industrial societies define and regulate the temporal structures of socio-economic life. It influences how industrialising countries are regulated, managed and controlled by those who oversee their 'development'. Thus, for example, the very essence of the globally constituted free trade agreement, policed by the WTO since 1995, is its dissociation from time and space. In tune with the globalization of clock time, all that is local, context-dependent, and seasonal becomes an obstacle to be overcome while particular histories and personal biographies are rendered irrelevant. Furthermore, absolute decontextualization is the ideal condition for money to flow freely and for capital and operations to be moved unencumbered where the circumstances for wealth generation are optimal. In such decontextualized conditions, real people living in particular places with specific needs are sidelined out of the frame of reference: they have no place in a decontextualized world.

C2 — the commodification of time

Time is money. This unquestioned assumption permeates the industrial way of life, underpins global economic activity and drives the development agenda. It has its root in 3000 years of interest and credit, going back to pre-Christian Babylonian times (LeGoff, 1980; Wendorff, 1980, 1991). For this belief to become internalized by Christian Western societies, two preconditions had to be fulfilled: the sin of usury had to be transformed into a positive economic principle and production had to shift from use value to abstract exchange value. For non-Western cultures other additional major obstacles in belief systems and traditions of conduct had/have to be overcome.

In his book *Time, Work and Culture in the Middle Ages* (1980), Le Goff writes on the problem of usury and time. He quotes a text from the 12th century that lays out very clearly the Christian position on trading with time.

> 'The usurer acts in contravention to universal law, because he sells time, which is the common possession of all creatures. . .
>
> Since therefore the usurer sells what necessarily belongs to all creatures, he injures all creatures in general, even stones. Thus, even if men remain silent in the face of usurers, the stones would cry out if they could, and this is why the church prosecutes usury.
>
> (G. d'Auxerre, 1160–1229, *Summa aurea*, III, 21; LeGoff, 1980: 289–290, footnote 2)

From this Christian perspective, the trade in time is theft because it is trade in something that cannot belong to individuals. As long as the notion of earnings on time was rejected outright, capitalism and the money economy could not develop (LeGoff, 1980). The commodification of time therefore relates to a shift from understanding the time–money relation as sin to viewing it as virtuous, rational action in the service of God and later in the service of economic growth and profit. Clock time, the created time to human design, was a precondition to this change in value and practice.

Clock time also underpins the shift in emphasis from use value to the utilization of time as abstract exchange value, from barter to the money economy. When we want to exchange something for money, a third value has to be introduced to mediate between the two. Unlike the use value, which is context- and situation-specific, this mediating exchange value has to be context-independent. The common, decontextualized value by which products, tasks and services can be evaluated and exchanged is time. Not the variable time of seasons, ageing, growth and decay, of fear and pain, joy and play, but the invariable, abstract time of clock where one hour is the same irrespective of context and emotion allowed work to be translated into money. Only in this decontextualized form, as Marx (1857/1973) showed, could time become commodified on the one hand and an integral component of the globalized market economy on the other. Any social organization that does not work on the basis of commodified time, therefore, operates outside the logic of globalized capitalism.

When time is money then time compression and rationalization schemes become economic imperatives. Taylorism, Fordism, flexibilization and just-in-time production have been logical developments emanating from this foundational premise. 'Time is money' further means that capital has a built-in clock that is constantly ticking away. This inevitably leads to careful calculations with respect to the length of time that equipment is used, labour is paid for, materials spend in warehouses before they are used in the production process and goods are stored and in transit and/or lie on shelves before they are sold. From such economic time calculations it is a short step for countries to increase their commodified temporal relations, for companies to reduce time costs by cutting jobs and/or moving production to the locations that promise the cheapest labour and for workers to transfer to locations that pay the best wages. The latter involves relocation from rural homes to urban centres. For women in service it means getting involved in global care chains, as outlined above (Anderson, 2000; Hochschild, 2000). Finally, when time is money any use of free time enhances profit. Dependence by industrial societies on the free time of social re/production, provided predominantly by women, and the free time extracted from nature for industrial agriculture are thus key components of socio-economic profit generation.

Any time that does not fit the industrial economic logic, which covers by far the largest proportion of humanity, becomes invisible. It either falls outside the economic framework of evaluation altogether, or it is filtered through and evaluated from that way of thinking about and evaluating the world, which is precisely the case globally with women's social re/productive activity in the family. Equally, this applies to Third World subsistence farmers, predominantly women, whose food production, services and reproductive activities in the household do not feature in their country's economic accounting. Their work is rendered invisible at the level of inter/national economics because their time is not exchanged for money. It is moved into the 'shadowlands' of the globalized economy, from where it is a few short steps only to being marginalized, devalued and in need of 'development'. In the light of this devaluation of their social contribution, it is not surprising that many women have chosen to follow the path of paid employment in which time *is* accorded a monetary value. Such a shift towards women's participation in the global labour market is recorded worldwide, even if this involves predominantly part-time work or women registering as unemployed rather than as housewives.[19] This has the effect, however, of further devaluing the non-remunerated work of social re/production.

C3 — control of time

With its commodification, industrial time has become a scarce resource and its control a central task for the global economy. At company level, this involves being faster than competitors on the one hand and shortening the time per operation and speeding up the turnover of resources on the other. Times when nothing happens — breaks and pauses, waiting and rest periods — are considered unproductive, wasteful, lost opportunities that need to be eliminated or at least minimised. Compression and intensification of processes are key aims in the quest for time control as a way to achieve increased efficiency and profit. The means by which this intensification is to be achieved are manifold and can involve the use of machinery on the one hand and the rationalization, mechanization and reorganization (sequence and order) of labour and production processes on the other. All these in turn are underpinned by a quantitative approach to time. One of the rationales for the industrial/ising

19 For Europe see especially, 'Best European Studies on Time' (European Foundation, 2001) and 'Gender Use of Time. Three European Studies' (European Commission 2000).

societies' approach to time compression is thus to be sought in the quantification, decontextualization, rationalization, and commodification of time and in the calculation of time in relation to money, efficiency, competition and profit. The control of time, however, is not exhausted by time compression. It includes in addition the slowing down and the re-arrangement of processes. Castells (1996) argues that time is not just compressed but processed and, clearly, both compression and processing are advances in the control of time.

Electronically based instantaneity is a logical extension of the modernist time project of creation, commodification, control and colonization. It constitutes the holy grail in the quest for increasing speed: compression down to point zero. It brings with it powers that had previously been the preserve of god(s): the supernatural power of exterrestrials to be everywhere at once and nowhere in particular (Virilio, 1991, 1995). The physical constraints of bodies in space are transcended by 20th-century developments in transmission. Movement of information has been dematerialized. This is accompanied by paradoxes that have been widely commented on (Bauman, 1998; Castells, 1996; Poster, 1990; Rifkin, 1987; Virilio, 1991, 1995): a precondition to mobility in cyberspace is the immobility of embodied beings. Structural relations and processes, which arise from the control of time, moreover, tend to be beyond the control of those involved since the combination of instantaneity of communication with simultaneity of networked relations no longer functions according to the principles of clock time and mechanical interaction. The increase in mastery, therefore, is accompanied by a decrease in control. Unintended consequences of networked instantaneity force operation in a no man's land beyond design and action capacity with far-reaching consequences for recipients across the globe, be they participants, protestors or innocent bystanders.

For different reasons, the lived and experienced times of nature, body and mind similarly elude such mastery. Rhythmic and wildly variable, lived and experienced, regenerated and given rather than exchanged and sold, these times are not suitable for harnessing to the money economy, and resist control and rationalization. And yet, the logic of industrial time is applied globally irrespective of the conflicts and environmental problems it causes (Adam, 1998). However, while some logics and aspects clearly take priority over others, none are completely negated in their displacement. All are mutually implicating at the same time as their meanings are refracted and their importance altered.

Looked at globally, the vast majority of peoples across the world live and give time beyond the grasp of the time control of global institutions and corporations. Defined as 'backward' and *un*productive the socio-economic relations of gifted time operate in a realm beyond the time economy of global capitalism. This is both a curse and an opportunity. On the one hand, it renders these gendered temporal relations invisible and obliterates their production from the official statistics, while on the other hand it opens up a space for action in which genuine alternatives are developed to the globally imposed economic norm. Spearheaded by women, these opportunities are seized by groups and movements of a social ecological and economic kind whose agenda are built around life-enhancing values, respect and socio-economic responsibility (Mitter, 1986; Rajput and Swarup, 1994; Sachs, 1993; Scott, 1995; Seager, 1993; Starr, 2000; Visvanathan *et al.*, 1997, and the extensive work of Shiva). However, despite these encouraging developments, there is no room for romanticism or complacency. As more and more women partake in the time economy of globalization, the net of industrial time with its un/intended consequences is ever widening, the reach expanding, further devaluing women and traditional cultures' base of expertise and power. We are dealing here with colonialism by temporal means.

C4 — colonization with and of time: past, present and future

There are two sides to the colonization of time: the global imposition of a particular kind of time on the one hand and the incursion into the time of distant others, successors and predecessors on the other. In the first case, Western clock time and commodified time have been exported across the globe and imposed as the unquestioned and unquestionable standard. This is colonization *with* time, which has already been discussed above. In the second, the global present as well as the past and future are brought under human control. This is colonization *of* time, of which I briefly want to outline some examples.

Electronic communication and financial flows at the speed of light have freed corporations from space and afforded them a global power that is rooted in their deterritorialization. Unencumbered by locality and territorial constraints, TNCs are disconnected from the lives of their immobile employees and the social needs of their host countries. Now/here and no/where become interchangeable. Money is both the lifeline and the exclusive measure of corporate value. With locality and place becoming increasingly irrelevant, the price of labour, tax breaks and other relocation enticements are becoming the prime determinants of physical location. The duty to contribute to daily life and 'the nation's' prosperity has evaporated under the new conditions of 'radical unconditionality' and 'unanchored power' where power has been disconnected from obligation (Bauman, 1998: 9). As living beings rather than abstract entities, the space-bound 'locals', in contrast, build up loyalties and commitment, nurture relationships and interests, develop specialist knowledge - all slow and long-term processes. When these long-term interdependencies are suddenly dissolved, social structures evaporate, leaving members of communities without the support and stability essential to communal life, or, as Bauman puts it, leaving to the locally bound 'the task of wound-licking, damage repair and waste-disposal' (Bauman, 1998: 8). If we add to this the role of the Bretton Woods institutions, which also operate as exterrestrials and, like the TNCs, carry 'no liability for their errors' (Korten, 1995: 171), we get a sense of the systematically expanding asymmetry of power.

From its very inception the economy has been focused on the future. The future is understood with reference to the threat or benefit it holds for the present. The economy inescapably operates in the sphere between present and future with a view to use the future to secure the present. To achieve that task, it borrows from the future to finance the present or it hedges against potential future disasters through saving and insurance. Thus, Giddens suggested in his Reith Lectures, that 'modern capitalism embeds itself into the future by calculating future profit and loss, and thereby risk, as a continuous process' (Giddens, 1999: 2, 2000: 24). The future is drawn into the activities of the present. Nowotny (1989/1994) conceptualizes those temporal incursions as 'extended present', as a future that is organised, regulated, tamed, safeguarded and foreclosed now. Thus, all non-sustainable use of resources such as fossil fuels, for example, entails taking from the future for use and depletion in the present. Equally, through their 'development' strategies, the Bretton Woods institutions draw heavily on successors' presents and futures.

> Rather than increasing their self-reliance, the world's low income countries, under the guidance of the World Bank and the IMF, continue to mortgage more of their futures to the international system each year.
>
> (Korten, 1995: 165)

Today, furthermore, most money is made on the speculative market that trades not with goods but with time (Boden, 2000). This involves bets on future prices of the stock market, currency prices, interest rates, even on the entire stock market indices. The trade in time, which is estimated at 18 trillion dollars for 1999, equals the entire stock of productive fixed capital of the world. In all these cases, a radical present orientation makes parasitic use of the future and forecloses successors' presents without their consent. Finally, with the genetic modification of food, science has achieved a temporal equivalent of spatial globalization. It has extended the scientific reach to the beginning and end of time. That is, to modify organisms with genetic material from other species, scientists draw on genetic bases that are shared by all life forms since the beginning of the evolution of life. However, the effects of those modified organisms in the environment, in contrast, are open to an indefinite, unbounded future: uncontrolled and uncontrollable.

On the basis of the four C's of industrial time — creation, commodification, control and colonization — it has been possible to identify some principles and processes of the time politics of globalization. What is important to understand is that these logics and processes are mutually supporting and enhancing. They work as a Gramscian (Gramsci, 1971) bloc. Importantly, they have arisen from a world of thought and practice that was (until recently) almost exclusively male and therefore work best in that world of scientific creation, of conquering, control and colonization. Today, this logic of industrial time is applied globally as a taken-for-granted norm, irrespective of whether or not it is appropriate and/or beneficial to the recipients and their respective environments. The hierarchy of values associated with this hegemonic patriarchal time renders invisible the social relations of time practiced by the majority of the world's people. As a result, it created (and still creates) 'shadowlands' of work and re/production in which women the world over dwell in disproportionate numbers.

Towards a time-literate feminist politic of globalization

> Political tyranny in every culture begins by devaluing the time of others. Indeed, the exploitation of human beings is only possible in pyramidical time cultures, where rulership is always based in the proposition that some people's time is more valuable and other people's time more expendable.
>
> (Rifkin, 1987: 196–197)

The globalization of trade, information, finance and 'development' is rooted in a particular relation to time that has emerged with industrial/ising societies' socio-economic adoption of clock time as public norm. With the heuristic of the four C's the pervasiveness of the taken-for-granted becomes palpable. Not just the cohesiveness of the logic but the attendant exclusionary practices become visible. While the resulting 'shadowlands' are in no way entirely peopled along gendered lines, women, as I have sought to demonstrate above, dwell there in unequal numbers. Moreover, the value put on whole cultures' time varies according to their position in the global power structure. It is determined by who is doing the developing and who is being developed according to which norms, values, definitions and models of best practice. It is therefore important to recognise the interdependence of the gender bias in terms of the power relations associated with the four C's of industrial time and the time-based relations of definition. This is because these relations render invisible and non-valuable the social contribution of the majority of the world's people while relying on that invisible work for the economic production of profit. To devalue and negate people's lived and experienced re/productive, non-profit-generating time is a political act of oppression. It can only be recognised as such, however, once the invisible begins to be explicated, once the temporal relations are foregrounded and debated.

There is much to be gained from the political mobilization around the social relations of time. We can begin to think in terms of rights and responsibilities to be fought for. First, we might want to think in terms of the right to time. Culturally and personally, this would entail the right to have times other than those associated with the four C's recognised as valid and of equal status to the industrial public norm. Time giving and long-term goals would have to be recognised on equal terms with the time of commodified exchange and ever shortening cycles of profit creation. Ownership of time as a basic human right would enable people to structure the temporal organization of their lives appropriate to context and conditions in accordance with their own and their dependents' needs. Secondly, we might consider as a right the re-appropriation of agri/cultural re/production. This would currently contravene the WTO's trade-related investment measures (TRIMS) and trade-related intellectual property rights (TRIPS). In food production it would involve, for example, farmers' rights to own and control their ancient crop varieties, seeds, and locally evolved and adapted breeds. And it would return to them as a right the construction of the long-term future and the capacity to think and plan in generations.

Both these rights are tied up with the long-term future. Western democratic political structures, however, have no mandate for the long-term future. Whilst in practice their actions always extend beyond the period of election, their jurisdiction and principle rights for action tend to be covered and bounded by the time and space (territory) for which they have been duly elected. In a world of globalized markets, networked instantaneity, transgovernmental institutions and long-term socio-environmental effects this established political mandate is no longer adequate to the task. At the very least it needs to be supplemented with political structures that encompass responsibility for the emerging global temporal relations and have as mandate the task to secure the long-term future, which has to be safeguarded not just for those who can give them their vote now but for the voiceless and 'voteless' generations of successors. Furthermore, the sphere of responsibility would have to extend as far as the effects of current economic and scientific actions can reach. For World Bank development projects, for example, this would mean taking responsibility for their long-term impacts: for the accompanying increase in poverty, mass starvation and national debt, on the one hand, and the decrease in self-sufficiency, on the other. For some of the key technologies associated with industrialization this would entail massively extending the current temporal depth of responsibility: for nuclear power it would mean accompanying the effects of the various forms of radiation involved to the end of their respective half-lives, for chemical pollution as far as the hormone-disrupting chemicals are acting up the food chain, for genetically modified food as good as forever. It would entail putting in place legal structures and litigation procedures that locate responsibility for long-term effects firmly with originators of the actions and their dependents.[20]

All of this, I want to suggest, is a feminist agenda. The feminist approach to invisible relations of power is a transferable skill that is eminently suitable to the globalization debates. Moreover, not only are women and their dependents most affected by the processes of globalization, they are also driving the alternative development discussions through 'glocal' alliances and allegiances.[21] Given that women are already highly sensitised to the conflicts and harm that arise with the

20 For more detailed accounts of these relationships and more extensive arguments on responsibility for the future see my 1998 *Timescapes of Modernity. The Environment and Invisible Hazards.*

21 Four global women's

conferences (the first three under the UN's International Women's Decade, 1976–85) represent only the tip of the iceberg of organised alternative visions: Mexico City (1975), Copenhagen (1980), Nairobi (1985) and Beijing (1995). See Visvanathan *et al.* (1997), especially Chapter 2 by Tinker.

global imposition of industrial time, it is their temporal expertise and knowledge that is needed to formulate such an alternative political agenda. And given that they are already practiced in time giving, re/production and the long-term perspective, at both the family and 'glocal' levels, it is women who are best placed to take on the transnational political offices associated with the rights of time and the global guardianship of the future.

author biography

Barbara Adam is Professor of Sociology at Cardiff University. She is founder editor of the journal *Time & Society* and has published extensively on the social relations of time.

acknowledgements

I would like to thank Sian Barry, Gabrielle Ivinson, Charles Thorpe, Chris Weedon and the *Feminist Review's* anonymous referees for their helpful comments on an earlier draft on what was easily my most difficult paper to date.

references

Adam, B. (1990) *Time and Social Theory*, Cambridge: Polity; Philadelphia: Temple UP.

Adam, B. (1993) 'Within and beyond the time economy of employment relations: conceptual issues pertinent to research on time and work' *Social Science Information sur les sciences socials*, Vol. 32, No. 2, pp.163–184.

Adam, B. (1995) *Timewatch: The Social Analysis of Time*, Cambridge: Polity; Malden, MA: Blackwell.

Adam, B. (1998) *Timescapes of Modernity. The Environment and Invisible Hazards*, London/New York: Routledge.

Adam, B. (1998/2001) '*When time is money: contested rationalities of time and challenges to the theory and practice of work*' (Keynote Paper for the Sociology of Work Group, ISA Montreal, July 1998), School of Social Sciences, Cardiff University, Working Paper Series, Paper 16.

Albrow, M. (1996) *The Global Age*, Cambridge: Polity.

Anderson, B. (2000) *Doing the Dirty Work? The Global Politics of Domestic Labour*, London: Zed Books.

Baker, S. (1994) 'Structural adjustment and the environment: the gender dimension', in P. Rajput and H.L. Swarup (1994) editors, *Women and Globalization. Reflections, Options and Strategies*, New Delhi: Ashish Publishing House, pp.313–341.

Bartky, I.R. (2000) *Selling the True Time. 19th Century Timekeeping in America*, Stanford, CA: Stanford UP.

Bauman, Z. (1998) *Globalization. The Human Consequences*, Cambridge: Polity.

Bauman, Z. (2000) 'Time and space reunited' *Time & Society*, Vol. 9, Nos. 2 and 3, pp.171–186.

Beck, U. (1992) *Risk Society. Towards a New Modernity*, London: Sage.

Beck, U. (1996) 'World risk society as cosmopolitan society? Ecological questions in a framework of manufactured uncertainties' *Theory, Culture and Society*, Vol. 13, No. 4, pp.1–36.

Beck, U. (1997) *Democracy without Enemies*, Cambridge: Polity.

Beck, U. (1998) 'The cosmopolitan manifesto' *New Statesman*, 20 March, pp.28–30.

Beck, U. (1999) *World Risk Society*, Cambridge: Polity.

Beck, U. (2000a) *What is Globalization?* Cambridge: Polity.

Beck, U. (2000b) 'The cosmopolitan perspective: sociology of the second age of modernity' *The British Journal of Sociology*, Vol. 51, No. 1, pp.79–106.

Beck, U. (2000c) 'Risk society revisited: theory, politics and research programmes' in B. Adam, U. Beck and J. van Loon (2000c) editors, *The Risk Society and Beyond. Critical Issues for Social Theory*, London: Sage, pp.211–229.

Beck, U. (2000d) *The Brave New World of Work*, Cambridge: Polity.

Beck, U., Giddens, A. and Lash, S. (1994) *Reflexive Modernisation: Politics, Tradition and Aesthetics in the Modern Social Order*, Cambridge: Polity.

Blyton, P., Hassard, J., Hill, S. and Starkey, K. (1989) editors, *Time, Work and Organisation*, London: Routledge.

Boden, D. (2000) 'Worlds in action: information, instantaneity and global futures trading' in B. Adam, U. Beck, and J. van Loon (2000) editors, *The Risk Society and Beyond. Critical Issues for Social Theory*, London: Routledge, pp.183–197.

Boserup, E. (1970) *Women's Role in Economic Development*, London: Allen & Unwin.

Bourdieu, P. (1979) *Algeria 1960*, Cambridge: Cambridge UP.

Brodribb, S. (1992) 'The birth of time: generation(s) and genealogy in Mary O'Brien and Luce Irigaray' *Time & Society*, Vol. 1, No. 2, pp.257–270.

Castells, M. (1996) *The Rise of the Network Society*, Oxford: Blackwell.

Castells, M. (2000) 'Information technology and global capitalism' in W. Hutton and A. Giddens (2000) editors, *On the Edge. Living with Global Capitalism*, London: Jonathan Cape, pp.52–74.

Chossudovsky, M. (1997), *The Globalization of Poverty*, London: Zed Books.

Collins Dictionary of Sociology (2000) Glasgow: Harper Collins.

Cwerner, S. (2000) 'The chronopolitan ideal: time, belonging and globalization' *Time & Society*, Vol. 9, Nos. 2 and 3, pp.331–345.

Davies, K. (1990) *Women and Time. Weaving the Strands of Everyday Life*, Aldershot: Avebury.

Dunne, J.S. (1973) *Time and Myth. A Meditation on Storytelling as an Exploration of Life and Death*, London: SCM Press Ltd.

Eliade, M. (1954/1989) *Cosmos and History. The Myth of Eternal Return* (transl. W.R. Trask), London: Arkana.

Elson, D. (1991) editor, *Male Bias in the Development Process*, New York: St. Martin's Press.

Elson, D. and Pearson, R. (1981) 'Nimble fingers make cheap workers: an analysis of women's work in Third World manufacturing' *Feminist Review*, Vol. 7, pp.87–107.

Elson, D. and Pearson, R. (1997) 'The subordination of women and the internationalisation of factory production' in N. Visvanathan, L. Duggan, L. Nisonoff and N. Wiegersma (1997) editors, *The Women, Gender and Development Reader*, London: Zed Books, pp.191–202.

Enloe, C. (1989) *Bananas, Beaches and Bases. Making Feminist Sense of International Politics*, London: Pandora Press.

Escobar, A. (1995) *Encountering Development: The Making and Unmaking of the Third World*, Princeton: Princeton UP.

European Commission (2000) *Gender Use of Time: Three European Studies*, Luxembourg: European Communities.

European Foundation (2001) *Best European Studies on Time*, Luxembourg: European Communities.

Fernández-Kelly, M.P. (1983) *For we are Sold, I and My People: Women in Industry in Mexico's Frontier*, Albany, NY: SUNY Press.

Forman, F.J. (1989) 'Feminizing time: an introduction', in F.J. Forman and C. Sowton (1989) editor, *Taking our Time. Feminist Perspectives on Temporality*, Oxford: Pergamon, pp.1–10.

George, S. (1984) *Ill Fares the Land: Essays on Food, Hunger and Power*, London: Writers and Readers Publishing Cooperative Society Ltd.

George, S. (1989) *A Fate Worse than Dept: A Radical New Analysis of the Third World Dept Crisis*, London: Penguin Books.

George, S. (1992) *The Debt Boomerang. How Third World Debt Harms us All*, London: Pluto Press.

Giddens, A. (1999) *Reith Lecture 2: Risk*, London: BBC (published in Giddens, A. (2000)).

Giddens, A. (2000) *Runaway World: How Globalization is Reshaping our Lives*, London: Profile.

Goldsmith, E., Khor, M., Norberg-Hodge, H., Shiva, V. et al. (1995) *The Future of Progress. Reflections on Environment and Development*, Dartington: Green Books.

Gramsci, A. (1971) *Selections from Prison Notebooks*, London: Lawrence & Wishart.

Guyatt, N. (2000) *Another American Century? The United States and the World after 2000*, London: Zed Books.

Hareven, T.K. (1982) *Family Time and Industrial Time*, Cambridge: Cambridge UP.

Hareven, T.K. (1991) 'Synchronizing individual time, family time, and historical time' in J. Bender and D.E. Wellbery (1991) editors, *Chronotypes. The Construction of Time*, Stanford, CA: Stanford UP, pp.167–184.

Heidegger, M. (1927/1980) *Being and Time*, Oxford: Blackwell.

Held, D., Mcgrew, A., Goldblatt, D. and Perraton, J. (1999) *Global Transformations*, Cambridge: Polity.

Hochschild, A.R. (2000) 'Global care chains and emotional surplus value' in W. Hutton and A. Giddens (2000) editors, *On the Edge. Living with Global Capitalism*, London: Jonathan Cape, pp.130–146.

Hutton, W. and Giddens, A. (2000) editors, *On the Edge. Living with Global Capitalism*, London: Jonathan Cape.

Irigaray, L. (1983) *L'Oubli de l'air, chez Martin Heidegger*, Paris: Les Éditions de Minuit.

Irigaray, L. (1989) *LeTemps de la Différence. Pour une revolution pacifique*, Paris: Librairie Générale Francaise.

Kern, S. (1983) *The Culture of Time and Space 1880–1919*, London: Weidenfeld & Nicolson.

Korten, D.C. (1995) *When Corporations Rule the World*, London: Earthscan.

Leacock, E. and Safa, H. (1986) editors, *Women's Work: Development and the Division of labour by Gender*, Hadley, MA: Bergin & Garvey.

Lechner, F. and Boli, J. (2000) editors. *The Globalization Reader*, Oxford: Blackwell.

LeGoff, J. (1980) *Time, Work and Culture in the Middle Ages*, Chicago: Chicago UP.

Luhmann, N. (1982) 'World-time and system history' in *The Differentiation of Society*, New York: Columbia University Press, pp.289–324.

Madeley, J. (2000) *Hungry for Trade. How the Poor Pay for Free Trade*, London: Zed Books.

Martin, H.-P. and Schumann, H. (1997) *The Global Trap*, London: Zed Books.

Marx, K. (1857/1973) *Grundrisse*, Harmondsworth: Penguin.

Mies, M. (1986) *Patriarchy and Accumulation on a World Scale. Women in the International Division of Labour*, London: Zed Books.

Mitter, S. (1986) *Common Fate, Common Bond: Women in the Global Economy*, London: Pluto Press.

Mohanty, C.T. (1993) 'Under western eyes: feminist scholarship and colonial discourses' in P. Williams and L. Chrisman (1993) editors, *Colonial Discourse and Post-colonial Theory*, London/New York: Harvester Wheatsheaf, pp.196–220.

Nash, J. and Fernández-Kelly, P. (1983) editors, *Women, Men and the International Division of Labour*, Albany, NY: SUNY Press.

Nishimoto, I. (1997) 'The civilisation of time' *Time & Society*, Vol. 6, Nos. 2 and 3, pp.237–60.

Norberg-Hodge, H. (1995) 'The pressure to modernise' in E Goldsmith, M. Khor, H. Norberg-Hodge, V. Shiva *et al.* (1995) editors, *The Future of Progress. Reflections on Environment and Development*, Totnes: Green Books, pp.91–108.

Nowotny, H. (1989/1994) *Time. The Modern and Postmodern Experience*, Cambridge: Polity (from the German (1989) Eigenzeiten, Frankfut a.M.: Suhrkamp).

O'Brien, M. (1989) 'Resolute anticipation: Heidegger and Beckett' in *Reproducing the World: Essays in Feminist Theory*, London/Boston: Routledge & Kegan Paul.

Poster, M. (1990) *The Mode of Information*, Cambridge: Polity.

Rajput, P. and Swarup, H.L. (1994) editors, *Women and Globalization. Reflections, Options and Strategies*, New Delhi: Ashish Publishing House.

Ransom, D. (2001) editor, *New Internationalist*, pp. 9–28 (Special Issue on the WTO).

Rifkin, J. (1987) *Time Wars*, New York: Henry Holt.

Robertson, R. (1992) *Globalization: Social Theory and Global Culture*, London: Sage.

Rogers, B. (1981) *The Domestication of Women: Discrimination in Developing Societies*, London/New York: Routledge.

Rowbotham, S. and Mitter, S. (1994) editors, *Dignity and Daily Bread: New Forms of Economic Organizing among Poor Women in the Third World and the First*, London/New York: Routledge.

Sassen, S. (1996) *Losing Control? Sovereignty in an Age of Globalization*, New York: Columbia UP.

Sachs, W. (1993) editor, Global Ecology. A New Arena of Political Conflict, London: Zed Books.

Scott, C.V. (1995) *Gender and Development: Rethinking Modernization and Dependency Theory*, Boulder, CO: Lynne Rienner Publishers.

Seager, J. (1993) *Earth Follies. Feminism, Politics and the Environment*, London: Earthscan.

Sen, S. (1994) 'Structural adjustments and gender. issues in developing countries' in P. Rajput and H.L. Swarup (1994) editors, *Women and Globalization. Reflections, Options and Strategies*, New Delhi: Ashish Publishing House, pp.51–63.

Shiva, V. (1989) *Staying Alive. Women, Ecology and Development, London*: Zed Books.

Shiva, V. (1991a) *The Violence of the Green Revolution*, London: Zed Books.

Shiva, V. (1991b) *Ecology and the Politics of Survival Conflicts over Natural Resources in India*, New Delhi: Sage.

Shiva, V. (1992) 'Structural adjustment and Indian agriculture' *The Ecologist*, Vol. 22, No. 6, pp.271–275.

Shiva, V. (1993a) *Monocultures of the Mind. Perspectives on Biodiversity and Biotechnology*, London: Zed Books.

Shiva, V. (1993b) 'The greening of the global reach' in W. Sachs (1993b) editor, *Global Ecology*, London: Zed Books, pp.149–156.

Shiva, V. (1995) 'Globalism, biodiversity and the Third World' in E. Goldsmith, M. Khor, H. Norberg-Hodge, V. Shiva *et al.* (1995) editors, *The Future of Progress. Reflections on Environment and Development*, Dartington: Green Books, pp.50–67.

Shiva, V. (2000a) *Stolen Harvest. The Hijacking of the Global Food Supply*, London: Zed Books.

Shiva, V. (2000b) 'The world on the edge' in W. Hutton and A. Giddens (2000b) editors, *On the Edge. Living with Global Capitalism*, London: Jonathan Cape, pp.112–129.

Shiva, V. and Moser, I. (1995) editors, *Biopolitics: a Feminist and Ecological Reader on Biotechnology*, London: Zed Books.

Singh, K. (2000) *Taming Global Financial Flows*, London: Zed Books.

Soros, G. (2000) 'The new global financial architecture' in W. Hutton and A. Giddens (2000) editors, *On the Edge. Living with Global Capitalism*, London: Jonathan Cape, pp.86–92.

Starr, A. (2000) *Naming the Enemy. Anti-corporate Movements Confront Globalization*, London: Zed Books.

Swantz, M.-L. (1985) *Women in Development. A Creative Role Denied*? London: C. Hurst & Company.

Swarup, H.L. and Rajput, P. (1994) 'Changing political economy of India within the global adjustment programme: some critical gender issues' in P. Rajput and H.L. Swarup (1994) editors, *Women and Globalization. Reflections, Options and Strategies*, New Delhi: Ashish Publishing House, pp.87–128.

Thompson, E.P. (1967) 'Work, time-discipline, and industrial capitalism' *Past and Present*, Vol. 38, pp.56–97.

Tinker, I. (1990) *Persistent Inequalities: Women and Development*, Oxford: Oxford UP.

Tinker, I. (1997) 'The making of a field: advocates, practitioners and scholars' in N. Visvanathan, L. Duggan, L. Nisonoff and N. Wiegersma (1997) editors, *The Women, Gender and Development Reader*, London: Zed Books, pp.33–41.

Tzannatos, Z. (1995) 'Women and labor market changes in the global economy: growth helps, inequalities hurt and public policy matters' *World Development*, Vol. 27, No. 3, pp.551–569.

Urry, J. (2000) *Sociology beyond Societies: Mobilities for the Twenty-first Century*, London: Routledge.

Virilio, P. (1991) *La Vitesse*, Paris: Éditions Flammarion.

Virilio, P. (1995) *La vitesse de liberation*, Paris: Galilée.

Visvanathan, N., Duggan, L., Nisonoff, L. and Wiegersma, N. (1997) editors, *The Women, Gender and Development Reader*, London: Zed Books.

Visvanathan, N. (1997) 'Introduction to "theories of women, gender and development"' in N. Visvanathan, L. Duggan, L. Nisonoff and N. Wiegersma (1997) editors, *The Women, Gender and Development Reader*, London: Zed Books, pp.17–32.

Volcker, P.A. (2000) 'The sea of global finance' in W. Hutton and A. Giddens (2000) editors, *On the Edge. Living with Global Capitalism*, London: Jonathan Cape, pp.75–85.

Wendorff, R. (1980) *Zeit und Kultur*, Wiesbaden: Westdeutscher Verlag.

Wendorff, R. (1991) *Die Zeit mit der wir leben*, Herne: Heitkamp.

Young, K. (1992) editor, *Gender and Development Reader*, Ottawa: Canadian Council for International Cooperation.

70 | global mobilities, local predicaments: globalization and the critical imagination

Avtar Brah

abstract

Analysing some of the key discourses of 'globalization' and their relationship to global/local processes of gender, the article makes a distinction between the 'global' and 'globalization', such that the latter is seen as only one dimension of the 'global'. Globalization is understood as comprising complex and contradictory phenomena with diverse and differential impact across distinct categories of people, localities, regions and hemispheres. Hence, the notion of being straightforwardly 'for' or 'against' globalization is problematized. The essay explores media response to a major global event – the bombing of the World Trade Center in New York and the Pentagon in Washington DC on 11 September – in terms of the 'agenda setting' role of the US's 'mainstream' national television news coverage in the aftermath of the first two weeks. A subsequent peace rally, the 'International Day Against War and Racism', held in Washington DC, is analysed as the site for the emergence of a new oppositional political subject in the current context. The article underscores the importance of addressing 'intersectionality' to a critical imagination.

keywords

gender; women; feminist imagination; global; globalization; global economy; international economy; Islam; media representations; 11 September and the bombing of Afghanistan; Taliban

(30–45) © 2002 Feminist Review. 0141-7789/02 $15 www.feminist-review.com

introduction

The dawn of the 21st century is replete with discourses of globalization. Globalization is high on the agendas of such entities as the governments of nation-states as well as the transnational institutions like the World Trade Organisation, the International Monetary Fund and the World Bank. The question of globalization is frequently raised in the mass media, and it is the subject of analysis in ever-growing reams of academic literature produced from within different subject disciplines. It is also the target of political opposition by a wide variety of pressure groups and NGOs all over the world. However, the meanings attached to the word 'globalization' in these different sites may vary quite substantially. It is crucial therefore to make a distinction between 'discourses of globalization' with their multiple, even disparate connotations *and* the historical and contemporary 'processes' that assume distinctive patterns in different parts of the world under the weight of 21st-century formations of capitalism (Brah *et al.*, 1999). I take this distinction as a point of departure in this article, as I address specific forms of 'globalization-speak' and their relationship to economic, cultural and political processes at this conjuncture. My aim is to raise some questions about the possible reconfigurations of 'humanity' as a collective political subject that is distinguishable from the universal subject of modernity.

global questions

The question of the 'global' itself is not new. Humans have migrated across the globe and formed settlements and groupings that go back many millennia. In these varying and variable contexts, they dreamt and imagined the shape of our planet, its topography, its fauna and flora, and its peoples. They travelled across mountains and seas, exchanged information, developed new technologies, bartered and traded, and discoursed about the meaning of life and the nature of the universes beyond our planet. Diverse cosmologies, philosophies, sciences, rituals, lore, arts, cultural traditions, and political institutions developed out of these ancient encounters. These developments across the globe comprise our collective human heritage. However, we have learned to convert the collective output of these human endeavours into commodities that are construed as the private property of designate sections of humanity. During the last six centuries in particular, this logic of commodity became generalized and the conquest and division of territories was accelerated through histories of slavery, colonialism, capitalism, socialism, genocides and holocausts, and democracy. Of course, these phenomena are not identical; indeed, some are diametrically opposed. Yet, whilst there is no direct one-to-one correspondence between these histories, they are relational formations. The interacting, complex and at times contradictory web of power dynamics embedded in these phenomena served to produce what has come to be known as the formations of 'modernity'. One of the key 'modern' forms to emerge from this crucible, and one that was not fully consolidated until the 19th century and did not proliferate globally until the 20th century, was a new technology of global governance: the nation-state. The global imaginary of this period was thus refracted through discourses and practices of the 'nation', the 'national' and the 'international' and these discursive formations became the staple of 20th-century economics, politics and cultural developments.

With many aspects of modernity now in crisis, especially since the demise of the Cold War, the shift of hegemonic global power to the US as its primary centre, and the emergence of a new international political order that incorporates certain 'Southern' countries such as Japan and China, we are increasingly faced with many new challenges. One important feature that distinguishes the current situation from the period of empires is that the conditions of the US's predominance are so intrinsically inscribed in the current differentiated pattern of global power relations that the US does not have to depend on the expansion of its territory to secure its status and power. If the history of formal empires was one of ongoing imperial rivalry, the network of G8, whilst marked by a degree of internal dissension, remains, overall, remarkably quiescent to the demands of US leadership. Such vestment of power in a single nation-state at a time when many features of sovereignty of the nation-state, as a general category of governance, are in relative decline, is part and parcel of the apparently contradictory processes underpinning early 21st-century forms of 'globalization'. There has been substantial academic debate (generally, though not exclusively, subsumed under discussions about 'the postmodern' problematic) concerning the inadequacy of political blueprints of modernity to deliver much of what they promised. As such we are now justifiably weary of the arrogant and self-referential claims of modernity's narratives of 'progress' and 'universalism' while the majority of humanity continues to suffer abysmal conditions. Equally, there remains as much, if not greater, need for critical scrutiny and vigilance of present day discourses of 'the free world', 'terrorism', 'fundamentalism' and 'democracy' — envisioned as they often are in the image of the rhetoric of G8 powers and marked by their economic and military muscle. The necessity for re-imagining the politics of 'common good', equality, and justice has never been greater.

Although the effects of 'globalization', with all their complexity and diversity, form a very significant part of the global question, they do not, however, fully exhaust it. After all, feminists have been debating the concept of 'global sisterhood' (problematic though the concept proved to be) long before the recent discourses of globalization assumed ascendancy. It is necessary therefore not to conflate the concept of 'the global' with 'globalization' even as they overlap and interject each other, not least since there remain still quite significant disagreements as to what precisely does the phenomena of globalization consist of and how it should be understood.

globalization: what art thou?

The globalization debate is wide-ranging, complex, and it is marked by major disagreements. It is beyond the scope of this article to address it in any significant depth. However, overall, there are those analysts for whom the global marketplace is the defining feature of globalization, ushering in an altogether new era in which the nation states are becoming increasingly redundant as people everywhere are subjected to the logic of the global market. Others remain sceptical about the overarching impact of the *global* economy and suggest instead that what is really happening is that the *international* economy is merely becoming segmented into *regional* blocks with national governments still retaining a powerful role (Hirst and Thomson, 1999). Yet others seem to emphasise the speed and unprecedented level of social change in all spheres — economic, political, cultural, and social (Held *et al.*, 1999; Held, 2000; Waters, 2001). There is also considerable difference of opinion about periodization. While some writers hold the view that the emergence of globalization may be traced back to the beginning of trans-Atlantic western voyages of the 15th century or even to earlier periods than that, others confine the concept of globalization as referring primarily to the last decades of the 20th century. For example, Cox (1996) limits the use of the term globalization to the period since the worldwide economic recession of the 1970s. From the perspective of the 'world-system' theory with its key proponents such as Samir Amin, Eric Hobswam, and Immanuel Wallerstein, on the other hand, capitalism has always been global in intent, no matter how far back its emergence is assumed to have occurred, and what tends to be known today as globalization is primarily a new phase of capitalist expansion. With this view, the new phase would seem to be a logical extension of capitalism's inherent thrust towards re-inventing itself in order to maximise profits in the service of the entrenchment of power and control in the hands of a tiny minority of the world's population. As an overall, general audit about the state of the world, this view is, of course, largely valid, but when we move from the mega-historical focus of the world-system theory to a closer inspection of the historically, geographically, politically and culturally specific and contingent features, it becomes apparent that in neither of these guises can globalization be understood as following an inexorable, evolutionary logic. There have been major discontinuities, sudden shifts and disruptions, variegated trajectories of geographical expansion or contraction, and many different configurations of distinctive temporalities. Hence, Held and colleagues (1999: 413), differentiate between 'four distinctive historical forms each of which reflects a particular conjuncture of spatio-temporal and organizational attributes' and draw out a four-fold periodization of: premodern globalizations, early modern globalizations, and contemporary forms of globalization. Globalization, then, would seem to be an umbrella term covering varied phenomena with differential effects across nation-states and different groups of people.

There is also the related issue of whether or not the use of the term 'globalization' has the effect of representing the processes named under this rubric as neutral when their effects are clearly partisan. Harvey (2001) takes up this position, arguing that the appellation 'late capitalism' is more appropriate and accurate in making sense of the radical transformations and the variety of globalizing tendencies that have shaped our lives since the Second World War. The use of these different terms is significant. This is the case not only because it is relevant to appreciate different theoretical, substantive, and political perspectives on the issues at hand, important though this is and, in any case, there is much on which these writers concur. My concern with terminology is to do with the role that differing discourses of 'globalization' play in the taking up of political positions. The discourse of being pro- or anti-globalization is a case in point. I shall return to this.

It is worth noting that certain aspects of global processes that the concept of globalization attempts to capture have been previously analysed under various other names. We may recall, for example, the studies of Thatcherism/Reaganism, the new international division of labour, feminization of the labour market, the role of multinationals, as well as, the research into restructuring of the global economy. This research unpacks socio-political and economic processes, which have been pivotal to the constitution of currently emerging regimes. In this regard, Cox (1996), citing Bernadette Madeuf and Charles Albert Michelet (1978), draws attention to a useful distinction between *international* and *global* economy. Provenance of classical economic theory, the concept of international economy is concerned mainly with the movements in trade, investment, and payments across national boundaries. These movements are regulated by nation-states and by international organisations created largely by nation-states. The concept of the world economy or the global economy, on the other hand, is used to analyse the sphere in which the governance of cross-border or transnational networks of production and finance could largely escape national and international regulatory powers. Evidently, the necessity of making this distinction became apparent by the 1970s following the radical changes occurring in the wake of the onset in 1973 of a generalised economic crisis across the world.

In the more advanced capitalist economies, manufacturing went into serious decline during the 1970s and there were high levels of unemployment — among the working classes in general but in particular amongst women, young people, immigrants, and those groups confronted with racism and discrimination. The growing erosion of the 'Fordist' mode of labour-intensive mass production associated with institutionalized forms of collective bargaining and redistributive policies of the state was further accelerated by the development of new technologies in production and communications. Capital and knowledge-intensive methods geared towards niche markets began to make their presence felt. As an example of this, we may take 'homeworking' as one of the few areas of employment related to manufacturing that experienced growth in Britain during the late 1970s and the 1980s. The adoption of strategies geared towards niche markets by large employers played a crucial part in providing impetus for expansion of employment in this field as they introduced the 'putting out' system whereby large firms transferred their costs to small firms who, in turn, tried to maintain profitability by making individual employees shoulder many of the employer's production costs. In Britain, South Asian women, particularly those of Muslim background, became a major target for this home-based form of paid work (Phizacklea, 1990; Brah and Shaw, 1992). The employment of women, especially immigrant and migrant women, and 'women of colour', in low-waged areas of the labour market such as homeworking, electronics, information industries and a variety of services was to account for the majority of jobs subsumed under the concept of 'feminization of work', although of course relatively better paid work in middle management also saw more women enter the scene (Jensen et al., 1988). The off-shoring of manufacturing jobs from the Northern Hemisphere to the South (made viable by new developments in production and communication technologies) under pressure of low-cost imports had the effect of drawing a disproportionate number of women in poor countries into the paid workforce. The electronics assembly sector and the garments industry were among the major beneficiaries of this low-waged female labour force.

The neo-liberal modes of governance played their part by fostering strategies of market deregulation and privatisation and by launching attacks on the role of trade unions, reducing state budgets for social welfare, and strengthening international competitiveness at all costs. Generally, wealthier countries began to invest far more within regional blocs such as the European Union or North American Free Trade Agreement (NAFTA). In the less developed capitalist societies, the onslaught of the 1970s and subsequent recessions and related political events was refracted through their social relation with the advanced capitalist world. With the decrease in investments and loans from the latter to the former, combined with the burden of servicing the existing debt to the rich capitalist countries, the less advanced economies shifted away from the policy of import substitution towards the production of export-oriented commodities. This meant a reduction in the production of goods for domestic consumption in favour of gaining foreign exchange. There were cuts in state expenditure and a removal of restrictions on the movement of capital (Nazir, 1991). The detrimental effects of these policies weighed most heavily on the poor, especially women and girl children. Far from being mere antecedents of the current phase of globalization, these are critical and continuing moments in its constitution, operations and transformation.

So, what are the main features of 'globalization' over which there is currently substantial agreement? These may be summarized as follows:

- By the close of the 20th century, there has been a proliferation of nation-states. However, the nation-state is no longer the sole site of sovereignty even as it still remains a critical player.

- Global cities such as London, New York, Los Angeles and Tokyo are crucial to the servicing and financing of international trade, investment, and headquarter operations.
- Contemporary globalization is characterised by distinct patterns of stratification. The global military hierarchy is dominated by the US. In the economic domain, the political hierarchy is between the Organisation for Economic Co-operation and Development (OECD) and non-OECD states, and within the OECD the largest economies – the G8 – have the greatest control of the global networks and infrastructures.
- Among OECD states, an unprecedented volume of national exports, employment, output and technology investment are controlled by multinationals, yet multinationals are only a part of the arrangements necessary for the implementation of globalization.
- There has been an explosion of global trade between North America, Asia Pacific and Western Europe following the upheavals of the 1970s such as the OPEC (Organisation of Petroleum Exporting Countries) oil crisis, the reconfiguration of Bretton Woods and the formation of the World Trade Organisation (WTO), and the development of new communications technology and neo-liberal deregulation.
- The liberalisation of the world economy is accompanied by multilateral, regional and global systems of regulation and governance with tighter mechanisms of multilateral economic and political surveillance, for instance through the WTO.
- There is a mutually reinforcing tendency between processes of regionalization such as the formation of the European Union and globalization.
- The combined use of older and new technologies in production and communications has tremendously increased and transformed the velocity and reach of social and cultural networks and interactions of all kinds.
- Global migrations, including the worldwide flows of refugees and asylum seekers, are a major process through which the new transnational political economy is being reconstituted.
- The majority of refugees and asylum seekers are entering the poor countries of the South rather than the richer North.
- The world is witnessing an environmental crisis of an order never seen before. (Carnoy et al., 1993; Sassen, 1996, 1998; Held et al., 1999; Giddens, 2000; Beneria, 2001)

Seen in their generality, these features seem abstract, as if they follow their own internal logic. But these processes are thoroughly marked by human agency. Globalization does not exist in some rarefied stratosphere. It always touches ground. It has regional and local impact and ramifications. It confronts us with predicaments about the meanings of locality, staying-put in a place, no less than those of mobilities, migration and displacement. It is neither a teleological expression of what went on before; nor is it some kind of hermetically sealed totality. Its effects are multifarious, negative as well as positive, and there is both continuity and discontinuity.

The effect of the enormous increase in trade between North America, Asia Pacific and Western Europe, for example, means that some previous partners in trade and commerce have now been sidelined, reconfiguring the old dichotomy of Third World/First World. The new topography of inequality emerges not simply due to 'uneven development' but also at a point where whole regions – such as large parts of Africa – are altogether excluded from the equation (Castells, 1998). Yet, such inequality is accompanied by the development of global elites who share similar life-styles in every big city of the globe, giving even a poverty stricken region the appearance of being globally linked as the elite go about their business accompanied by the latest high-tech accoutrements, selling consumer dreams to a population unable to realise those dreams. Their raised aspirations are then likely to be disciplined by repressive political regimes in those countries – often propped up by support from the rich democracies – carrying out the structural adjustment programmes dictated by transnational institutions such as the International Monetary Fund or the World Bank. In the advanced economies, a wider section of the population may benefit from the material fruits of globalization, but here too there are sections of the populations – the unemployed, the underemployed, women, the racialised or otherwise discriminated against etc – who are institutionally excluded from the high table of 'global feast'.

In theorising the gender ramifications of globalization, it is critical that we do not see gender as an add-on feature of a core dynamic. Saskia Sassen's work on the global economy is singularly useful in this regard. She argues that gender is a 'strategic nexus' within the 'strategic dynamics and transformations' associated with the contemporary global economy. We have already noted how gender has served as a strategic nexus between subsistence economies and capitalist enter- prise in export-oriented agriculture, in the processes underlying the dismantling of older forms of manufacturing production, and in the creation of gendered forms of offshore labour markets. In global cities, which Sassen and others argue are crucial sites for the 'materialization of global processes and for the valorization of corporate capital', the bulk of the day-to-day jobs of the services complex, dominated by finance, are low paid. These jobs are likely to be held by women, immigrants, and people of colour, and of course these are overlapping categories. Although not always recognised as such in a great many discourses of 'globalization' this work is an essential part of the infrastructure necessary for coordinating, implementing, and running the global economic system. As Sassen notes:

> Much of what we still narrate in the language of immigration and ethnicity is actually a
> series of processes having to do with: (1) the globalization of economic activity, cultural
> activity, and of identity formation; and (2) the increasingly marked racialization of labour
> market segmentation so that the components of the production process in the advanced
> global information economy that take place in immigrant work environments are
> components not recognized as part of the global information economy.
>
> (Sassen, 1998: 87)

The current economic and political developments have witnessed expansion of high-income households with their new lifestyles dependent upon an easily available large supply of low-waged workers. The figure of the immigrant woman from distant corners of the earth as domestic help in a middle-class professional household in a number of Western societies is an instantiation of such processes. It is not that domestic help in professional households was unknown in the 20th century. In the countries of the 'South' poor women are frequently employed in middle-class homes. In Britain, Irish immigrant women have often been employed in domestic service. But Filipino women doing the same work in Britain is a more recent phenomenon. The historical links of imperial countries to their former colonies for the purpose of recruiting low-wage labour is becoming far less tenuous as the mobile labour supply itself becomes globalized in its origin as well as destination. As the clamour of xenophobia, racism and anti-refugee/asylum seekers rhetoric grows apace, the governments of many receiving countries fail to address the growing confrontation between the circulation of capital, commodities, cultural signs and products, on the one hand, and the circulation of people, on the other. The gender-specific effects of the increasing militarization of the world, the traffic in women and girls for prostitution from certain parts of the world to others, the issue of mail-order brides, global market for domestic work, and so on (Enloe, 1990; Pettman, 1996; Kofman et al., 2000) — all raise critical questions for feminists.

global spaces, local places and feminist imaginations

This would seem to be an appropriate stage at which to revisit my earlier concern about terminology. The multiplicity of popular, political, and academic discourses of globalization with their differing and sometimes opposing meanings suggest that it is difficult to make any blanket statements in favour or against globalization. In the interest of historical specificity, we might designate the processes associated with strategic transformations that have occurred since the post 1960s period as 'contemporary (late 20th- to early 21st-century forms of) capitalist globalization' (CCG). As I have already noted, processes of CCG are multiaxial and multidirectional. They represent complex articulations of socio-economic, political and cultural dimensions. Their effects are varied and differential across diverse groups of people, hemispheres, regions and localities. For example, a United Nations report shows that between 1995 and 1999, the world's 200 richest people doubled their wealth to more than one trillion dollars ($1000 billion) whilst 1.3 billion people in the world were living on less than one dollar a day. As regards consumption, the richest fifth accounted for 86% and the poorest fifth just 1%. Almost 75% of the world's telephone lines are in the West, which has only 27% of the world's population (Charlotte Denny and Victoria

Brittain in *The Guardian*, 12 July 1999). Thus, the gap between the rich and the poor continues to expand. Correspondingly, there is a growing concentration of economic, military and political power in the hands of a minority. Its consequences are there for all to see.

But how do we address the vast myriad of concerns and predicaments raised by this historical moment? There are times such as the present — a few weeks after the bombing of the World Trade Centre in New York and the Pentagon in Washington, two key symbols of globalization, on 11 September 2001 — when one political discourse can become so hegemonic that it may appear hugely difficult to interrogate or displace it. On the other hand, there are always alternative discourses and practices, no matter how marginalized they may appear at that moment, which can provide resources of hope. In what follows, I briefly explore some issues raised by 11 September. I begin with a few comments on the first two weeks of the US's 'mainstream' television news coverage of the events. This focus on mainstream national TV news is largely because of its availability to virtually every household in the US, so its content can offer some indication of its effects in terms of what media studies analysts would call its 'agenda setting' role and its importance in providing 'inferential structures' for subsequent news coverage as well as for shaping public opinion.

To my dismay, there was an almost total absence of any significant television debate during this early period concerning the issues behind the act of violence. This media and popular response may in part be ascribed to the effects of shock and the feelings and emotions associated with a very specifically American trauma related to 11 September. However, this would not fully account for the repeated chorus from politicians and media commentators calling for revenge and war on 'terrorists and all those who hide, support and abet them'. Afghanistan became an early target for revenge in the eyes of those in favour of an immediate military response. In the face of this verbal avalanche, virtually no dissenting voices received an airing on mainstream national television. The incident was called an attack on 'civilisation', a concept that reverberates with eurocentric connotations. Although the victims of the bombing are said to have come from 80 different countries ranging from India and Argentina to Zimbabwe, this point did not come to the fore for some time, while the media in the US unleashed its fury at the temerity of what had been 'done to America'.

In the midst of all this, a very disturbing scene from a British documentary — of a crouching Afghan woman covered from head to toe in a light blue burqa, and being publicly executed with a pistol in a sports stadium in Afghanistan — was shown on American television to demonstrate the 'barbarity' of 'the evil terrorists who hate the US'. During the weekend of 29/30 September, the documentary was shown in full at different times to catch a wider audience. Titled 'Beneath the Veil', it is anchored by the British journalist Saira Shah who, together with the television crew, entered Afghanistan under cover. The programme was first broadcast earlier in the year on Channel Four in Britain amidst considerable publicity. It was billed as showing the 'truth' of Afghanistan. Through inflection of her own Muslim ethnicity, especially when she intersperses her commentary with autobiographical anecdotes about family links with Afghanistan, Saira Shah could be seen as providing added credence and authenticity to the programme. What is immensely problematic about this documentary, however, is that from the outset it figures the 'Afghan woman' in such a way that it leaves little scope for the articulation of Afghani female agency, such that by the time we get to the actual scene of the woman being killed, it becomes extremely difficult to dissociate this merciless and deplorable act from the long-standing Western representational regime of the 'barbaric other' in general and the 'barbaric Muslim' in particular.

The documentary evacuates the historical context of the civil war in Afghanistan in which the 'Taliban' were armed, propelled into power, and initially feted as heroes — 'Soldiers of Islam' — by Western powers against the then socialist regime in Kabul that was supported by the then Soviet Union. Apparently, Osama bin Laden was a key figure in this insurgency, 'aided and abetted' directly or indirectly by the CIA (Strauss, 2001). In the ensuing events, ethnicity and religion were called into play in the mobilisation of Pathan ethnicity of the majority of the Afghan population against that of the numerical minority of Tajiks, Hazaras, and Uzbeks. But after the Cold War ended, Afghanistan was abandoned by the world powers. The Taliban, a political category and identity that emerged in the refugee camps during the Afghan civil war, came to power in 1995. They were given little material support for reconstruction of the country decimated by war. On the contrary, as religious militancy gained ground, partly due to poverty and lack of even the most basic amenities of everyday life, sanctions were imposed by the USA and its allies, which further exacerbated the situation of a people already devastated by war. Without providing the viewer with some understanding of the complexity underlying this background — on the contrary the programme seemed to suggest that the poverty was *caused* by the Taliban — the documentary's portrayal of the Afghan woman as a victim of 'uncivilised, cruel, patriarchal, religious zealots' easily articulated with the stereotypic imagery of the 'terrorists' and 'fundamentalists'. This left little space for a critical feminist stance that could condemn the unnamed woman's murder without demonising Muslim populations as a whole. It is not surprising, therefore, that this deeply painful and horrific scene became a sound bite of a stick with which the British and US media pundits could beat 'the terrorist barbarian'. It is possible that there were some 'feminist' intentions behind the documentary. It shows women activists inside Pakistan and Afghanistan, whose political actions provide a different and more hopeful narrative: one that contests both patriarchal practices in Afghanistan at the same time as it defies demonising of all Muslims. However, this reading was rendered tremendously difficult under the representational weight of the dominant image.

In the aftermath of the bombing, there has been 'visual (read racial) profiling' of those who 'look Middle Eastern'; mosques have been attacked, racial abuse hurled, and individuals threatened, assaulted and even killed. On the other hand a considerably different representation of Muslims is gradually emerging. Clearly, there is need for analytical and political imagination that can allow us to mourn and grieve for all those who are killed everywhere in these wars of the 21st century but, which also provides scope for critical intervention.

Such a lead was provided on 29 September by participants in the 'International Day Against War and Racism' held in Washington DC and San Francisco. The Washington rally was organised under the aegis of an umbrella coordinating network called Act Now to Stop War and Racism (A.N.S.W.E.R). I viewed it live on C-Span, the current affairs channel that broadcasts many of the proceedings of the Congress and the Senate. Although the audience figures for C-Span are very low compared to those for popular television, nevertheless channels such as these are also a technology of the 'global', and in this instance became an alternative political space. The organisations represented on the platform were many and varied, including: Women for Afghan Women (just formed); SATI (South Asian women's group against domestic violence); The Women Fight Back Union; Mexican Support Network (consisting of both 'documented' and 'undocumented' workers); Collective For Lesbian, Gay, Bisexual and Trans-Gender Rights; Pastors for Peace; Action for Community and Ecology; AFSCME (part of the labour movement); Black Voices for Peace; Campaign for the Release of Mumia Abu Jamal; Healthcare Now Coalition; Kensington Welfare Rights Group; School of the Americas Watch; Plymouth Congressional Church; SNCC and the Black Panther Party; George Washington University Action Coalition; Hunter College Peace Initiative; and, the musical band Pam Parker Group. The proceedings were appropriately conducted in both English and Spanish.

What was inspiring was to see a new collective political subject being constituted as speaker after speaker made connections across many different experiences, forms of differentiation and social divisions. The speakers expressed grief for the dead and sympathised with all the bereaved. A friend of a woman whose partner — a window cleaner — had perished in the attack reminded us that the work of the World Trade Center or the Pentagon is carried out not only by the high officials or professionals, but also a large number of low-paid support staff, many of whom are immigrants. The best memorial for the dead, it was argued, was to organise for equality and equity in jobs and access for all to high-quality free education and healthcare. There should be an end to racisms of all kinds; to discrimination on the basis of religion, creed, gender or sexuality, and a stop to ecological destruction and its fatal effects. Concerns were raised about civil liberties by the government's decision to cede an almost carte blanche discretion to the CIA, the FBI and other related agencies in the use of strategies and tactics for tracking 'terrorists'. The reliance of contemporary economies and societies on oil, which often results in the support of undemocratic regimes by the world powers, was captured in the slogan: 'No Blood for Oil'. The role of politicians, opinion formers, and the media in 'whipping up war frenzy' and 'driving the war machine' was addressed with a cautionary note that the most likely effect of the frenzy would be a reduction in social spending for the welfare of the people. Attention was drawn to the plight of the world's disadvantaged and the dispossessed whose work lubricates global economies. The need for solidarity across the globe was emphasised, but it was with the understanding that the effects of global processes are always experienced as mediated predicaments in specific localities.

New technologies that are the key components of cultural globalization have been put to good use by anti-war activists. As the campaigns for peace gather momentum, individuals and organisations have taken to the virtual freeways communicating on the Internet, mounting petitions, posting essays, commentaries, leaflets, news about what is happening locally, setting up campaigns, calling meetings, holding teach-ins and generally demonstrating the value of new information technologies for collective action. To the extent that the conditions underpinning CCG favour multilateralism, there is scope for the intervention of non-state actors and subjects, even though currently the 'global alliance' has not protected the Afghan people from the onslaught of bombs and missiles that began on 7 October. Women are developing cross-border affiliations and are speaking up for representation in different international and global forums. Like the Latina woman speaking at the Washington DC rally, they are raising issues excluded by conventional legal discourse such as the rights of 'undocumented workers' whose mobility and 'flexibility' or contingent labour global capital sorely needs but nation-states disavow. But, the figure of the Latina woman speaking with confidence about the situation of her fellow 'documented' and 'undocumented' workers does not stand simply as a symbol of economic exploitation. She signifies much more than that — a novel transnational political subject marked by the multiplicity of her constitution in terms of her gender, class, ethnicity and so on. This political subject is simultaneously diasporized and localized.

In other words, 'the space of the global' can be a space for imagining and negotiating alternative transnational conceptions of the person as 'holder of rights' that are distinct from the current notions of citizenship. It can be a place for all manner of cultural and political creativity.

These events have highlighted with renewed force the importance of the long-standing debate as to how consent is socially and culturally manufactured. The old feminist adage that 'woman', and by extension 'human' is not a homogeneous category has lost little of its import and many aspects of the feminist debates of the 1980s and 1990s concerning inequalities, inequities and other 'differences' between women remain pertinent. Scope for interventions that challenge the basis of these inequalities is wide and open. Given the deepening of global inequalities as capitalism becomes further entrenched, Marx's concept of 'generalized commodity production and circulation' and 'exploitation' holds considerable analytical purchase even though the conditions under which capitalism operates today are radically different, and both class and its associated 'structures of feeling', to mobilise Raymond William's memorable phrase, or 'habitus', to use Pierre Bourdieu, have been critically transformed. But to invoke Marx's is not to forget that there are regimes of representation, modes of experience, discursive formations and issues about selfhood, subjectivity and identity that cannot be captured or appropriately addressed within the framework of exploitation. Nor does it mean that I buy into old 'class centricism'. On the contrary, it is the feminist concept of politics of location that animates my thinking. The feminist discourse of 'politics of location' (Mohanty, 1992; Kaplan, 1994) signals a move away from 'centricism' towards critical engagement with the interrelationships of socio-cultural, economic and political processes as they articulate in our biographies and collective histories. That is to say, it foregrounds positionality of 'dispersal *and* simultaneous situatedness' across different axes of differentiation, such as gender, ethnicity, racism, sexuality, class and caste. I believe that to think through, within, and across *intersectionality* of these varying *modalities* of power is indispensable to a critical feminist imagination.

The question of power, of course, is complex. Structuralist notions of power have been successful in drawing attention to its systemic, patterned and recursive forms. This view of power, with its primary focus centred upon the binary opposition of domination/subordination, has been fruitfully reconfigured by Foucault. His theorization of the micrologies of power that do not always radiate from top to bottom and cannot be reduced to the effects of class alone is crucial to re-thinking agency, as is his view that power is not merely coercive, but is also productive. But, Foucault, in my view, would always have to be refigured through the subtle and sustained feminist attention to the theorization of subjectivity — whether through appropriations of psychoanalysis, semiotic readings, or other perspectives (de Lauretis, 1984; Flax, 1990; Mani, 1999; Weedon, 1999; Gedalof, 1999; Lewis, 2000; Brah and Coombes, 2000). My emphasis on 'analytics of intersectionality' derives in large part from both a conceptual and political necessity. Where axes of differentiation intersect is precisely that *nexus* where our subjectivities and positionalities are 'hailed' into subjects through multiaxial performance of power. It is the site of irreducible polyvocality and polyphony. This time-space of 'difference' and the Derridean 'differance' in the sense that I have addressed elsewhere (Brah, 1996), makes it possible for new meanings, discursive formations, subject positions, and political projects to ensue.

The critical imagination at work in the rally at Washington DC represents what is possible even in the face of an extremely difficult situation. But I neither wish to sentimentalize nor homogenize this political time-space. The individuals and groups present at the rally were an extremely heterogeneous category of people. I am sure that their views are far from identical on every issue. It may be important to reiterate here a distinction I have made elsewhere (Brah, 1996) between political identity as conscious agency designed to produce consensus along common goals *and* subjectivity. Out of the social and subjective heterogeneity at the Washington rally emerged a collective political subject that does not disavow 'differences' but operates within its interstices. It speaks not as a transcendental figure but through embodied subjects. Inevitably, like any political subject, this one also will be interrogated by processes of subjectivity — its contradictions, repression, projections, dispersal, fragmentation, and fantasies. It is impossible therefore to directly read off psychic motivations or investments of participants at the rally from the public discourse they have helped inscribe. But the public discourse itself marks a new subjectivity that invokes commonality and difference as relational configurations instead of oppositions. That is to say, a recognition of another's 'difference' without 'Othering'.

In the light of a plethora of, to my mind, convincing critiques of the modernist concept of the 'human', there may be greater purchase in valorizing a non-transcendental and non-logcentric idea of humanity that foregrounds a view of power as permeating all social, psychic and cultural landscapes. This reconfigured political subject — in its full heterogeneity and difference — may signal a somewhat more hopeful future for the projects of connectivity and affiliation in our times. The question of the global, then, becomes one about how we imagine and realise our relationship to one another as individuals and collectivities, and to 'non-humans' including the living earth and the various known and unknown universe(s). On this view, the 'non-human' cannot function as humanity's 'outside'. On the contrary, it is its immanent symbiotic and critique.

author biography

Avtar Brah teaches at Birkbeck College, University of London. Currently she is in the USA, as a Visiting Fellow of the Society for the Humanities at Cornell University for the academic session 2001/2.

note

The discussion of the events of 11 September covers the period up to mid October 2001.

references

Brah, A. (1996) *Cartographies of Diaspora, Contesting Identities*, London & New York: Routledge.
Brah, A. and Coombes, A.E. (2000) *Hybridity and Its Discontents*: Politics, Science, Culture, London & New York: Routledge.

Brah, A. and Shaw, S. (1992) *Working Choices: South Asian Muslim Young Women in the Labour Market*, London: Department of Employment, Research paper no. 91.

Brah, A., Hickman, M. and Mairtin Mac an Ghail (1999) editors, *Global Futures: Migrations, Enviornment and globalization*, London: Macmillan.

Carnoy, M., Castens, M., Cohen, S. and Cardoso, F.H. (1993) *The New Global Economy in the International Age; Reflections on our changing world*, Pennsylvania State University Press.

Castells, E. (1998) *End of Millenium*, Vol. 3 of the Information Age: Economy Society and Culture, Oxford: Blackwell.

Cox, R.W. (1996) 'A perspective on Globalization' in *Globalization: Critical Reflections*, Mittleman, J.H. editors, London: Lynne Rienner.

de Lauretis, T. (1984) *Alice Doesn't: Feminism, Semiotics, Cinema*, Bloomington: Indiana University Press.

Enloe, C. (1990) *Bananas, Beaches and Bases: Making Feminist Sense of International Politics*, Berkely: University of California Press.

Gedalof, I. (1999) *Against Purity: Rethinking Identity with Indian and Western Feminisms*, London and NY: Routledge.

Giddens, A. (2000) *Runaway World: How Globalization is reshaping our lives*, London, NY: Routledge.

Harvey, D. (2001) *Spaces of Hope*, Berkely: University of California Press.

Held, D. (2000) editor, *A Globalizing World? Culture, Economics, Politics*, London and New York: Routledge.

Held, D., McGrew, A., Goldblatt, D. and Perraton, J. (1999) *Global Transformations: Politics, Economics, Culture*, Cambridge: Polity.

Hirst, P.Q. and Thomson, G.F. (1999) *Globalization in Question: The International Economy and the Possibilities of Governance* (2nd edn), Cambridge: Polity.

Kaplan, C. (1994) 'The politics of location as transnational practice' in I. Grewal, and C. Kaplan, editors, *Scattered Hegeminies*, Minneapolis and London: University of Minnesota Press.

Kofman, E, Phizacklea, A., Raghuram, P. and Sales, R. (2000) *Gender and International Migration in Europe: Employment, Welfare and Politics*, London and New York: Routledge

Lewis, G. (2000) *Race, Gender, Social Welfare*, Cambridge: Polity.

Mani, L. (1999) *Contentious Traditions*, USA: Indiana University Press.

Mittleman, J.H. (1996) editor, *Globalization: Critical Reflections*, London: Lynne Rienner.

Mohanty, T. (1992) '...Locating experience' in M. Barrett, and A. Philips, editors, *Destablising Theory*, Cambridge: Polity Press.

Pettman, J.J. (1996) *Worlding Women: Feminist International Politics*, London and New York: Routledge.

Phizacklea, A. (1990) *Unpacking the Fashion Industry*, London: Routledge.

Sasssen, S. (1998) *Globalization and its Discontents: Essays on the New Mobilities of people and Money*, NY: The New Press.

Sassen, S. (1999 [1996]) *Guests and Aliens*, New York: The New Press.

Strauss, B.R. (2001) *Vengeance, Blowback and President Bush*, blowback.wpd.http://www.financial express.com/fe20010922/ed3.html.

Waters, M. (1995, 2001) *Globalization*, 2nd London and New York: Routledge.

Weedon, C. (1999) *Feminism, Theory, and the Politics of Difference*, Oxford: Blackwell.

70 | interview with Naomi Klein

Lyn Thomas

Born in Montreal in 1970, *Naomi Klein* is an award-winning journalist and author of the international best-selling book, *No Logo: Taking Aim at the Brand Bullies*. Translated into 16 languages, *No Logo* was described by *The New York Times* as 'a movement bible.' *The Guardian* newspaper short listed it for their First Book Award in 2000. In April 2001, *No Logo* won the Canadian National Business Book Award, and in August 2001 it was awarded the *Le Prix Médiations*, in France. For the past six years, Naomi Klein has travelled throughout North America, Asia, Latin America and Europe, tracking the rise of anti-corporate activism. Naomi Klein lives in Toronto.

Lyn: Really my first question was how you see globalization developing at the moment, whether you see any changes in the kinds of processes that you analysed in *No Logo* or whether you think it's very much still progressing on the lines you described in the book.

Naomi: Well, I don't really talk about it in terms of globalization — it's not a phrase that I find particularly useful and I don't use it very much in the book. And I use it even less now. Because I think it frankly confuses what it is that we're talking about. Because globalization isn't a new process. And if we think of it in terms of integration and trade between nations, it's at least as old as colonialism. Certainly what I'm talking about in the book is corporatization — in other words corporate power, the annexing of the public sphere by the private. I wouldn't say that the process has changed dramatically since *No Logo* was published by any means. However, my own understanding of economics has deepened since the book was published. Because it was a couple of years ago that I finished writing the book.

Lyn: Yes, sure. The next thing really is really whether you would comment on the ways in which women are particularly affected and differently affected by the process of corporate power.

Naomi: I'll get to that but first I think it helps to define the debate. What people are responding to globally in terms of mass protests is essentially the lie of globalization, the broken promises. The promise of globalization is the promise of increased equality, a levelling of the playing field globally, and an increased democracy, increased freedom — that's the promise. The reason why people are responding so strongly has to do with the fact that this promise has not been kept. Not only has it not been kept but in fact this economic project — which is not globalization, it's a set of economic policies which you can call neo-liberalism, or turbo-capitalism — is actually creating inequality and exacerbating inequality and decreasing freedoms for many people. By neo-

(46–56) © 2002 Feminist Review. 0141-7789/02 $15 www.feminist-review.com

liberalism I mean the familiar agenda of deregulation: cut taxes, privatize, deregulate, chase economic growth and increased profits at all costs. And, we are told, the process will trickle down to eradicate poverty, solve all our environmental problems (laugh) and bring more democracy in the process. I mean, that's the theory, that's the ideology. That's what I think we mean when we say 'globalization'. And we should be really clear that that's what we're talking about.

Lyn: So you basically are finding the term 'globalization' unhelpful because it's...

Naomi: I find it profoundly unhelpful. Yes. And I really think that part of the process of moving forward for this kind of movement has to involve rejecting that phrase 'globalization' and rejecting the characterization of the movement as an anti-globalization movement. It's not helpful for us because it's a vague term and it's far too easy to then paint this movement as protectionist.

Lyn: Yes. And anti-progress.

Naomi: Yes exactly. So I do think we're talking about a very specific set of policies and in fact an ideological belief in the powers of trickle-down economics. And so we need to name that really clearly and measure it against its promises. And provide alternatives that are not protectionist and that are not anti-progress. Another way of thinking about globalization is to think about it as a system that involves the rapacious, never satiated logic of privatizing every aspect of life — which is what's needed to constantly increase growth and expand the market. And that I think is an idea that runs through many aspects of the resistance movements to neo-liberalism. Some of it is the ground I covered in *No Logo* — in terms of the privatizing of ideas, because that's what branding is. It's turning ideas, our most powerful ideas, into commodities. You know, it's important to understand that the stage that we're at in the expansion of the market is not simply about moving more goods, as it is often posited, but creating new areas that are now goods that were not previously goods, like ideas, like water, body parts, genetic material, like seeds...

Lyn: Air.

Naomi: Exactly. That's a really good point. With carbon trading. We see this now, because some of the highest-stake trade disputes involve intellectual property: patents, copyrights, trademarks. This is where globalization is being fought, on intellectual property. So we need to understand this agenda as a rapacious process of privatization and commodification in the sense of creating new areas of ownership that were not previously within the market at all. This is a big reason behind the betrayed promise of this system because so many people and ways of life are being displaced by this commodification. So instead of more equality what we have is forgotten people, we have forgotten continents. And instead of development we have the dismantling of the social safety net that we had, done in order to facilitate investment. And instead of more democracy we have governments handcuffed by debt and structural adjustment dictates. We are facing a World Trade Organization that allows multinational corporations to sue national governments for failing to deliver market access. Understanding this process means understanding the logic of capitalism. So clearly what is happening, and I think it's tremendously positive, is that capitalism is coming out of the closet. And this is particularly significant in a North American context I think, also in a British context, less so in a European context where the phrase capitalism never completely disappeared. But in North America, you know, people stopped saying the word because it was just the way the world worked.

What does that mean for women? Well, essentially this movement is a convergence of every movement under the sun including the women's movement, and a kind of re-focusing and an understanding of a shared framework in which all these issues are unfolding, and that is allowing for new coalitions and some ability to work through divides, including splits between say environmentalists and labour unions. But at the same time, there's something I have confronted a lot. Since the publication of *No Logo* I've been to countless conferences about the future of the Left, etc. etc., and there's the resurgence of a man of a certain age (laugh) that sees this discussion of economics and capitalism and is sort of breathing this sigh of relief that says, 'Oh, good we don't have to worry about gender and race and all of those so-called special interests any more because everyone has finally realized the supremacy of the market and class'.

Lyn: Yes, indeed. Well, and that was one of the things that made us think about this issue because to me that's a description of some of the academic work that's been done on these kind of issues...

Naomi: ... and it's one of the reasons that I wanted to talk to you because it's been coming up more and more in the work that I do and I feel that I didn't distance myself enough from it in the book. I really do want to distance myself from that because if we really understand this global system as a system that is exacerbating inequality as opposed to eradicating poverty as it promises then we also have to understand that this system is exacerbating pre-existing inequality. Therefore it's affecting women particularly, especially women of colour around the world, and the statistics bear that out in a very dramatic way. Women no matter where they live in the world are still earning 75 cents on the dollar, but more dramatically women make up 70% of the world's poor...

Lyn: ... and they're very much in these invisible work forces.

Naomi: Yes. And privatization of previously uncommodified areas also affects women, much more deeply, because it tends to be women's knowledge that's stolen with the patenting of seeds and traditional medicines, and it's women's body parts that are being trafficked. At the same time it's women's work — and that's been the same for years — that's not counted in any traditional economic measure. This then lays the ground work for the sort of hyper exploitation of women's labour

1 'Workfare' or welfare to work programmes target single mothers, obliging them to work without the benefits of unionization or minimum wage in order to receive benefits. Such programmes have been introduced in the US since 1996 and have since become a central plank in the privatization of social welfare programmes in Western countries. In the UK they were introduced under the slogan 'New Deal'. Such programmes have had particularly serious consequences for single mothers and people living with impairments or illness.

2 'The Fourth World Conference on Women: Action for Equality, Development and Peace', organized by the UN, took place in Beijing in 1995. In 2000 a 'Beijing +5 and beyond' special session of the UN's General Assembly met in New York.

3 The World Social Forum aims to act as 'a new international arena for the creation and exchange of social and economic projects that promote human rights, social justice and sustainable development'. The Forum's January 2001 conference in Porto Alegre, Brazil, was timed to coincide with the meeting of the World Economic Forum in Davos, Switzerland.

whether in the sex trade or in the *maquiladoras* or in homework of various kinds. And through 'workfare' programmes.[1] So, I mean, it's been a real problem that the analysis of globalization has not included a profound enough understanding of where gender and race and geographic location fit into this process of privatization and stratification...

Lyn: And that's something you would see as an area that feminist researchers should be addressing?

Naomi: Yes. But I think that there is a huge body of knowledge out there already and in fact that the women's movement globalized before pretty much any other movement. And in many ways you know the Beijing conference[2] was a precursor to the explosion of civil society activism that we're seeing now globally. I think that there's a recognition within the international feminist movement that there needs to be a deeper understanding of where macro-economic policy fits in to the marginalization of women globally, and that at the same time the macro-economists have to tap into all this research that already exists really, so it's a process of meeting in the middle. But we're not that far off because there are these bodies of knowledge that just aren't intersecting enough.

Lyn: Yes, yes. Exactly. Yes, so really it sounds very much as if you're saying that you think that the struggles against corporatization and corporate power have really developed out of feminism and other new social movements and have learnt quite a lot from them. And that needs to continue...

Naomi: I think that the moment we're in now is drawing on social movements of the past and present — it's finding new intersections to develop a coherent analysis. But so far when attempts have been made to develop that coherent analysis, feminist theory and the globalized feminist movement have been marginalized again. We saw this in Porto Alegre — the World Social Forum.[3] But I do think that even since then there's been growing awareness that recognizing the power of capital does not mean saying that gender and race no longer matter, quite the opposite, they matter more than ever. At least I hope that is happening.

Lyn: Yes. In *No Logo* you argued that feminisms and other new social movements had really been quite misguided in the 80s and perhaps...

Naomi: I tried to be clear in the book that I was talking about a very specific incarnation of a Western feminist movement which was quite specific to North American and I think to some extent to European university campuses which were extremely postmodern and narrow in their obsession with media representation. You know, in terms of fitting in feminist analysis within a broader macro-economic context, it was just off the map. I really did try to choose my words extremely carefully in the book and to state very clearly that this isn't a rejection of feminism — in fact it's a return to the roots of feminism because this was actually in my opinion an aberration — an aberration from the history of the feminist movement and an aberration within the global feminist movement, which never stopped focussing on economics. It's not that people weren't making the arguments — they were — it's just that they weren't being heard within the more privileged mainstream of feminist discourse. And I think that was a problem not only within the feminist movement but a general problem for left academics, who were really quite scandalously cut off from real world urgent struggles.

Lyn: Do you think this is still a problem?

Naomi: I think that there's been — there has been a shift in the recent past. I don't know — I think that the academic world is frankly playing catch up at the moment and this is good, it's about time. This is reflected in an endless stream of conferences about globalization and there is a clear desire to reconnect amongst many academics with real world struggles. And I think you see this with someone like Andrew Ross at NYU who was like the poster child of postmodernism, but who became very involved in 1995 with the anti-sweatshop movement in the States — and he has regrounded his theory. So, I don't see it as just as an issue of feminist academics I think it was an issue for left academics in general...

Lyn: And you feel that there are some signs of change, perhaps as education itself is privatized. I realize that in many ways it's already happened in America, but here it's in the process of being privatized and that's certainly focusing the minds... But you do perceive there is an increased interest in addressing some of these issues.

Naomi: Yeah. And to be clear, I think it's a reaction to the resurgence of youth activism that is extremely grounded in material reality. Left political parties that lost their way are also trying to find ways to connect with this activism, as well they should. And I think there are a lot of people who that challenges, you know, a lot of people who were calling themselves left and were not engaged with real world struggles. I think a lot of people are in the process of meeting that challenge and, yeah, I do see that as a North American — I can't speak for Britain unfortunately — I see it, and I also have to say that I get an extremely distorted view of reality because I spend a lot of time at those academic conferences, so it seems to me that there is a great deal of work going on.

Lyn: OK.

Naomi: But at the same time some of it involves this resurgence of the classical Marxist analysis that is trying to use this opportunity to reject a gender analysis — so there's a tension there. But I feel confident that people are very energized by all the action that is going on and want their work to connect with it and the young activists I know are by no means rejecting feminism or anti-racism.

Lyn: So — I mean in terms of different kinds of anti-globalization or anti-corporatization movements do you see, you know, new developments and do you think things are changing in terms of feminist interventions in these struggles?

Naomi: Well, I think it's funny because I often think it's less about changing the movement than the movement changing its perception of itself. There is this idea that we have to build the movement from scratch. I think probably more accurately what we have to do is to recognize the movements that already exist and try to better connect them. When you look closely you realize that means that the communities that are truly engaged in powerful struggles are communities of colour, certainly in North America, against police violence, police brutality, immigration crackdowns. So I would say that yeah the movement is changing but I think that in some ways that change is simply — as the analysis deepens and there's greater understanding of the connections between race and gender and class and migration patterns, environmental issues — that what we start to see is that there are pockets of resistance everywhere. Our task really is to make those inter-connections clearer — networking — as opposed to building a movement from scratch.

Lyn: Yes. Pockets of very different kinds of resistance depending on the national context and regional context.

Naomi: Yeah. Yeah. I think so. And I don't think we're doing nearly a good enough job of connecting. I was in Britain recently when the race riots happened or whatever you want to call them, and it's interesting that the issues behind them seemed to be totally disconnected — from the so-called Left... And sometimes this is presented as a recruitment problem (laugh): 'We need to go do better outreach for our movement'. And I think that that's the fundamental problem — that what we need to do is to completely re-think about where we start. And I think that where you start is where people are already resisting and are already mobilized.

Lyn: Yes. And in a sense resisting the media model of these struggles and resistances which is really to focus on the big mass protests in major cities. It seems that when there's a lot of media attention they're more likely to write about that than, say, trade union groups, or workers' groups, or more local movements. And the focus on the big demos.

Naomi: Yes. In the US it's also about movements against the explosion of the prison system, police violence, immigration crackdowns. I mean these are where the most intense struggles are taking place. And...

Lyn: On the ground.

Naomi: On the ground. Yes.

Lyn: Perhaps even more importantly than the mass demonstrations although they obviously have a role, an important role. Do you agree?

Naomi: Well, I think that all of these struggles are weakened when the connections aren't made. And I think we're in this situation right now where we have these two activist solitudes — the global protests, the mass convergences, that are taking on these macro trade policies or financial institutions, and then you have the local struggles. They are about the effects of neo-liberalism on the ground. The flip side of the increased flow of goods is the crackdown on peoples, on migration — and migration is the flip side of industrial agriculture and World Bank mega dams, for example. These connections are there to be made and I think that everyone is weakened by the failure to make those connections. Again, locally it's demoralizing as well to simply just cite the policies as opposed to the ideology behind the policies. And then there is this problem that this so-called anti-globalization movement sometimes seems more and more cut off from day to day struggles. So I think that that there are these two activist tracks that clearly have to meet in the middle. I think that is starting to happen and there is a growing understanding of this in the discussions certainly in North America. But there needs to be a localizing of the anti-globalization movement. And we need to stop calling it an anti-globalization movement (laughs).

Lyn: Yes. Because that makes it easier to label it and criticize as well.

Naomi: Yes. And then I think that within the context of a movement that really is a 'movement of movements' that's grounded in communities and day to day struggles, of course, there's a role for mass demonstrations. There's always a role for mass demonstrations but the problem with the mass demonstrations we've been having is that they are becoming an end in themselves. Instead of demonstrations of something. Something that is less obvious. So much energy goes into getting people on buses, getting them somewhere, getting them to Genoa, getting them to Quebec City. When really the most powerful movement is a movement that doesn't have to move, because it's everywhere.

Lyn: Yes, yes. That's very interesting. Thank you.

Naomi: The other thing I want to mention is — that if we do think about this movement in a different way, not just simply as these mass convergences, then it is also clear that it is, I think, overwhelmingly women who are the unsung leaders, if you want to call them that because it's not a traditional leadership structure, but from what I've seen — and it's not comprehensive...

Lyn: And in some ways as you said women are suffering more and the gender inequalities and other kinds of inequality are being exacerbated. Though you also see them reacting and resisting very strongly.

Naomi: Yes, we see that in the unions in free-trade zones and maquiladoras, and we see in the movement of women who are leading the fight against the Narmada Dam in India, for instance, and that it's women like Vandana Shiva who are leading the struggle to protect traditional medicines, seed varieties, against the privatization patenting forces. And also fighting for the rights of domestic workers and migrant workers and sex workers all over the world. So also I think that some of the best theorists of this movement are people like Saskia Sassen, who is looking at the connections between colonialism and migration, for instance. And the most profound questionings of how we measure economic growth and progress come from women like Marilyn Warring, in New Zealand. It's women who have been at the front lines of this incredible process of popular education that is pretty unglamorous.

Lyn: I suppose that one of the ways in which *No Logo* has contributed is as part of that process. Because it's reached a mass readership. It seems very positive that it's a book that young people will read — and that's my sense of this and it seems a very positive thing.

Naomi: Yeah. Most of the letters I get are from people in their late teens, and I think that the contribution probably of the book has been in making the connection between some of this theory and youth culture. And young people's lives and the language of branding which is our shared language. So it's provided something of a window — not for people who are already hardened activists but for people who are looking for a doorway — they have to start somewhere. And so what I've been trying to do since the book has come out is to develop ways to make sure that that doorway leads somewhere. And I've started to do this with the website[4] which has become much more of an activists' forum, not a forum about the book but as a forum for people who talk about this global activists' network and share information, stay connected, get connected to other people who are thinking about the issues. Because the biggest frustration for me was the amount of letters I was getting from young people who were not politically active but wanted to become politically active. And who had read the book. And I felt this responsibility to respond to everyone but wasn't able to so that's what we've been trying to sort out.

Lyn: And you've had a great number of letters from young people?

Naomi: Yeah. A huge number of letters because the book is on a lot of course lists now. And it tends to be people in their teens I suppose who take the time to write me and they ask questions about what they can do and how they can get involved.

Lyn: And that's quite encouraging, isn't it?

Naomi: Yes. I'm very encouraged but not just about this but in general I think the success of the book has everything to do with the success of this movement. The fact that's it's growing and there's greater and greater interest, and also that the media coverage has been so bad, there is a hunger for any kind of contextualized information.

Lyn: Well, indeed, yes. Having just gone through the coverage of the May the 1st events[5] here, which was really quite extraordinary.

4 The website address is: http://www.nologo.org/

5 On May 1, 2001, demonstrators against global capitalism protested

Naomi: Yes, the backlash was extraordinary. It's a little difficult for me because I sort of feel distanced from the book in the sense that my ideas have really developed a lot since it was published. So I try to use the speaking that I do to reflect that, and the interviews that I do. I tend not to be writing about branding as much.

Lyn: But you still feel that the book has played a key role. That brings me on really to the last question. This is something that I'm sure that people ask you all the time. And indeed I've seen people asking you this kind of question about the contradictions involved in the success of *No Logo* and the way you yourself become, get packaged as it were by the media and so on, as a celebrity. It obviously has connections with celebrities within feminisms as well. And I just wondered whether you felt that really was a problem, and whether gender has played a role in that as well. And how you feel it can be combated, I suppose?

Naomi: It's very complicated. I try not to worry about it all that much because I'm not somebody who is obsessed with purity — I'm aware of contradictions. *No Logo* itself is all about contradictions and the fact that we need to use the language of our shared culture to combat corporate power. And I'm not afraid of that, and I think that there's a tendency on the left sometimes to opt for purity over engagement. We are all aware of how co-optation works. You can become so keenly aware of it that it almost can prevent us from acting, from engaging other people. So the truth is that I feel very fortunate that I have the opportunity to speak publicly about these issues and my integrity is in what I say within those forums, what I do with those forums. I'm not going to turn down the opportunities of speaking publicly about my beliefs. But I realize that sometimes the only reason why I'm given the opportunity is because I'm a young woman and for five minutes that makes it interesting. I've seen the way a lot of the other women I've been talking about are marginalized because they're a few years older than me so that makes their views somehow less interesting in this media culture. So I am aware of how transient this moment is. In terms of the celebrity stuff, I think that I just try to give interviews responsibly. This is the first interview I've done with a British publication in six months. That's because I came to Britain for one week, I think it was last November, to do some lecturing and there was this flurry of media coverage some of which I was very uncomfortable with, particularly the pin-up revolutionary and all of that, so I just stopped doing interviews in Britain. It's been really easy. Because for me the only reason to do that stuff is just to lead people to the book but they already know about the book now. But for me it's kind of a question of knowing when to stop.

Lyn: And you have your — you publish in *The Guardian*.[6]

Naomi: Yes. Exactly. And I have control over what I say.

Lyn: And you have a serious column, etc. You have a serious column in *The Guardian*.

on the streets of London and in many other locations world-wide. In London hundreds of demonstrators were held by police for several hours in Oxford Street.

6 *The Guardian* is a liberal broadsheet newspaper published in the UK.

Naomi: Right. I try not to play into celebrity culture in the writing I do, to focus on serious content, not be frivolous, or self-obsessed (laugh) — if I can say that, without seeming too self-obsessed. I can, in some ways, control how I'm viewed. I can reject personality profiles, and I have turned down a whole bunch of offers to either do a film or a series or whatever by various British production companies.

Lyn: So do you get a lot of requests for things like personality profiles?

Naomi: I get a lot of requests for those types of interviews. And so — I don't know, it's like an intuitive thing, of knowing when. I feel very lucky that I have a forum in *The Guardian* to write about these issues. Maybe if I didn't it would be more important to me to do interviews and rely on other people to try to get my ideas across. But I feel right now, the book is out there in a far more mainstream way than I ever expected and I have a forum to write about the issues that I care about. So in terms of getting the celebrity stuff under control, and frankly I feel that there was a moment when it was not in control, I can do that by trying to opt out. So people can write about me and compare me with Noreena Hertz — but I'm not participating in that in any way. I'm not part of the discussion — I'm not at the parties, I'm not doing the thing, you know.

Lyn: So that's the way you're conducting it. Exercising your own power. Yes.

Naomi: Yeah. And by trying to challenge the media perception of me as a kind of brand. I don't know what exactly people think they're going to get from me but I think they often don't get what they are looking for. I don't play up a glamour thing, I don't cater to it really. I had the funniest moment with a photographer once, it was in Canada for this magazine and it was an article that was really not about the book, it was about the kind of phenomenon of the book — it made me very uncomfortable. During the photo shoot, the photographer and the journalist wanted to go to the business district and they asked me to kick a building, right, so that would be the pose. (laughing) And it was just so funny, that's why I say I think that I disappoint people when they actually meet me, because I'm not a *Charlie's Angel* activist — and so I just said to these guys, 'Wouldn't it be great if you actually had this *Charlie's Angel* anti-corporate activist? But you actually just have me and I'm not going to kick that building.' So I think I have more control over it.

Lyn: And these are things that happened to famous women. It just reminds me a bit of Simone de Beauvoir and what Toril Moi describes as the 'book reduced to the woman' topos. It seems as if it's more possible to resist now than it was in the 1940s.

Naomi: I could be deluding myself. I can't control the extent to which things take on a life of their own. But I can control my participation and I try to be strategic about what I do and basically my strategy is very simple — I do media interviews when the book comes out in a country, because I do want people to read the book,

I didn't write a book for people not to read it. But in terms of the speaking I do, usually the speeches I do are with activists' groups and they're tied to specific campaigns so there's not any kind of idea that I'm leading people to the promised land, it's more 'I wrote a book about this movement and if you want to get involved, it's right here'.

Lyn: So you're supporting the movements?

Naomi: That's how I am comfortable using the celebrity nonsense. So during the protests in Quebec against a free trade area in the Americas, I set up a bunch of media, and that had nothing to do with me and nothing to do with the book but it was about the free trade area of the Americas. And I'm doing the same thing in Britain this November around the next World Trade Organization round and the general agreement on trade in services. If we're in the middle of a campaign I'll debate anyone, I'll talk to anyone, I'm not going to self-marginalize, and say, 'no, no, no.' There are moments when you try to use media interest to get issues across. I'm certainly not against doing that. So I think it's just a question of managing it. But I'm learning as I go.

70 | celling black bodies: black women in the global prison industrial complex

Julia Sudbury

abstract

The 1980s and 1990s have witnessed an explosion in the population of women prisoners in Europe, North America and Australasia, accompanied by a boom in prison construction. This article argues that this new pattern of women's incarceration has been forged by three overlapping phenomena. The first is the fundamental shift in the role of the state that has occurred as a result of neo-liberal globalization. The second and related phenomenon is the emergence and subsequent global expansion of what has been labelled a 'prison industrial complex' made up of an intricate web of relations between state penal institutions, politicians and profit-driven prison corporations. The third is the emergence of a US-led global war on drugs which is symbiotically related and mutually constituted by the transnational trade in criminalized drugs. These new regimes of accumulation and discipline, I argue, build on older systems of racist and patriarchal exploitation to ensure the super-exploitation of black women within the global prison industrial complex. The article calls for a new anti-racist feminist analysis that explores how the complex matrix of race, class, gender and nationality meshes with contemporary globalized geo-political and economic realities. The prison industrial complex plays a critical role in sustaining the viability of the new global economy and black women are increasingly becoming the raw material that fuels its expansion and profitability. The article seeks to reveal the profitable synergies between drug enforcement, the prison industry, international financial institutions, media and politicians that are sending women to prison in ever increasing numbers.

keywords

war on drugs; globalization; prison industrial complex

(57–74) © 2002 Feminist Review. 0141-7789/02 $15 www.feminist-review.com

introduction

> My mother got twelve years. She's in Foston Hall. They can give people those long sentences
> just for knowing drugs are in the house. He sentenced her to 12 years for knowing. She
> wasn't even involved and he knew that. But he said she knew it was in the country and if
> had got through, she would have benefited from it, from any money. He said one only has to
> read the papers every day to know the trouble it causes once it gets in the pubs and clubs,
> what it does to people... There was a recorder in the cage and she was saying: 'Why did you
> do it?' They convicted her on that (Janet, HMP Holloway).

Janet[1] is an African–Caribbean woman in her mid-twenties serving a seven-year sentence for importation of Class A drugs. She was six months pregnant when she was arrested at Heathrow airport and brought to HMP Holloway, England's oldest and most notorious women's prison. After having her son, she was transferred to the Mother and Baby Unit where I interviewed her. In this 'compassionate' penal environment, designed to punish the mother but not her innocent child, Janet and son are confined to a 6 by 8 foot cell with a bed, toilet and closet from 8pm to 8am. During the day, they have intermittent access to a creche, playroom and roof garden where the baby can breathe fresh air under wire mesh designed to prevent escape attempts. When her son reaches nine months, Janet will be transferred to another unit where she can keep him for a further nine months, at that stage, they will be separated while she serves the remainder of her sentence. While Janet was sentenced to a 'lenient' seven years because of her guilty plea, her mother, who was not involved in the drug trade, was sentenced to 12 years because of her failure to report her daughter to the police.

Janet, her mother and her son represent three generations caught up in an ever expanding network of penal repression and profit that increasingly defies national borders. The past two decades have witnessed dramatic increases in women's incarceration accompanied by expansive prison building programme in Britain as well as the rest of western Europe, North America and Australasia. At the same time, there has been a shift in the nature of confinement as the private prison industry has been embraced by New Labour and Conservatives alike, and the deprivation of liberty has become an extremely profitable enterprise. This article will argue that the explosion in women's incarceration is the hidden face of neo-liberal or 'corporate' globalization and cannot be understood without reference to three overlapping phenomena. The first is the fundamental restructuring of national economies and social welfare provision that has occurred as a result of the globalization of capital. The second and related phenomenon is the emergence and subsequent global expansion of what has been labelled a 'prison industrial complex' made up of an intricate web of relations between state penal institutions, politicians and profit-driven prison corporations. The third is the emergence of a US-led global war on drugs, which is symbiotically related and mutually constituted by the transnational trade in criminalized drugs.[2] These new regimes of accumulation and discipline, I will argue, build on older systems of

1 Between 1999 and 2001 I interviewed 50 women in prisons in England, Canada and the US. All names of women prisoners are pseudonyms.

2 The 'threat' of drugs can be seen to be socially constructed insofar as some drugs with

addictive properties and damaging social consequences including violence and theft (tobacco, alcohol) are sold to the public legally under government license, and others (heroin, cannabis, cocaine) are criminalized. In addition, substances that are illegal in one context (alcohol during Prohibition), may be enjoyed legally in another. Others may be simultaneously legal and illegal (medical marijuana in California). Referring to 'criminalized' rather than 'illegal' drugs reminds us that 'the criminal', like 'the crime' she commits are products of penal regimes that shift over time.

3 Writing about gender and race transnationally generates problems of naming, since racial terms have different meanings depending on location. In this article, I use 'black' as the common term for women of African, Caribbean and Asian origins in Britain only; since 'black' in the US and Canada refers only to women of African descent, I use 'women of colour' to refer to women of African, Asian, Latin American and indigenous communities transnationally. I also use the term 'women of the global south' since this is now widely used by activists to refer to women in what is often, and problematically called 'the Third World'.

racist and patriarchal exploitation to ensure the super-exploitation of black women and women of colour[3] within the global prison industrial complex.

the global boom in women's imprisonment

Since the early 1990s, increases in the prison population in England and Wales have sparked a boom in prison construction, leading commentators to comment on 'the largest prison building program since the middle of the 19th century' (Morgan, 1999: 110). While women make up a small proportion of those incarcerated, their rates of imprisonment have multiplied faster than men's, causing feminist activists to call for drastic measures to counter 'the crisis in women's prisons'.[4] Between 1985 and 1998, for example, the number of women in prison more than doubled, from 1532 to 3260 (Prison Reform Trust, 2000). The prison service has responded by contracting with private corporations to build and operate new prisons, and by re-rolling men's prisons for women. Recent government initiatives designed to slow the increase in the use of incarceration, such as Home Detention Curfews, have had little impact on the number of women sentenced to prison, which continued to grow during the year to April 2001 by 9%, compared to 2% for men.

The British pattern is mirrored elsewhere. In the US, where the prison and jail population reached two million in the year 2000, women's incarceration is also spiralling upwards at a greater pace than that of men. While the number of men in US prisons and jails doubled between 1985 and 1995, women's imprisonment during the same period tripled (Department of Justice, 1998). In 1970, there were 5600 women in federal and state prisons, by 1996, there were 75 000 (Currie, 1998). In Australia, a surging women's prison population, accompanied by pressure from activist organizations, forced the Parliament of New South Wales to commission a Select Committee on the Increase in Prisoner Population (Bacon and Pillemer, 2000). The Select Committee was instructed to investigate a 20% increase in men's and 40% increase in women's incarceration (Parliament of New South Wales, 2001). In Canada, the increase in federally sentenced women prisoners, accompanied by pressure from penal reform organizations, has led to the construction of five new federal prisons for women (Hannah-Moffatt and Shaw, 2000). In Ontario, spiralling numbers of prisoners have fueled the construction of three 1600-bed superjails where a growing women's population will be warehoused within US-style, austere co-ed facilities.

Aggregate rates of increase in prison populations under-represent the impact of the prison boom on black women, women of colour and indigenous women. In all the countries mentioned above, oppressed racialized groups are disproportionately represented. For example, in New South Wales, while all women's imprisonment increased by 40% in five years, aboriginal women's incarceration increased by 70% in only two years. In Canada, aboriginal people comprise 3% of the general population and 12% of federal prisoners, a figure that increases to over 60% in provinces like Saskatchewan and Alberta (Canadian Criminal Justice Association, 2000). African Canadians are also disproportionately policed, prosecuted and incarcerated (Commission on Systemic Racism in the Ontario Criminal Justice System, 1994). In the US, Latinas and African-American women make up 60% of the female prison population. And despite their small numbers in the population, Native Americans are ten times more likely than whites to be imprisoned (Rojas, 1998). Finally, 12% of women prisoners in England and Wales are African–Caribbean British passport holders[5] compared to 1% of the general population (Elkins et al., 2001). In addition, British prisons hold numerous women from West Africa, the Caribbean and Latin America, either as immigration detainees, or serving sentences for drug importation. The crisis of women's prisons can therefore be read as a crisis for black women and women of colour worldwide.

the emergence of the prison industrial complex

Activist-intellectuals in the US have traced the emergence of what has been labelled the 'prison industrial complex' to the economic transformations of the 1970s (Davis, 1998; Goldberg and Evans, 1998). As advances in technology enabled corporations to transport information and capital between distant geographic locations in fractions of a second, new forms of globalized capital began to appear. US-based corporations downsized their unionized Western workforces and relocated manufacturing operations to locations in the global south where labour was cheap and labour and environmental protections minimal. Multinational trade agreements such as NAFTA and GATT and the establishment of Free Trade Zones hastened the process, opening the doors to the unhindered super-exploitation of predominantly young women of colour from Tijuana to Manila. The impact of massive downsizing in the US on urban African-American and Latino communities was catastrophic. Redlining and racist violence had kept African-Americans and Latinos out of the 1950s suburbanization drive that had allowed many working class white families to move out of the inner cities, restricting the former to urban ghettos where they were warehoused with few opportunities for mobility (Oliver and Shapiro, 1995). As job cuts hit these communities, they were devastated by pandemic rates of unemployment, a declining tax base and resultant cuts in social, welfare, educational and medical provision. The result: spiralling rates of poverty, drug addiction, violence and social dislocation. These conditions were not met passively. The Black Liberation Army, Black Panthers, Young Lords, Chicano Power and American Indian movement were the organized voice of the resistance that sprung from these oppressive conditions. However, these movements encountered brutal repression and criminalization. The FBI's Counter Intelligence Program (COINTELPRO) identified the Black Panthers as THE number one threat to the security of the US and targeted activists such as Assata Shakur, Pam Africa

4 'The Crisis in Women's Prisons', Press Release, Leeds Metropolitan University, April 7, 1999 http// www.lmu.ac.uk/ news/press/archive/ apr99/prisons.htm.

5 British officials have changed the way in which they report ethnic origin in order to downplay the number of black women and men in prison. By excluding non-British passport-holders, the Home Office Research Development Statistics unit has 'reduced' the proportion of African Caribbean women prisoners by 51% to 12% of prisoners, compared to 1% of the general population (Elkins et al., 2001). However, this is revealed to be a sleight of hand if one considers the large number of black British residents who hold 'commonwealth' passports.

and Angela Y. Davis for neutralization via trumped up charges, massively publicized manhunts and incarceration in maximum security institutions (Churchill, 1990). The scene had therefore been set for the mass criminalization of African-Americans, Native Americans and Latinos. In the white imagination, black protest was synonymous with lawlessness and violence. While overt Jim Crow racism had waning public acceptance in this post-Civil Rights era of Martin Luther Kingesque integrationist policies, criminalization provided a new camouflaged racist language in which code words such as 'criminal', 'drug dealer' and 'welfare queen' could be used to refer obliquely to the racialized 'enemy within' (Davis, 1998: 66). *Criminalization therefore became the weapon of choice in dealing with the social problems caused by the globalization of capital and the protest it engendered.*

Joel Dyer argues that three components make up the 'perpetual prisoner machine' that transforms criminalized populations in the US into fodder for the prison system and has caused the prison population in the US to increase ten-fold in 20 years (Dyer, 2000). The first is the consolidation of large media corporations that rely on violent and crime-oriented content to grab ratings and that have created a dramatic rise in the fear of crime in the US population at large. The second is the increasing use of polling and market research by politicians to align their platforms with 'popular' views about policy areas, leading to 'tough on crime' rhetoric on both sides of the electoral spectrum. This rhetoric is translated into policies such as mandatory minimums, truth-in-sentencing and three strikes that cause more people to serve prison sentences, for longer terms, and leads to spiralling prison populations. The third is the intervention of private prison corporations such as Wackenhut Corporation and Corrections Corporation of America, which provide a way for governments to expand their prison estate without having to spend the initial capital cost of prison construction. The mutually profitable relationship between private corporations and public criminal justice systems enables politicians to mask the enormous cost of their tough-on-crime policies by sidestepping the usual process of asking the electorate to vote for 'prison bonds' to raise funds to build publicly operated prisons. Instead, they can simply reallocate revenue funds from welfare, health or education into contracts with privately run-for-profit prisons. Since the 1980s, the private sector has allowed prison building to continue, even where public coffers have been exhausted by the prison construction boom. It has been rewarded with cheap land, tax breaks and discounts in sewage and utilities charges, making prison companies a major beneficiary of corporate welfare. These three components constitute the 'political and economic chain reaction' that we have come to know as the prison industrial complex: *a symbiotic and profitable relationship between politicians, corporations, the media and state correctional institutions that generates the racialized use of incarceration as a response to social problems rooted in the globalization of capital.*

the PIC goes global

Although the prison industrial complex (PIC) emerged in the US, the past 15 years have witnessed its transformation into a global phenomenon. Multinational prison corporations have fueled this expansion through an aggressive strategy of pursuing foreign markets through sophisticated marketing techniques. Targeting British politicians has proven particularly fruitful. During the 1980s, Labour and Conservative politicians were invited to the US for tours of flagship private prisons where the new steel and glass buildings and latest technological advances in surveillance appeared to offer a striking advance over Britain's decaying penal estate. The glossy rhetoric of the 'new corrections' where prisoners were called 'residents', prison guards 'supervisors' and cells 'rooms' was favourably compared to the brutal and dehumanizing prison culture in Britain that had long proved resistant to reform. Prior to this time, both sides of the House of Commons were opposed to prison privatization. Politicians tended to view the denial of freedom as too serious an undertaking to be entrusted to private interests and subjected to the vagaries of the profit motive. However, these carefully orchestrated visits led to a sea-change. As Sir Edward Gardner, Chair of the all-party penal affairs group commented after a visit to the US in 1986: 'We thought it was stunning. These places didn't feel like prisons and didn't smell like prisons. There was nothing we could find to criticize.' (Young, 1987: 3).

In 1987, a Home Affairs Select Committee visited four adult and juvenile jails run by the Corrections Corporation of America and the Radio Corporation of America. The Select Committee subsequently recommended that corporations should be invited to bid for contracts to build and manage custodial institutions, initially as an experiment. A key to the recommendation was that privatization would *dramatically accelerate* the prison-building program, which was hindered by lack of public funds (Speller, 1996). Gradually, key British politicians and administrators were won over to the possibilities for cost cutting, modernization and prison expansion offered by the corporate agenda. Privatization was presented as a panacea to the problems facing the prison service: overcrowding, old buildings, high annual costs, resistance to reform and a rigid prison guard culture reinforced by the powerful Prison Officers Association. Between 1991 and 1994 the mutually profitable relationship between Conservative politicians and the prison industry culminated in a series of Acts which allowed for corporations to design, construct, manage and finance new prisons and to bid to operate existing prisons. By 1997, when New Labour came to power, Britain had become a profitable location for multinational prison corporations, producing revenues of over £95 million for the five leading private incarcerators, Premier Prison Services (a joint venture of Wackenhut and Sodexho), Wackenhut (UK) Ltd., UK Detention Services (a joint venture of Corrections Corporation of America and Sodexho), Securicor, and Group 4 (Prison Privatisation Report International, 1998a; Sudbury, 2000). Although Labour had condemned the Conservative privatization programme, pre-election promises to return prisons to the public sector were short lived (Prison

Privatisation Report International, 1996). Within a year of election, Home Secretary Jack Straw announced that privately run prisons would only return to the public sector if the latter could outbid their private competitors, and that new prisons would be built under the Private Finance Initiative (Prison Privatisation Report International, 1998b).

While Wackenhut Corporation, Corrections Corporation of America and others have reaped enormous profits in the US since the 1980s, their profits have recently been compromised. A radical popular prison movement, and a series of high profile legal cases have pushed the US prison industry into a period of crisis as shares go into freefall.[6] Critical Resistance, the Prison Moratorium Project and the Black Radical Congress' 'Education not Incarceration' campaign have mobilized popular support and media coverage in questioning the logic of ever increasing incarceration. At the same time, private prisons corporations have proven vulnerable to the 'Jena' effect, whereby a case of malpractice turns the tide of popular and political sentiment and corporations are left with legal costs and empty facilities due to cancelled contracts.[7] Potentially damaging incidents of prisoner abuse, sexual assault, violence and protests are generated by the very conditions that make prisons profitable: low paid non-unionized staff, low staffing ratios and sparse provision of activities for prisoners (Yeoman, 2000). Although corporations engage in a process of damage limitation, whereby they seek to suppress public knowledge about such incidents, close scrutiny by prison activists has severely limited their ability to do so. As domestic profits come under threat, foreign operations play a key role in maintaining corporate viability. New prisons in Marchington, Olney and Peterborough therefore play an important role in maintaining the viability of the multinational prison industry as it seeks new markets in South Africa and further afield (Martin, 2001). Women and men serving time in British prisons thus fuel stock market profits from London to New York, reinforcing the logic of incarceration with the logic of capitalist accumulation.

6 Between 1998 and 2000, Corrections Corporation of America (aka Prison Realty) shares fell from $40 to $2, Wackenhut shares fell from $30 to $9 (Martin, 2001).

7 In September 2000, the State of Louisiana agreed in federal court to cease contracting with privately run juvenile facilities after an investigation found that boys in Wackenhut's Jena facility had been abused with pepper spray and tear gas and denied basic needs from underwear to food (Martin, 2001).

the war on drugs wages war on women

> With the entering of the New Year, I want to give you the gift of vision, to see this system of Modern Day Slavery for what it is. The government gets paid $25,000 a year by you (taxpayers) to house me (us). The more of us that they incarcerate, the more money they get from you to build more prisons. The building of more prisons create more jobs. The federal prison system is comprised of 61% drug offenders, so basically this war on drugs is the reason why the Prison Industrial Complex is a skyrocketing enterprise.
>
> (Smith, 1999)

In 2000, two African-American women were among the prisoners granted clemency by outgoing President Clinton. Dorothy Gaines and Kemba Smith's cases had been highlighted by organizations including Families Against Mandatory Minimums, the

Kemba Smith Justice Project and the Million Woman March as evidence of the egregious injustices occurring as a result of the 'war on drugs' and the particular impact on women. Kemba Smith's case in particular attained national attention and was widely reported in the mainstream press.[8] Kemba was a student at Hampton College, a traditionally black college in Virginia. She became involved with a young man, Khalif Hall, who, unknown to her, was a key figure in a large drug operation. Kemba stayed with Hall despite abuse and threats to kill her because she was afraid for her family and herself and because she had become pregnant. Shortly before the drug ring was apprehended, Hall was shot and killed. Kemba pleaded guilty to conspiracy to distribute crack cocaine, but hoped Hall's abusive behaviour would be taken into account. Instead, she was held responsible for the full 255 kilos involved in the offense, although she personally was not found to have handled the drugs, and was sentenced to 24.5 years in prison. Kemba, like Janet and her mother (above) have been targeted by a transnational war on drugs that emerged in the mid 1980s in the United States and has since been aggressively exported around the globe. While the shadowy figure of the drug dealer or trafficker tends to be envisioned in the popular media as male, increasingly women are the low level 'footsoldiers' within the transnational drug trade who are most vulnerable to arrest and punishment.

The current war on drugs was announced by Ronald Reagan in the early 1980s and formalized in the 1986 Anti Drug Abuse Act. The Act made a critical break with the concept of drug users as a medical population in need of treatment, and instead targeted them as a criminal population. It also utilized the erroneous assumption that users would be deterred from their habit and dealers and traffickers incapacitated by punitive and extensive use of penal sanctions. By removing those involved in the criminalized drug trade from the streets for long periods of time, it was assumed, syndicates would be severely damaged in their ability to get drugs to the streets.[9] Since 'liberal' judges could not be trusted to hand down sufficient sentences to deter and incapacitate those involved in the drug trade, the Act removed discretion and imposed mandatory minimum sentences. Thus treatment programmes and community service were effectively barred in cases involving drugs, and sentence length related not to the role of the defendant in the offense, but to the weight and purity of drugs involved. In the US, African-American women and Latinas are disproportionately affected by mandatory minimums. Since the only way a lesser sentence can be given is in cases where the defendant provides 'substantial assistance' in the prosecution of another person, women, who tend to be in subordinate positions within drug syndicates and thus have little access to information are usually unable to make such an agreement. The crack-cocaine disparity also feeds the disproportionate impact on women of colour. The mandatory minimum sentence for crack cocaine is one hundred times harsher for crack than for powder cocaine. Since crack is cheaper, and has flooded poor inner city neighbourhoods, African-Americans and Latinos receive disproportionate

8 Kemba Smith's case is a composite of factors which make her both representative of and different from the majority of women incarcerated as a result of the war on drugs. As an African-American woman, young mother and victim of domestic violence, she is typical enough to become a symbol of the anti-war on drugs campaign. As a middle-class, articulate student, she is clearly untypical, yet her class status strengthens the message to 'middle America', that this could happen to 'your daughter'.

9 This has not been the case, instead, criminalization and targeting by law enforcement artificially inflate the price of drugs, so that manufacturing, trafficking and selling them become immensely profitable and increasingly associated with violence. This mutually profitable relationship between law enforcement and the drug trade has been labelled the 'international drug complex' (Van Der Veen, 2000).

sentences when compared with white powder cocaine users and dealers (Waters, 1998).

While the war on drugs has had a dramatic impact on US communities of colour, it has reached far beyond US borders.[10] From the mid-1980s, the war on drugs increasingly played a key role in US foreign policy decisions as the Reagan and Bush administrations pushed a US drug agenda on the global community. Initial efforts focused on the G7 countries as the Reagan administration used US economic clout to push for international compliance with US drug policy. In 1988, the Toronto Summit endorsed a US-proposed taskforce, which in turn led to the 1988 United Nations Convention Against Illicit Traffic in Narcotic Drugs and Psychotropic Substances (Friman, 1996). The Convention contained a number of controversial conditions that ran counter to the policies of other member states. By requiring states to criminalize drug cultivation, possession and purchase for personal use, maximize the use of criminal sanctions and deterrence and limit early release and parole in drug-related cases, the Vienna Convention represented the transnational spread of the US punitive 'law and order' agenda (Albrecht, 2001). By signing the Convention, member states signed onto the logic of incarceration, pledging to use criminal justice sanctions in place of medical or social solutions and turning decisively away from legalization.[11] By the mid-1990s, Canada, Australia, New Zealand, Taiwan, South and Central America, the Caribbean and African countries including Nigeria and South Africa were fully fledged partners in the US-driven transnational war on drugs.

The Americanization of drug policy is evident in the British approach to criminalized drug use, trafficking and retail. While the 'British System' of prescribing heroin or methadone to addicts, dating to the 1920s, indicates a medical approach to drug use, it exists uneasily alongside recent developments that draw on the US model of criminalization and incarceration. UN conventions are not the only way in which US drug policy is exported abroad. Indeed, British politicians on both sides of the house have 'gratefully accepted and sometimes sought' the 'benevolence, advice, influence and leadership' of the US on drug matters (Bean, 2001: 90). US–British synergy on drug policy comes about as a result of exchanges of research findings, fact-finding missions to the US by politicians and administrators, international conferences and visits by 'specialists' to Britain. An infamous case involves Drug Enforcement agent Robert Stutman's 1988 visit to Britain. Addressing the Assistant Chief Police Officers Conference, Stutman 'scared the hell' out of the participants with his apocalyptic visions of the crack epidemic in the US and its inevitable migration to Europe as the US market became saturated. Stutman's account was based on an unpublished report and anecdotal evidence. Nevertheless, a 1989 Home Affairs Committee Report echoed Stutman's unsubstantiated argument that there is 'no such person as a fully recovered crack addict' and that crack, by its very nature, called for a penal, rather than a medical response (Bean, 2001). Stutman's presentation had

10 In Latin America, the war on drugs has been a military war. Since 1989, Colombia has seen deployment of US military personnel, financial assistance for policing, provision of attack helicopters and weaponry to assist in the fight against 'narcoterrorists'. This fight has been closely associated with counter-insurgency measures against left wing guerillas such as the FARC and ELN and has thus fuelled a bitter civil war. US counter-drug measures have also included spraying of crops with herbicides including Agent Green, which indigenous groups claim has destroyed the rainforest and polluted the water table. For the impact of the war on drugs on Colombian women, see Sudbury (2001).

11 Although Dutch coffee shops selling cannabis and the British practice of prescribing to heroin addicts have gone largely unaffected by the 1988 Convention, they are in opposition to and theoretically threatened by its provisions.

immediate and racialized effects. From the late 1980s, the press ran reports of crack infiltrating British cities. Crack became a foreign threat, an enemy brought into Britain by Yardies, with African–Caribbean communities as the Trojan Horse enabling the foreign infiltration. As a result, resources were pumped into law enforcement activities such as Operation Dalehouse and the Crack Intelligence Coordinating Unit, specifically to increase the surveillance and policing of black communities. Coinciding with the entrenchment of 'Fortress Europe', the crack threat was also a justification for a heightened suspicion of black British women and men entering Britain after vacations abroad, as well as Caribbean nationals entering to visit family and friends. With such targeted policing and customs attention, the numbers of African–Caribbean women and men apprehended for possession, sales and importation of both class A and lesser drugs increased dramatically. In some instances, retail of crack was largely inspired by police operations and protection of informants, as is the case in a northern city where a senior police officer admitted that undercover police buyers stimulated demand that disappeared once the police operation was over (Joyce 1998). While the belief that Britain was on the verge of a US-style 'crack epidemic' was found by the mid-1990s to be a 'media inspired panic' (Joyce, 1998: 181), the pattern of targeted surveillance has continued unabated. As public funds are poured into the high-tech policing of black suspects, a self-fulfilling cycle is generated whereby increased arrests in the black community reinforce the public fear of African–Caribbean drug dealers and traffickers, legitimate the continuation of racially discrepant policing practices and generate additional resources for the police.[12] The impact on black women has been devastating. While in 1980, 4.4% of women serving time in prisons in England and Wales were incarcerated on drug-related offenses, by 2001 that figure had risen to 39% (HMSO, 1982; Elkins et al., 2001). Between April 2000 and April 2001 alone, the number of women sentenced to prison as a result of the war on drugs grew by 20% (Elkins et al., 2001).

As the risk of apprehension at Heathrow, Toronto or New York increases, drug syndicates find it increasingly profitable to use black women and women of colour as low level 'mules' to carry drugs through customs. Women are seldom involved in the planning and organization of drug trafficking, nor are they party to the large profits involved (Harper and Murphy, 1999). Male dealers may believe that women will be less likely to come under suspicion of carrying drugs and more likely to receive lenient sentencing if they are apprehended. However, black women are not the recipients of such chivalrous behaviour, since they do not fall under the benevolent patriarchal protection of the white men who judge them. Nicole, a 29-year-old black British woman incarcerated with her daughter at HMP Holloway explained:

> The judge when he sentenced me said he's going to use me as an example. Because he knows I've been set up, but he has to give a message the world: 'Don't bring drugs'. He used me as an example because he knew I was pregnant. I was set up by a friend of mine, if you

12 In winter 2000, the Metropolitan Police received £800,000 to carry out Operation Crackdown, targeting low level dealers of crack and class A drugs on council estates in boroughs with large black populations. The operation led to surveillance of 700 private properties, over 80 raids and 1000 arrests ('1000 arrested in London Class A drugs offensive', Press release, Metropolitan Police 01/03/2001). An evaluation of the operation found that it had 'little discernible impact' on London's crack trade, which quickly adapted to meet continuing demand (Rose 2001).

can call him that. And they knew that. But still he said that's why they're using women to bring drugs to the country because they think that the system is not going to be as hard on women as on male prisoners. He said that's not the case.

The women I interviewed became involved in the transnational drug trade through three paths: economic need, threats and coercion, and deception. Faced with poverty and often without a second income to support the family, many women make the choice to risk carrying drugs, sometimes believing it will be a one-off. Interviewees often had specific financial goals, such as an emergency medical bill, or school fees for a son or daughter. Marta, a Jamaican mother of four serving a five-year sentence at HMP Winchester explained:

> They do it mainly for the kids, to support the kids. You have a mother who has four or five kids, two is very sickly, every time she visit the hospital or the doctor, you have to pay to register, you have to pay for medicine, you have to pay for an X-ray. Everything costs money. So anything comes up they're going to jump at it, the easiest way to make money.

Marta is typical of women who import out of economic necessity. Knowing little about the punitive criminal justice system that awaited her in Britain, she took a calculated risk based on the limited options available for her to ensure the survival of herself and her children:

> I was self employed doing a bit of selling. I was married but my husband wasn't supportive after sending the kids to school and the money kept going down. I never knew nothing much about drugs, the only form of drugs I know is ganja, we call it weed. That's the only hard drugs I've known of in my life until I come here. And I was just asked by somebody to carry some baggage for $100 000 Jamaican dollars and I just jump at it, thought it could really help out. They said there is no risk involved, they make it look so easy, just carry the drugs and collect your money and that's it and come back. They didn't show me the possibility that I could get caught, just do it.

While Marta was not told explicitly that she was importing drugs, the fee involved made it evident to her that the package was illegal. In contrast, Maureen, a middle class North Londoner of Jamaican ancestry and mother of six was unaware of the contents of her luggage. While on a visit to her father in Jamaica, she was approached by an acquaintance who asked her to carry coconuts, rum and cans of coconut cream to England. She was apprehended at customs and cocaine was found in the cans:

> I'm so embarrassed. I haven't told no-one. I keep going over in my head, what have I done wrong? What happened? Was I set up? Was I being duped? I don't know what happened to me. I told them the truth and they didn't believe me. I know so many people who lie to them and they get off, they get a few years. Its not fair. And then again the jury was all white and it was a verdict of 10 to 2.

Maureen's case, she believes, was exacerbated by a customs officer who mistook her for another detainee and stated that she was carrying £9500, rather than the few hundred pounds she actually had with her. In the face of racialized stereotypes of African—Caribbean drug traffickers, Maureen's class status is erased. She is processed through the criminal justice system as 'just another' courier, found guilty by a predominantly white jury and given a mandatory minimum sentence.

While it may be tempting to draw a bold line between guilt and innocence in these two cases, the reality of women's involvement in importation is far more blurred. In many instances, importing was part of a complex emotional relationship between a male dealer or trafficker, often himself a minor player in the drug trade, and a lover/partner/'mule'. Diane, a biracial Canadian 25-year-old, is serving the second half of a five-year sentence for importation at the Elizabeth Fry halfway house in Toronto. As a young woman, Diane left home and moved into a women's shelter because of her abusive relationship with her father. While she was there, she entered into a relationship with a Grenadan man who was subsequently arrested for drug dealing. While he was incarcerated, Diane visited him regularly and he discussed marriage with her. Shortly after his release, she gave up her job and started importing drugs for him, not knowing at the time that his previous courier had been arrested and incarcerated. She was not paid in cash for the trips she made, but occasionally, he would buy her expensive gifts such as jewelry and a computer:

> He looked at it this way, he was paying the rent, he was paying for the food, he was paying the bills, if I needed anything I'd ask him for it. If I needed a new pair of shoes. But it was hard for me to ask him for anything because I don't like asking anybody for anything. I never got any money.

Diane and her partner were married before she was finally arrested and incarcerated at Grand Valley State, Kitchener. During the first few days of her sentence, she met the first courier and also learned that her husband had already moved in with another girlfriend. Nevertheless, she refused to trade information for a shorter sentence out of loyalty and respect for his paternal role:

> I had been told don't implicate him because he's still on parole, so he'd do more time than I would, because he'd go back to jail to finish the remainder of his sentence, plus a new charge. So I figure I can't do that to him because I'd be taking the kids away from their father. And altogether I was with him for $7\frac{1}{2}$ years.

Diane's case illustrates the complex web of emotion, economics and abuse that often draw women into criminalized activities. In her study of battered African American women, Beth Richie argues that 'gender entrapment' best describes the way in which black women are incarcerated due to their involvement with a coercive and violent male (Richie, 1996). While Diane was not subjected to physical violence, her partner's controlling behaviour in relation to the money that she generated through importation, the deception with regard to his other girlfriends, and his apparently cynical use of marriage as a means of controlling her labour form a web of abuse and exploitation. By controlling the labour of his 'stable of mules' through promises of love and commitment, Diane's partner generates wealth for himself without either taking the personal risk of importation, or paying the going rate of several thousand dollars per trip. This web of economic/ emotional exploitation was a factor in the stories of many of the women I interviewed. As Marta explained:

> Men do it [import], but they tend to prey on the women more. Because they know that the woman in Jamaica, they care for their family, especially their kids. They would do anything to make sure their kids is looked after. So they mainly prey on the woman, especially single woman. You have men do it, but the number isn't as large as the woman.

Women's subordinate role in heterosexual relationships and their role as the primary and often sole carers of children combine to devalue their labour in the drug trade. The low value of women's labour in the drug trade is demonstrated by the women I interviewed who reported being 'set up' as decoys so that their arrest would distract customs officials from a larger shipment coming through. Paid anywhere from zero to a few thousand pounds for carrying a shipment worth upwards of £100 000, women form a cheap and replaceable army of labourers. As one is incarcerated, another, like Diane, quickly fills her place.

the global feminization and racialization of poverty

While transnational drug policies play an important role in channelling women of colour into prisons from Cape Town to Toronto, women are not without agency and do, of course, make choices within the options available to them. As the global economy has been transformed, however, these options have become increasingly limited. In the global south, this economic transformation has driven a shift in the role of the state. Firstly, governments have been formed to scale down their role as providers of a social-welfare fabric as international financial institutions have driven neo-liberal economic reform. In Jamaica, policies introduced since the mid-1980s by the Jamaican Labour Party working closely with the US, IMF and World Bank, have led to cutbacks in public sector employment, the scaling back of local government services, health and education, increases in the cost of public utilities as state-owned companies are sold to the private sector and a dramatic decline in real wages. Such cuts hit women particularly hard as they carry the burden of caring for children and sick or elderly relatives (Harrison, 1991). Marta's experience exemplifies the increasing economic pressures facing women:

> Things in Jamaica is very expensive. Its hard for a single woman with kids, especially anywhere over three kids, to get by without a good support or a steady job. It doesn't mean that I didn't have an income. I did have an income, but having four kids and an ex-husband who doesn't really care much. I had to keep paying school fees and the money kept going down. I did need some kind of support. That's why I did what I did. We don't get child

support in Jamaica, three-quarters of the things that this country offers for mothers here we don't have it. This country gives you a house, they give you benefits, we get nothing in Jamaica. We have to pay for hospital, not even education is free. Primary school used to be free under one government hand, but under another government it has been taken away. You're talking about high school, you're talking about fifteen up to twenty thousand dollars a term, for one kid to go to high school. Its difficult in Jamaica.

Secondly, while the state has cut back its role in social welfare, it has stepped up its role in subsidizing foreign and domestic capital. Free Trade Zones established in Kingston, Montego Bay and elsewhere offer foreign garment, electronic and communications companies equipped factory space, tax exemptions, a cheap female workforce and, for the busy executive, weekends of sun, sea and sand.[13] Foreign-owned agribusiness and mining companies have also been encouraged, displacing traditional subsistence farming and causing migration from rural areas to the cities, which now account for 50% of the Jamaican population. As the economy has shifted, women working in the informal economy as farmers and 'higglers' find themselves unable to keep up with the rising costs of survival. While younger women may find employment in the tourist industry as maids, entertainers or prostitutes, or within the Free Trade Zones assembling clothes or computers for Western markets, working class women in their thirties and older have fewer options. Even where these women do find employment, low wages, driven down by multinational corporations in search of ever greater profit margins and kept low by governments unwilling to set a living minimum wage for fear of losing foreign investment, mean that they cannot earn a sufficient income to support their families. The failure of the legal economy to provide adequate means for women's survival is the key incentive for those who chose to enter the drug trade as couriers.

The feminization of poverty in the global south is mirrored by conditions among black people and communities of colour in the West. As Naomi Klein argues, the flight of manufacturing jobs from the West to the global south has led to the Macdonaldization of jobs in North America and Europe, with part-time, casual, low-wage jobs the norm in the new service and 'homeworker' economies (Klein, 2001). At the same time, successive governments, whether espousing compassionate conservativism or the 'third way', have pursued market-led economic reforms which have dramatically reduced public services, introduced widespread privatization and raised the cost of living. The result is the disenfranchisement of working class and black communities and black women in particular as the state sheds its social welfare responsibilities. In Britain, as in the US and Canada, this has entailed a dramatic reform of welfare, and the targeting of single mothers in particular as a drain on the public purse. It is this impoverishment that acts as the motor to women's involvement within the retail end of the drug trade and their subsequent targeting by the criminal justice systems of these countries. Working class women, and in particular women of

13 'Jamaica: Island of Opportunity' www.vega-media.com/ jamaica/ Jamaica.html

colour therefore bear the brunt of both the punitive and economic regimes of neo-liberal globalization. The devaluation of their labour within the criminalized economy of the international drug trade is closely interrelated to their superexploitation within the formal sectors of the global economy (the Free Trade Zones and minimum wage tourism and service sectors). Both are made possible by the radical feminization and racialization of poverty that is an essential part, rather than an unfortunate offshoot, of the corporate maximization of profits in the global arena.

conclusion: towards resistance

As the new millennium ushers in an era of unchecked capital accumulation and massive and widening divides between information-rich elites and disenfranchised majorities, feminists and anti-racists need to respond by infusing our praxis with the new politics. The new social movements of the 21st century are more likely to be found shutting down Niketown in San Francisco or battling the WTO in Seattle than at a take back the night rally or consultative meeting on institutional racism. While women of the global south and disenfranchised communities of the north have been active in vibrant anti-globalization protests, feminist scholars have been slower to identify corporate globalization as central to their concerns. Gradually, a body of knowledge is being developed that can serve as a valuable resource for feminist and anti-racist organizers as well as anti-globalization activists. Research into sex tourism, the trafficking of women, women as workers in the Free Trade Zones and homeworkers in the garment industry and women in the global food chain have all demonstrated the centrality of black women and women of colour to the new global regimes of accumulation (Kempadoo, 1999; Phizacklea, 1990; Shiva, 2001; Ching Yoon Louie, 2001). Less attention has been paid to the repressive penal regimes that underpin these processes. The prison-like conditions under which women labour in the Free Trade Zones, with restricted access to restrooms, forced overtime and punitive sanctions for union activities and pregnancy, have generated considerable outrage among researchers and activists alike (Klein, 2001). The confinement of increasing numbers of women in the prisons and jails of the global north, where they are subject to separation, sometimes permanent, from children, sexual abuse, medical neglect and forced labour has, however, been muted.

Perhaps the explanation for this muted response lies in a failure to connect women's incarceration to the social, economic and environmental concerns generated by the new global economy. The prison has traditionally served the purpose of separating those who have 'offended' from the social body politic. Prisoners are therefore seen as 'criminals' whose behaviour is qualitatively different from that of 'normal' people and must therefore be analysed using different tools, hence the existence of criminology as a distinct discipline. Yet if the complex web that has led to the massive increases in women's (and men's) imprisonment documented in this article is to be understood and challenged, prisons must be liberated from the criminologists and criminal justice professionals, and brought under the scrutiny of anti-globalization, feminist and anti-racist scholars and activists. Prisons serve a vital role in suppressing dissent and invisibilizing disenfranchised populations. They therefore maintain the viability of corporate globalization and mask its devastating effects on global majority communities. Prisons also play a direct role in capital accumulation since their operation generates profit for corporations engaged in building, equipping and operating them as well as those employing prisoners as cheap labour. Increasingly, black women and women of colour are the raw material that fuel the prison industrial complex: as scapegoats of tough-on-crime rhetoric, targets of drug busting operations that generate millions for police, customs and military budgets, or workers sewing and assembling electronics in prison workshops. There is a need for a new anti-racist feminism that will explore how the complex matrix of race, class, gender and nationality meshes with contemporary globalized geo-political and economic realities. It must be transnational in scope and womanist in its integrated analysis of gender—race—class and in locating black women and women of colour at the centre. As the gendered and racialized bodies that turn prison cells into profit margins, women of colour play a vital role in the global prison industrial complex. As activists, inside and outside of the prison walls, we are a critical part of the forces that are challenging its parasitic existence. The challenge for scholars and activists alike is to make visible the women hidden behind prison walls and to dismantle the profitable synergies between drug enforcement, the prison industry, international financial institutions, media and politicians that are celling black women in ever increasing numbers.

author biography

Julia Sudbury is Associate Professor of Ethnic Studies at Mills College, Oakland, USA, and author of *Other Kinds of Dreams: Black Women's Organizations and the Politics of Transformation* (Routledge 1998). She was formerly director of Sia, a national development agency for the black voluntary sector based in London and coordinator of Osaba Women's Center in Coventry.

references

Albrecht, H.J. (2001) 'The international system of drug control: developments and trends' in J. Gerber, and E. Hensen (2001) editors, *Drug War, American Style: The Internationalization of Failed Policy and Its Alternatives,* New York and London: Garland Publishing.

Bacon, W. and Pillemer, T. (2000) 'Violence blamed as women fill prison', *Sydney Morning Herald,* www.smh.com.au/news/001/08/national/national1.html, January 8, 2000.

Bean, P. (2001) 'American influence on British drug policy' in J. Gerber, and E. Hensen (2001) editors, *Drug War, American Style: The Internationalization of Failed Policy and Its Alternatives*, New York and London: Garland Publishing.

Canadian Criminal Justice Association (2000) *Aboriginal Peoples and the Criminal Justice System*, Ottawa.

Ching Yoon Louie, M. (2001) *Sweatshop Warriors: Immigrant Women Workers Take on the Global Factory*, Cambridge, MA: Southend Press.

Churchill, W. (1990) *Cointelpro Papers: Documents from the FBIs Secret Wars Against Domestic Dissent*, Boston: South End Press.

Commission on System Racism in the Ontario Criminal Justice System (1994) *Racism Behind Bars*, Toronto: Queens Printers.

Currie, E. (1998) *Crime and Punishment* in America, New York: Henry Holt and Co.

Davis, A.Y. (1998) 'Race and criminalization: black Americans and the punishment industry' in J. James (1998) editor, *The Angela Y. Davis Reader*, Malden, MA: Blackwell Publishers.

Dyer, J. (2000) *The Perpetual Prisoner Machine: How America Profits from Crime*, Boulder, CO: Westview Press.

Department of Justice (1998) Women in Criminal Justice: A Twenty Year Update, http://www.usdoj.gov/reports/98Guide/wcjc98/execsumm.htm, accessed July 13, 2001.

Elkins, M., Gray, C., and Rogers, K. (2001) *Prison Population Brief England and Wales April 2001*, London: Home Office Research Development Statistics.

Friman, H.R. (1996) *Narcodiplomacy: Exporting the US War on Drugs*, Ithaca and London: Cornell University Press.

Goldberg, E., Evans, L. (1998) *The Prison Industrial Complex and the Global Economy*, Berkeley, CA: Agit Press.

Hannah-Moffatt, K. Shaw, M. (2000) *An Ideal Prison?: Critical Essays on Women's Imprisonment in Canada*, Halifax: Fernwood Publishing.

Harper, R., Murphy, R. (1999) *Drug Smuggling: an analysis of the traffickers 1991–1997*, London: Middlesex Probation Service.

Harrison, F.V. (1991) 'Women in Jamaica's urban informal economy' in C.T. Mohanty, R. Ann and T. Lourdes (1991) editors, *Third World Women and the Politics of Feminism*, IN, USA: Indiana University Press.

HMSO (1982) *Prison Statistics England and Wales 1980*, London: HMSO.

Joyce, E. (1998) 'Cocaine trafficking and British foreign policy' in E. Joyce and M. Carlos (1998) editors, *Latin America and the Multinational Drug Trade*, Basingstoke: MacMillan Press.

Kempadoo, K. (1999) editor, *Sun, Sex and Gold*, New York: Rowman and Littlefield Publishing.

Klein, N. (2001) *No Logo: Taking Aim at the Brand Bullies*, Toronto: Vintage Canada.

Martin, W. (2001) 'Privatizing prisons from the USA to SA: controlling dangerous Africans across the Atlantic' *ACAS Bulletin*, Winter, No. 59, http://acas.prairienet.org/Wackenhutv5.htm.

Morgan, R. (1999) 'New Labour "law and order" politics and the House of Commons Home Affairs Committee Report on alternatives to prison sentences' *Punishment and Society*, July 1, No. 1.

Oliver, M., Shapiro, T. (1995) *Black Wealth, White Wealth: a New Perspective on Racial Inequality*, London and New York: Routledge.

Parliament of New South Wales (2001) Select Committee on the Increase in Prisoner Population, www.parliament.nsw.gov.au, accessed July 4.

Phizacklea, A. (1990) *Unpacking the Fashion Industry: Gender, Racism and Class in Production*, London and New York: Routledge.

Prison Privatisation Report International (1996) 'Labour to Halt New Private Prisons', London: Prison Reform Trust. June.

Prison Privatisation Report International (1998a) *'UK profits'*, Nov/Dec.

Prison Privatisation Report International (1998b) *'Labour's prison U-turn complete'*, June.

Prison R.T. (2000). *Justice For Women: The Need for Reform*, London: Prison Reform Trust.

Richie, B. (1996) *Compelled To Crime: The Gender Entrapment of Battered Black Women*, London and New York: Routledge.

Rojas, P.M. (1998) 'Complex facts', *Colorlines*, Vol. 1, No. 2, pp.13.

Rose, D. (2001) 'Opium of the People', *The Observer*, www.observer.co.uk/focus/story/ 0,6903,518495,00.html.

Shiva, V. (2001) *Yoked to Death: Globalization and Corporate Control of Agriculture*, New Delhi: RFSTE.

Speller, A. (1996) *Private Sector Involvement in Prisons*, London: Church House Publishing.

Smith, K. (1999) 'From the Desk of Kemba Smith', www.geocities.com/CapitolHill/Lobby/8899/pen. html, December 13, 1999.

Sudbury, J. (2000) 'Transatlantic visions: resisting the globalization of mass incarceration' *Social Justice*, Vol. 27, No. 3: pp.133–149.

Sudbury, J. (2001) 'Globalisation, Incarcerated Black Women/Women of Colour and the Challenge to Feminist Scholarship' *Women's Studies Network: (ed) 2001 Millenial Visions Issues for feminism*, Cardiff University Press.

Waters, M. (1998) *'Congressional black Caucus blasts president's crack/powder cocaine sentencing recommendations'*, Press Release, www.house.gov/waters/Pi_980722_cocaine.html, July 22. 1998.

Yeoman, B. (2000) 'Steeltown Lockdown', *Mother Jones*, May/June.

Young, P. (1987) *The Prison Cell*, London: Adam Smith Institute.

Van Der Veen, H. (2000) *The International Drug Complex*, Amsterdam: Center for Drug Research, University of Amsterdam.

70 | remotely sensed: a topography of the global sex trade

Ursula Biemann

abstract

Voluntarily or not, women are moved in great numbers from Manila to Nigeria, from Burma to Thailand, and from post-socialist countries to Western Europe: female geobodies in the flow of global capitalism. The recently released 53-minute video essay *Remote Sensing* by the Swiss artist and video director Ursula Biemann traces the routes and reasons of women who migrate into the global sex industry. Taking a geographical approach to trafficking, the video develops a particular visual language generated by new media and satellite technologies, which traces the migration of women in the age of digital images.

All stills are taken from the video that was shot in the Philippines, Thailand, California, and the German—Czech border.

keywords

gender; sextrade; trafficking of women; borders; geography; representation; migration

(75–88) © 2002 Feminist Review. 0141-7789/02 $15 www.feminist-review.com

It has become increasingly difficult to find a model of cultural representation that would live up to the complexity of the present discourse of gender and visual culture in the context of globalization. Over the last few years I have recognized the need to locate gender and other categories of identity, such as ethnicity and nationality, within the context of the wider transformations of the public sphere, particularly urban reality. In this endeavour, geography proves to be a useful and attractive arena to articulate questions of the moving subject in relation to space and location. Globalization is a very gendered process: an evergrowing proportion of migrant people looking for work are female. However, beyond a simple feminization of migration we notice that women's labour is being sexualized, that is to say, global processes actually address women directly in their sexuality. The worldwide migration of women into the sex industry or more specifically the burgeoning trafficking in women can be read as a structural part of pancapitalism. Rather than taking a human rights approach on the issue, I am using the theoretical framework of geography because it allows for an examination of female

migrancy, mobility and routing in relation to specific sites, while at the same time permitting an integration of their psychological and material experience. In other words, I am interested in the practice of linking geo-politics to an understanding of how subjects are produced.

Geography is understood as a visual culture in this context. Satellite media and other geographic information systems' are generating profuse quantities of topographic images to be interpreted for scientific, social and military use. Increasingly they make their way into our daily lives, inform the way we think about the world and code our concept of globality. I make it my project to explore how these satellite visions of globality are producing a sexual economy in which it has become thinkable to reorganize women geographically on a global scale.

counter-geographies

Spiralling down from an orbital view the video essay *Remote Sensing* takes an earthly perspective on the topography of the global sex trade. It is a project of

countergeography that engages in migration and cross-border circuits, illegal and illicit networks as well as alternative circuits of survival, where women have emerged as key actors. The digital documents generated for the video essay trace the routes and reasons of women who travel across the globe to enter this gigantic Fordism of service that is the sex industry.

Trafficking hinges on the displacement of women, their costly transportation across topographies from one cultural arrangement to another, from one spatial organization to another, from one abandoned economy to a place of greater accumulations. It is the route that counts. The agents charge money for the vehicle and for the escort who knows the path and the border geography, the contacts and the bribes. Female bodies are the new cargo in these transactions across boundaries that generate massive amounts of footloose capital, abstract global capital that is nevertheless so physical for some. The travel money will go back into bonding women to do unpaid sex work for the trafficking ring. It is a common

practice of debt-bondage that places women in the contexts of the historical spaces of the brothel and the colony.

There are numerous structural and political reasons why women move, and are being moved, into the global sex industry. The Mekong region has traditionally been a burgeoning basin for the trafficking of women who criss-cross borders in all directions since the liberalization of the socialist countries. Thailand is no longer just a sending country, but has also become a country of transit and destination. While Thai women migrated in the 1970s to Europe and North America or have been promoted to the higher echelons of the sex industry catering to foreign tourists, there is a need to supply new women and girls to the lower class brothels in Thailand. This market segment draws on the young rural female population in and neighbouring countries like Burma, Laos, and Vietnam. China goes through a different predicament. The prolonged period under the one-child policy has caused a major gender disparity in the present generation. Many Chinese men who do not find wives will acquire them abroad. In Taiwan, on the other hand, women prefer a

modern life in the city and male farmers have a hard time attracting a wife who wants to live a hardworking rural lifestyle. They also have to import females from the Philippines by the tens of thousands for unpaid agricultural labour and every year 100 000 Southeast Asian women are shipped into the Japanese entertainment industry, which equals Japan's defence budget in volume.

The commodification and displacement of female bodies in South East Asia generates impressive figures, but my work does not situate itself in the production of factual information. The questions I have to ask myself as an artist and video maker are: How can I dislocate and recontextualize a much belaboured question such as the marketability of women and the objectification of female sexuality? How can a video, rather than simply arguing against capitalism and affirming rigid gender identities, reflect and produce the expansion of the very space in which we write and speak of the feminine? There is a need to investigate the interplay between the symbolization of the feminine and the economic and material reality of women. To reproduce closed, privatized and restricted images of women is confining the feminine further. Some women take the route into sex work voluntarily, others not, it is true, but there is a large grey zone in between these two conditions, a vast field of negotiation, on which I focus my attention. The process of re-signification, which I undertake in my video practice, then, is not only an incessant struggle against the effacement of the diversification and differentiation of the feminine, it is also an analysis of the gendered dynamic inscribed in social and material landscapes. Of course I would like to see the space in which we write our lives, our bodies and sexuality as a heterogeneous one but in the course of creating this space, I am bound to look at the existing technologies and networks of knowledge that operate in delimiting and formalizing it.

> *Bandana Pattanaik (GAATW)*: I think seeing them as victims creates a lot of sympathy and therefore people find it easier to accept. If I'll say that I have been forced into prostitution, people say, oh poor thing, let's help her, she is in a really bad situation. But if somebody says I chose to become a prostitute that's very difficult to accept or to understand. Why would you chose to be a prostitute? So many times it's framed in this either/or debate. Either you are a victim or you are an agent. Either you have chosen to be a sex worker or you have been forced into prostitution. And I think there are such large grey areas in between.

While all of my videos to date elaborate on the relations of gender, technology and transnational capitalism, *Remote Sensing* engages maybe most explicitly in a critique of visualizing technologies, particularly the orbital omniscient view of satellite imagery. Taking up a feminist critique that has claimed the importance of the viewing structures and apparatuses for the power relations established by the gaze, there is a need to displace and interrogate the images and to reintroduce a situated way of seeing and knowing. Geographic information systems (GIS) propose an abstract and highly accurate view of the world from the top down. GIS are

HONG KONG
SUNRISE : 6:08 AM
SUNSET : 6:42 PM
MOONRISE : 8:54 PMI@
MOONRISE : 7:42 AM
CIVIL TWILIGHT : 5:47 AM 7:04 PM
TIDAL: 10:43 AM(2.1M)I@11:47 PM(1.8M)

香港天文台

criticized by feminist scientists for applying binary and mutually exclusive categories that are unable to hold and interpret a great variety of conflicting information. They are also completely unable to think in relational terms and reveal the gendered meaning of data. Cartography is insufficient, then, to map the subjective path of people on the move.

A major objective of *Remote Sensing* is to propose a mode of representation that traces the trajectory of people in a pancapitalist world order wherein the space between departure and arrival is understood as a transnational one, i.e., a potentially subversive space which does not adhere to national rules, but nevertheless a complex material and social space that is formed by economic relations. All this is from a gendered perspective. Remotely gazed at from the orbital perspective, transnational sexuality comes into full sight. In this topography of the global sex trade, the female bodies get sensed and identified, evaluated and re-routed according to their assigned function. The moving women

appear as data streams in the video, scans and X-rays portrayed over landscapes passing by, their anatomical and demographic data are recorded, their routes appear in electronic travel schedules on the screen. They are the embodiment of the abstract financial flows that feed the global economy.

Remote Sensing visualizes the multilayered meaning of geography where the mobilization and the sexualization of women is linked to the implementation of new technologies, often in contradictory ways. While the Internet facilitates the migration flow, particularly for women via the bride market, border reinforcement technologies on the other hand hinder and push it into the illegal sector.

Heat and movement sensors, infra-red and roentgen cameras, digital and genetic control mechanisms are developed and put to use along the Eastern and Southern borders. Parallel to this, European migration politics are quite explicit in their practice of directing migrant women straight into the sex industry without giving them any future option to switch to another trade. For non-European female

SERIALIZED REROUTING
21923996/MS 23NOV98
RESTRICTED PASSAGE
900889 38989009802
BULGARIA / RUSSIA
USBEKISTAN / KIRGHISTAN
304990100
02089009100
MARRIAGE MIGRANT
CABARET DANCER
PROSTITUTE
DOMESTIC WORKER
36499097800
PERMIT L
1222128720
UNIVERSITY DEGREE
1222128720

Temperature (Celsius)
36.4 9.1 -10.2-45.5-72.7

applicants, the Swiss government only issues 'cancers' visas' which hinge on cabaret contracts. The automatic channelling of migrant women into sex work is an index of their status under national rule but it also speaks of the place of sex in that national space where laws protects the flourishing sexual life of male citizens as a privilege and source of power. Two-thirds of the 500,000 women entering Europe's entertainment industry every year are from Eastern post-socialist countries. The social change in these sending countries since the 1990s and the migration politics of the receiving countries both impact the flow of women into the sex trade. Even though the official policy is to fight human trafficking and to help women getting out of the sex trade, the fact is that the number of trafficked women is steadily increasing. Technologies of marginalization always affect women, and particularly economically disadvantaged women, in their sexuality because powerful players like states, scientific complexes, and military institutions tend to create a sexuality that eroticizes hierarchies.

> *Aida Santos (WEDPRO)*: The history of the American involvement in prostitution and trafficking should not be missed in the history. In the 40's the Americans came and established their bases in the Philippines. The presence of the US Army and Navy contributed dramatically to the rise in prostitution and trafficking, in the sense that when you have an institution like twenty-one military bases scattered all over the country in a situation of poverty and where women's status is very low, families are willing to send off their kids to work and the elder daughters are bound by tradition to help their families and send their siblings to school, you've got very rich soil for exploitation. And that's what happened in the former US baselands. The Marines are still coming here for training and when the big carriers dock in the harbour, 10 000 servicemen go on shore. In the small town near the subic base of Olongapo there are 6000 women registered in a bar.

27 000 prostitutes are servicing the US military bases in Korea today

Since the infrastructure for the entertainment industry was already in place, many of the Rest and Recreation areas created for the US soldiers during the war in Vietnam and Korea have been turned into sites of prostitution and sex tourism. Most of the women who came to the baselands expected to find restaurant jobs, but as it turns out, waitresses do not have a regular salary but work on a commission basis only. Unless they go out with the customers and provide personal entertainment and sexual services, they will not earn a living. Some of the former bases have been transformed into assembly plants for outsourced production paying wages that do not cover their living costs so that many women are bound to gain a complementary income by prostituting. Whether it is an offspring of military camps or a by-product of Western off-shore operations, women are displaced and drawn into the global economy through sexual labour. Sexual difference becomes a primary structural factor in understanding a migration-bound economy.

Another reason for the trafficking of women is that movements of exile, migration and international business have created the need to supply 'familiar' services abroad. So Filipinas are routed to Lagos in Nigeria to cater to Chinese businessmen, Thai women are trafficked to Paris to serve French-born Chinese and Cambodian immigrants, and girls from Nicaragua are dispatched to Southern California to supply camps of Mexican agricultural workers while others are kept in mobile trailer brothels that circulate in the Chicano suburbs of Los Angeles. The clandestine becomes an obscure form of living the locality of culture, a location that remains suspended and transitory. There is no arrival. The existence of these women is marked by a constant mobility, their time is scheduled, their space is confined, civil rights and sexual governance are suspended. The non-status of their existence speaks of a geographic ambivalence, and it is not surprising that these bodies are usually suspended from the cartographic discourse even though they have become an important part of illicit border transactions and underground economic circuits and increasingly represent a major source of foreign currency for national households. The video makes an effort to track and register the movement of these women and to infuse meaning into the mapping of their trajectories. Why is it so important to trace their paths through space? I think because these very bodies are in fact the site of numerous conflicts. Clearly, they represent a phantasmatic femininity that has been ruled out from Western consciousness but continues to thrive in the a-national space in which the fleeing temporality of their presence and their non-adherence to a national programme are major criteria. Their service needs to be secured materially but denied in the official ideology. While their civil status is suspended, their figurative representation reveals another phantasm deeply rooted in the bourgeois projections onto permanently seductive postcolonial places. Silk dresses and an Asian gentleness mask the drastic economic imbalance in which the hard bargain between the sexes takes place in capitalist society.

In the course of the global dislocation of women and the sexualization of their labour, a new geography is being mapped by the recruitment of women among minorities and slum communities, their transportation along trafficking routes and across borders, abroad and off-shore for labour in the global sex industry. This geography maps the alternative circuits of survival in the margins of a pancapitalist reality.

While the powerful players certainly lay the foundation for the global trafficking of women, we have to recognize that most trafficking operations are not conducted by mighty syndicates. They work in small units, relatives or acquaintances who recruit girls in slum neighbourhoods, frequently there are bi-national couples who have good contacts to the source country. Women often feel that these agents are not exploiting them but actually providing a valuable service in their desire to

ROUTE≫ PASSENGER 30088324/MS 03JUN00
DEPARTURE 6.20PM LOIKAW / KARENNI
≫CROSS... BORDER TO THAILAND
AT 11.5PM ...A MENG FANG BAN
M.TH.EN / B...-NA / SAKHOTAI /
TAK...HAENG ... KAMPHENG PHAT
AR...AL IN ...KHON-SAWRAN 9.20PM
CHI...AI ...ARTURE BUS 2.55PM
≫BANGKOK ARRIVAL 12.30PM
11JUN00 BANGKOK 10.10AM CHECK-IN TIME
ARRIVAL HONG KONG 1.45PM TRANSIT
DEPARTURE 3.30PM SA3405H//085

move to richer countries or to the cities for a modern and more exciting life, helping them to trade a slum existence for the glamour of a Bunny Club. And even if they feel lonely and exhausted, they are still able to send money home, not only supporting their family but generating hard cash for their governments.

Siriporn Skrobanek: We respect these women because many are illiterate, cannot speak a word of English but still have a strong will and encounter the whole world. And many of them can survive and struggle in their own way.

70 | at your service madam! the globalization of domestic service

Helma Lutz

abstract

This article deals with the question of new domestic servants. It sets out to describe a 'new' phenomenon manifesting itself all over Europe, that is the comeback of domestic workers and carers for children and the elderly in many households. It then proceeds to explain the establishment of an informal labour market in the private sector, which arises amid today's revolution of information technology.

Research sources on the current situation are scarce compared to historical studies. This is particularly true for Germany and even more for the Netherlands. The present situation differs from its earlier appearance mainly in that domestic workers today are migrant women from Eastern Europe, from Asia or South America.

The article aims to show how studying this phenomenon raises relevant questions both on an empirical and a theoretical level for gender studies as well as for migration studies. It pleads in favour of an intersectional analysis by taking into account class, gender and ethnic differences within the context of globalized labour markets and transnational migration movements.

keywords

domestic workers, globalization, gendered migration, identity, Germany, The Netherlands

(89–104) © 2002 Feminist Review. 0141-7789/02 $15 www.feminist-review.com

the law of globalization?

In a conversation between Will Hutton and Anthony Giddens discussing the character of globalization, Hutton says the following: '...the growth in personal household services is the result of the emergence of two-earner households who *have to buy in* services because *the woman* is *no longer* at home' (Hutton and Giddens, 2000: 5,6; italics H.L.). I find this a remarkable sentence for two reasons.

Firstly, Hutton's point of departure is a situation where 'the woman' is a housewife and the natural provider of services at home. This conceptualization of female labour has been criticised by feminists for more than two decades: according to this kind of definition care work and housework are not considered 'work' in the *real sense*, but as *lovework* (Arbeit aus Liebe) which is performed as part of the natural female role (see Bock and Duden, 1977). If 'the woman' leaves this domain and becomes an earner — a deviance from the former normal situation — her household tasks are not redistributed among male and female partners but, according to Hutton, quite a different automatism arises: they 'have' to be bought in.

Secondly, it is striking that after decades of debate about social inequalities and differences in social positioning, a universal statement about 'the woman' can still be made. While Hutton's statement is rather concerned with the *partial* situation of professional (white) middle-class women in the West, there is no mentioning of the fact that 'the (professional) woman' buys in the work of another woman, the domestic worker and that, consequently, globalization generates a new category of difference between women: at the start of the 21st century amid the transition from industrial capitalism to information capitalism (Castells, 1996), hundreds of thousands of women enter 'domestic service' all over the world. This paper addresses the phenomenon of domestic servants or maidservants, their experiences and the paradox of the informal, archaic labour market that has arisen amid today's revolution of information technology. The now widely used term 'domestic worker' or 'servant' derives from a very different historical situation in the past and, therefore, is an 'old theme', but in the context of globalization and the transnationalization of life-courses, new aspects come to the fore. I will start by looking at (dis-)continuities of the servant question. I will then focus on gender studies, as domestic work is a very sensitive issue for this discipline. The 'new domestic workers' are predominantly migrant women; I will thus turn to the area of migration studies. Finally, I will summarise some major problems of this issue in the frame of global developments. While domestic service is a theme on a global scale and a topic of many studies in the United States and Britain, I will focus on the German and the Dutch situation where research has only recently started.

the new domestic servants

For a long time during the 20th century it was expected that technological progress would eliminate the need for assistance from humans in households. However, today, at the threshold of the 21st century, the numbers of domestic helpers working in European households in the Era of Technology are very similar to what they were a century ago. How can an activity that had certainly been deleted from the register of occupations by the end of World War II have made such a vigorous comeback in West European households? The simplest answer that is used by mainstream sociologists and economists (see the quote above by Hutton) is that professional working women today need help in coping with the double burden of family care and career. The reasons had been different 100 years earlier. Back then, domestic staff was part of the prestige of bourgeois families. Research on continuity and discontinuity in aspects of maid service in the 20th century reveals many changes. Today's maids are migrant women from Asia, Africa, Latin America and Eastern Europe. They emigrate to the centres of the wealthy world to support and sustain their families back home. This trend reflects not only the world-wide feminization of migration (see Koser and Lutz, 1998; Phizacklea, 1998) and the international labour market's globalization but also the shift of exploitation and dependence from a national to an international context. The maids issue has evolved from one of class to one of ethnicity and nationality.

Unlike in the past, no reliable sources today quantify domestic service — yet another paradox in our world controlled by technology. For Germany, Simone Odierna (2000) calculated 2.4 million sub-minimum types of jobs in private households without any social security. In their study of Bremen, Marianne Friese and Barbara Thiessen submit that one out of every eight households uses hired help (Friese and Thiessen, 1997).[1] These authors expect growth in this field of employment.

1 Unfortunately, numbers on the Dutch situation are absent.

We know little about the people doing this work, except that over 90% of them are women. They range from working-class German women, through Turkish migrant women, ethnic Germans from Eastern Europe, to Poles, Czechs and Russians, as well as women from Asia and Latin America. The vast differences between the estimates suggest that many women do this work either semi-legally or illegally. Polish women in Berlin, for example, use the leeway provided by the German–Polish agreement and the relative geographic proximity to their home country to enter without visas as tourists and leave the city again after two months. Five or six share an apartment, work for several households and easily pass their work on to acquaintances or relatives from Poland (Irek, 1998). The resulting rotation system is thus based on a jointly operated informal commuter network. In the 1990s, the Polish women were the highest paid domestic servants in Berlin. Next came the Latin American women. At the bottom of the hierarchy were women from the former Soviet Union, the Ukraine, Byelorussia and other East European countries. The heterogeneity of their tasks, which range from cleaning, washing and cooking through caring for children, the elderly and the infirm, to assisting at family celebrations and corporate events, corresponds to the heterogeneity of their employment situations (from a 2-h a week cleaning job to the 24-h on-call service of the live-in maids) and finally with the ethnic heterogeneity of the women recruited for this work.

World-wide agencies offer maids or domestic workers via the Internet. Commercial agencies compete with religious organizations (mostly Catholic), which operate in places such as Latin America and Southeast Asia and arrange travel, as well as charitable care for those concerned in the host country.[2]

These women are less organised than their counterparts in all other female occupations. Neither the employees nor the employers are interested in giving up the clandestine character of the work (for different reasons, however), because they fear negative legal and social consequences.[3] At best, we know that the Filipinas have organized all over the world. Cash transfers from the ones working overseas are the country's main source of foreign exchange; one-quarter of the 70 million inhabitants of the Philippines is now supported by women working overseas.[4] (For a similar situation in Malaysia see Chin, 1999). Nowadays, Filipinas are admitted as domestic helpers in many highly industrialized countries — as for example in Italy, Spain and Greece in Europe. They also enter Belgium, the Netherlands, France and the United Kingdom sometimes as au-pairs or without work permits. The Babylan Association (Network of Filipinos in Europe) estimates that ca. 500 000 Filipinas are presently in Europe (Ratzinger *et al.*, 1996). The largest share is believed to be in Italy, where most are live-in maids (Parrenas, 2001). Many leave their own children with relatives, in boarding schools, or they themselves employ a maidservant for their children's care.

Throughout Europe the situation varies immensely between countries. However, in their report 'Migrant Domestic Workers: A European Perspective' submitted to the European Commission's Equal Opportunities Unit, Anderson and Phizacklea (1997) note many similarities (see also Anderson, 2000). In the past decade the sector has expanded immensely. The majority of domestic workers in all countries are migrant women, although the dominant groups vary by country: North Africans in France, Spain and Italy; Peruvians and Dominicans in Spain; Albanians, Eritreans and Ethiopians in Greece and Italy; Poles and other East Europeans in Greece, France, Germany, Italy and Spain. The differences between the countries are due to very different legislation provisions. In particular, South European countries like Italy, Spain and Greece have released work permits and visa regulations for domestics, while these are completely absent in Germany, the Netherlands and the Nordic countries. All countries have ethnic hierarchies legitimised by racist stereotypes that determine remuneration.

Anderson and Phizacklea report the following common problems for domestics: unpaid hours; low income, often less than the minimum wage; denial of wages in cases of dismissal following trial or probation periods; refusal by employers to

2 Representatives of the Catholic Church are the main agents in businesses which operate world wide (see also Andall, 1998).

3 There were attempts in Britain, however, to develop pressure groups. On 30 and 31 October 1999, a European meeting in London adopted a 'Charter of Rights for Domestic Workers' (see www.solidar.org).

4 Today, the trading good 'maid' is the most important product for export to the Philippines. Of the ca. 8 millions of Filipinos in foreign countries 70% are women who ensure foreign exchange income of 8 billion US dollars. These numbers were mentioned by a Filipino labour economist in a documentary broadcast by the Dutch Television (NL3) on 26 November 2000. See also Wichterich 1998: 94—98.

arrange legal resident status (for tax reasons, etc.); control and sexual harassment; pressure to do additional work (for friends and colleagues); excessive workloads, especially where in addition to caring for children and elderly people they are responsible for all other household chores; and finally the very intimate relationship between the domestic helpers and their employers (Anderson & Phizacklea, 1997). Researchers all over Europe expect the demand for domestic workers to rise considerably in the years ahead. The factors include both the rapidly ageing population in Europe and the insufficiency of state care provisions for children, the elderly and the infirm in many countries. Throughout Europe, only 18% of all elderly men care for their infirm wives, whereas 54% of all elderly women care for their husbands (due partly to differences in their respective average life spans).

Remarkably, the change in middle-class lifestyles has contributed to this sector's growth as well: childcare is demanding, cleaning with environmentally friendly products is time-consuming, standards of cleanliness have risen, people have more pets and so on (Gregson and Lowe, 1994).

Although we have little evidence for it, it can be assumed that in countries such as the Netherlands or Germany, which have prevented official admission of domestics, au-pairs are employed as maids. Currently, the majority of au-pairs in Germany come from East European countries, trying to stay as long as possible (often overstaying the one-year residence permit) and use this opportunity to put a 'foot in the door' to Western Europe (Hess, 2000; Puckhaber, 2000 for Germany; Henkes, 1999 for the Netherlands). Their 'salary' is the pocket money which the International Au-Pair organization guarantees. It seems important to note that the au-pair system was originally not established to satisfy the need for workers, but as a support of the international exchange. From the few studies on this topic it can be deduced that nowadays the au-pair system is (mis-)used by employers for the performance of maidservants' tasks.

domestic servants in historical perspective

In the following, the maid question is dealt with from a historical perspective; this is for two reasons: first, in contrast to the current situation, there are numerous socio-historical studies on working-class women domestic workers in the 19th and 20th centuries that have been published in the last 20 years everywhere in Europe. They form a great corps of research sources for comparison. In most of the current studies, the historical term 'maidservant' or domestic servant is used, probably because it is still not clear if and how this new phenomenon differs from the former one. In other words, the qualification of the phenomenon as 'new' challenges the comparison with the old one. Second, historical studies can serve as framing background for the analysis of the actual situation. With its help, the question of reproduction or modernization of social inequalities can be posed. Moreover, in a historical review the question is to be asked if the current connection of the phenomenon with migration is new.

In the following historical comparison, I will refer exclusively to two studies addressing maidservants in different places over time. Both reveal that maidservants in the past — unlike today — were largely young, single women of age 14 and older who came from poor families in rural areas.

In her study about the emergence of women's work, Marianne Friese delineates the rise of the domestic service proletariat in Bremen during the 19th century. In this period, the 'transformation of the rural servants into urban domestic workers', as the trend was known, led to 'feminization of domestic workers as a characteristic of urbanization and industrialization' (Friese, 1991: 201). This also indicates that domestic servants have not always been exclusively women. On the contrary, until the middle of the 19th century the work was predominantly done by men in many European countries.

Unlike in the present, municipal and church records document the occupational rise of maidservants meticulously. Despite the relatively heterogeneous social environment, a civilising mission was the dominant discourse of the day, involving sophistication and civic re-education of the girls from rural areas. By the end of the century, demand increased for more professional maidservants. Training institutes were established, inspections introduced (also for employers to keep a register of domestic staff), complaints were admitted in civil courts, and sickness insurance funds for domestic servants started, as well as interest groups. The first one was the maidservants association founded in Leipzig in 1848. There were national conventions of domestic servants in 1899, and the first trade union of maidservants, laundresses and charwomen was established in Nuremberg in 1906. The objectives included abolition of the servant class and adjustment of legal rights according to the civil code, shorter working hours, better food and treatment, special employment agencies and the right to a month's notice. Their demands were met with immense reluctance.

The number of domestic servants, which was a million in the German empire about 1900, was slowly reduced in the course of the following decades as a result of the First World War and the economic recession. Tens of thousands of young women let themselves be recruited to America, or for example, to the Netherlands through the placement of the advisory board for emigration.[5]

A very interesting Dutch study (Henkes, 1998) discusses the historical trend during the inter bellum years of German maidservants who travelled to the Netherlands after being recruited through emigration information centres from 1920 onward. From 40 000 in 1934, their number dropped to 3500 following the Nazi invasion in May 1940. German maidservants received preference over Dutch ones because of their 'virtuosity and ability to adjust quickly.' This trend chagrined their Dutch

5 One of the blind spots in historical research concerns the employment of ca. 500 000 women workers from Eastern Europe as maids and nannies in Nazi Germany. Significantly, not a word is mentioned

about this forced
nursery labour in the
current debates on
compensation
payments for forced
labourers.
Annekatrein Mendel
has written an
impressive work
(1994) on the
subject based on
interviews with
contemporary
witnesses. There are
also occasional
references that
mention German
nannies passing
Jewish children off
as their own to save
them from
deportation (see the
interview with
Charlotte Knobloch,
the second
candidate for
chairing the central
council of German
Jews, *Die Zeit*, 52,
1999).

counterparts, who had formed unions to get their employers to agree to certain conditions. German maidservants, however, received praise from their employers for 'hearing, seeing and keeping silent.' In her study Henkes describes these migrant women's problems, which resemble those of today's female migrants in many respects. These women's life stories reflect a dramatic change in their images from cherished treasures to German traitors during and after the war. Their positions in domestic service allegedly predisposed these women to 'spy against the Dutch people.' The study refuted this myth. This example reveals that aside from gender, *nationality* may determine their social standing when politically expedient.

In conclusion, it can be said that the analysis shows continuities as well as discontinuities in the current and the former situation. In spite of all the historical differences, the following similarities between the old and the new maid question are given: The historical development of the *feminization* of the domestic servant's work is still relevant. The current studies show that (a) the people convened are women; (b) most of them think of this work as a period of transition. In contrast to 'old' domestic servants, maids today are older (often married and mothers) and they do not do the work in order to bridge the time between school and marriage that is to say to have a household of their own, but often in order to cope with a familiar financial crisis, the provision of a family, the education of their children, etc. (see Parrenas, 2001; Irek, 1998; Nyberg, 1999); and finally, the majority of those who arrive in Europe are not from working class backgrounds.

The existing studies reveal that the maids of the 21st century are *better educated* than their predecessors. Among them there are female teachers, students, lawyers, doctors and nurses. If women want to work in a foreign country, they are expected to have received a 'training' in their home country, to speak foreign languages (mainly English) or to have at least the skill to find their way around in a foreign country (see also numerous websites, on which maids are offered with photos and descriptions of their character traits and personalities). Despite their professional training skills they cannot earn enough to make a living in their own countries. Thus, they migrate to countries where they are needed. However, their professional expertise is not wanted there either; instead, what is needed are capacities that women seem to possess everywhere and that are ascribed to either their nature or their gender-specific socialization: the skill of cleaning and caring, of dealing with the most intimate sphere discreetly, of making a home, nourishing the children of their employers as well as their own, and of caring for old people patiently.

By taking a look at the current situation, it can be assumed that the *professionalization* of the work of the domestic servant is no relevant option today, because the professions providing private service are already professional-ized: there are nursery-school teachers, old people's nurses, professional cleaning teams, etc. Although their salaries are low, they are scarce and often not affordable for those who wish to employ them. Thus, the existence of the current domestic phenomenon should create an awareness towards the fact that the welfare state shows a lack in provision; or it takes premises for granted that are not valid in reality. This last aspect has to be seen in close connection with the question of gender-specific allocation of the housework. At this point, the 'old' demand of the women's movement that housework and the work of reproduction should be increased in value socially and that the division of labour in the household should be more equal, comes to mind.

A German study on time budgeting in the 1990s (Künzler, 1995) reveals that despite all emancipation rhetoric, men's participation in household chores and childcare has remained consistently low for decades. Although a slight increase in the participation of men in the housework could be seen in the Netherlands, there is no evidence of an equal participation (see van der Lippe, 1993). This situation raises empirical and theoretical questions for feminist research and possibly for redefining the public–private paradigm.

domestic servants as a challenge to gender research

The bipolarity of private and public life in modern societies has long played a central role in gender research. It is based on the impression that certain functions and operations are withdrawn from the public sphere (*privare* means to steal) and enclosed in the private one. According to Arendt (1981), women and slaves have been relegated to the private sphere since antiquity. The observation of 'separate spheres' means that operations and characteristics are localized publicly and privately and categorized by gender. Where professional work and politics are ascribed to the public sphere, they become a male domain, while the sector comprizing reproductive labour is classified as female. Gender research has challenged this circumscription and the corresponding gender codes ('the private sphere is political'). It has systematically highlighted women's unrecognized reproductive work and men's wage labour (there is a woman behind every working man). The research has indicated the implicit gender contract that not only differentiates between professional work and care work by gender but also enforces hierarchical distinctions evaluated according to the male standard.

The domestic servants issue both confirms and challenges the gender contract thesis at the same time. Large numbers of women in Western industrialized countries have entered the work force without bringing about the required change in outlook and organization in patriarchal professional contexts. Women remain responsible for care anyway and thus acquire a double burden or seek domestic help privately. Maria Rerrich describes this situation as a collision between 'two ongoing situations among distinctive groups of women' (Rerrich, 1993: 100).

According to Rerrich, this issue is explicitly not a women's issue but subject to debate throughout society; she calls for 'repoliticizing the private sphere' (Rerrich, 1993, 1997). Young (1998) considers the phenomenon an aspect of the internationalized, globalized labour market regulated by supply and demand, which has to be dealt with on the level of regulations.

Other womens studies researchers explicitly contradict this perception. They mention a refeudalization (Kurz-Scherf, 1995: 189) or modernized exploitation and violence in which equality by convention or otherwise is not forthcoming. As in most cases employment contracts and consequently resident status are restricted, the employer has more rights than the female employee from the outset.

While Rerrich assumes that the invisibility of jobs in the private sphere benefits many women working illegally by shielding them from discovery (Rerrich, 1997: 20), Becker-Schmidt (1992) and Phizacklea (1998: 34) note this twilight zone's disadvantage: live-ins in particular have minimal freedom to manoeuvre. 'What is 'home' to affluent white women has an entirely different meaning for her domestic staff, who experience it as a place of social alienation and exploitation' (Becker-Schmidt, 1992: 221). If they can afford it, live-in domestic servants therefore rent common dwellings, where they meet during their free time and find refuge or social safety and comfort (see for example Campani, 1993). More recent reports reveal that some live-in domestic servants, like their predecessors around the turn of the 20th century, suffer from sexual harassment by their male employers. Everywhere in the world rape takes place in private rather than in public. In both the past and the present the women concerned have found resistance against such practices virtually impossible, as the burden of evidence rests with the victim. It is further noted (Anderson and Phizacklea, 1997; Anderson, 2000) that domestic workers frequently complain of being controlled by their female employers, ranging from harassment and constant supervision of their work and other psychological manipulation to physical violence. However, some studies indicate that domestic workers devise individual strategies to compensate for their disadvantage in the dependence relationship, for example by appealing to the sense of guilt of their female employers to gain a material and psychological advantage. Alternatively, they may use moral negotiation to alter interpersonal balances of power (Özyegin, 1996; Henkes, 1999).

From these studies it becomes obvious that gender studies researchers take contradictory approaches to the analysis of domestic workers. While some focus on the exploitation of domestics, others underline the agency of the women involved.

In general, it can be said that gender studies have waited far too long to address the issue. Private and public spheres can no longer be analyzed adequately as separate gendered spaces but merit consideration as a continuum with regard to ethnic, not just class-specific aspects. The operating spaces and instruments designated as private and public need to be reassigned. Furthermore, it can be argued that theories of labour location in the 'public', separating the cultural from the political, the private from the public, reproduction from production, have to be revised; those notions have contributed to the academic invisibility of domestic workers.

Seen from this perspective, the private sphere as a work place seems to be predestined for an intersectional analysis of social positioning and social space in which the categories of ethnicity, class, gender and nationality must be combined.

This plea raises not only new questions for gender studies, but also challenges migration studies to abandon cherished concepts. The virtual disregard for gender as a determinant of migration trajectories and networks brings me to my next issue.

women as pioneers in globalized economic relationships — a new perspective on migration research

Analyzing the labour market's globalization at the threshold of the 21st century reveals that the broad supply enabled employers to demand specific levels of training and skill of the individuals they hired. The majority of international studies emphasise that western female employers benefit from the world market's hierarchical structure and the unequal terms of trade (Bakan and Stasiulis, 1995; Phizacklea, 1998; Chin 1999; Anderson, 2000; Parrenas, 2001). Friese (1995) attributes the present employment of thousands of East-European university graduates as domestic servants in Western Europe to the new devaluation of women's education. Migration research refers to this pattern as the brain drain (the exodus of the educated from the countries of origin), which turns into brain waste in the destination countries. These women engineers, physicians and lawyers, who are unable to find jobs in their own countries, help support their families by resorting to their apparently 'natural skills' at the *risk* of losing their social standing.

However, this phenomenon can also be understood differently. The study by Irek (1998), who examined the roles of Polish women workers on Berlin's informal labour market and interviewed 300 charwomen, indicates that these women certainly have not just bowed down with the weight of bad living conditions. Many of them became entrepreneurs and formed their own hierarchical networks, exploit their fellow countrywomen and establish their own small businesses in Poland. These women have been invaluable for Poland's most recent economic miracle. Thus, they did not remain in the country where they — as they put it — were 'condemned to slave labour', work that those left behind were not supposed to know about. They regarded this activity as a transformative instrument and primarily as a means toward an end. Many justified it by explaining that they did this work for their husbands in Poland for free, whereas they received wages in Berlin.

Some researchers, therefore, stress that these women are not passive beings, victims or marionettes driven by circumstances, but agents of change. They are, according to Morokvasic (1991, 1993), pioneers who cross borders and are very willing to travel and take risks to connect the sending and the receiving countries and establish a new global migration space. In addition to helping support their families, they promote transnational lifestyles and multiplication of consumption and communication.

In her study on domestic servants from the Dominican Republic in New York and Madrid, Nyberg (1999) describes such a transnational way of life. These women form an economic, communicative and mental transatlantic network between their home, the promised land of the United States and the alternative of Spain. Tighter border controls and admission restrictions do not lead them to abandon individual and family projects but encourage them to seek out places of temporary abode and to expand their radius of operation. In parts of the world afflicted by crises, planning is an unknown concept, and opportunities are elsewhere.

With caution one can probably say the following: The fact that women's socialization includes learning to be flexible, to tolerate humiliation and social degradation seems to make this kind of migration easier for women. The feminization of migration exists mainly in the private service sector (see also Hillmann, 1996; Phizacklea, 1998). Further research has to reveal why women seem to be more inclined to join this trajectory than men.

As Phizacklea (1998) has already mentioned, the old models of migration theory or those of related network approaches cannot sufficiently explain the gender aspects of domestic service. This becomes especially obvious when trans-national motherhood is dealt with: As was said before, many of the new domestic servants leave their children behind with either a paid substitute mother or with the children's grandmother. Their care can in no way be analyzed with the concepts of motherhood that exist in Western industrial countries. The physical closeness, seen as healthy and 'normal' in the Western upbringing of a child, are not given, because most of the women are not allowed to take their children with them. Parrenas (2001) calls this form of motherhood, which develops in the case of long parting, 'commodified motherhood': the tie between mothers and children is mostly expressed through material goods, financial aid and the payment for a good education. The psychological results, for example personal alienation, are often underestimated by the mothers. On the other hand, non-Western constructions of motherhood do not measure a good mother according to her direct involvement, or her symbiosis with her child, for this function can be handed over to other 'social mothers'. It is true that mental and consumption relevant transnational spaces are created. The respective sending and receiving states are, however, interested in the maintenance of national ties. While the latter use legal requirements, as restrictive residence permits for their national purposes, the former use systems of rewarding in order to guarantee the maintenance of the women's loyalty towards their home country. In the Philippines the 'best domestic servants of the year' are awarded with a national decoration (by the President), and they are sent into the wide world as 'soldiers of the nation'.

the traps of the global care chain

Domestic work is one of the most insecure forms of employment and is mainly performed by women. In a recent article, Arlie Russel Hochschild identifies the phenomenon of 'global care chains' by mapping out the migration paths of carers and servants around the world; she then asks what the response to this development should be from a critical modernist perspective. Her solutions are ambiguous and many of them, like the suggestion 'to reduce incentives by addressing the causes of migrant's economic desperation' (Hochschild, 2000: 142) have proved unsuccessful for decades.

In my view, the analysis of the current situation first and foremost highlights *dilemmas*. It also shows that globalization has very different faces, not just on different continents, but also within a political entity like the European Union. Notwithstanding the efforts for the establishment of a common European migration policy, there are important differences between nation-states. While some countries have implemented an official recruitment policy for domestic workers, others are far from acknowledging the very existence of (the need for) domestics. In Germany, while there is a vivid debate on the launching of a 'green card' for the desired information technology workers, there is no such discussion on domestics. Neither the government nor the unions are willing to deal with this question at all. As a response to recent media reports on this phenomenon the police raided private households and illegal domestics were deported. Although no single government in Europe is willing to deal with this issue on a broad public level, there are active NGOs who try to introduce this topic on to political agendas. However, we are far from having the right strategies, let alone solutions. Comprehensive research, which makes it possible to analyse the situation all over Europe, is still missing. In my concluding remarks, I wish to emphasise some of the paradoxes of the current situation.

The question of the global care chain is a troubling one. As feminists, we must confess that campaigns like the 'salary for housework' campaign or the demand for equal distribution of household tasks among male and female partners in the household — hot issues in the 1970s and 80s — have failed. Due to globalization, house- and carework is a cheap product that can be 'bought in': the impoverished and completely de-regularized labour markets of the world offer a large reservoir for these services. The global care chain has become an aspect of the international division of labour. In some countries of East Europe, Asia or South America domestics have been 'promoted' to be the main 'export product'. Such a situation opens the door to modernized exploitation and establishes a 'postindustrial household structure with preindustrial values' (Parrenas, 2001: 80). New forms of difference and hierarchies in the relations between women have emerged. However, an analysis that stops here ignores the agency of the domestic workers concerned. These women are obviously prepared to take great risks. Like many other migrants, domestic servants have to repress the anticipation of dangers and problems in favour of the expected positive results; they seem to trust their own problem-solving capacities. It may well be that their educational background helps them with the realization of their plans. The fact that this work is often regarded as temporary makes the establishment of collective action more difficult but not impossible (see note 4 and Parrenas 2001: 243). As is already known, many maids want to re-migrate as soon as they have earned enough money or found a (new) partner so that they can start a new life. However, in the course of time, financial dependencies and new consumption patterns in their families back home develop. These reasons repeatedly lead to the continuation of their stay. Moreover, emotional ties develop in relationships where children are taken care of, which cannot easily be broken (see Parrenas, 2001). While providing a home for their employers, domestics become providers for their families back home. Within this connection of the global and the local, multiple identities emerge. It is questionable, however, if the women can really raise their status. As the old-age pension of these women is not regulated, it can be assumed that new long-term dependencies develop, for example on their daughters' incomes whose education was paid by the absent mothers. As long as domestics are denied membership and citizenship in the receiving countries, options are restricted to their home country (Parrenas, 2001). What this future will be like is a question that cannot be answered. The successful return to their home country as described in Irek's study is as possible as impoverishment through disease or loss of income after return.

The analysis of the domestic workers phenomenon brings numerous structural as well as identity questions to the fore. Characterising the global care chain as either 'good' or 'bad' and distinguishing between pure 'winners' and 'losers' of globalization, in this case, is not helpful either. Nevertheless, I see the need to generate a public discussion, especially in the field of gender studies.

author biography

Helma Lutz is a reader at the University of Münster, Germany. She is a sociologist and educational scientist and combines women's studies with migration studies. She currently conducts the first larger study on 'new domestics' in Germany, financed by the VW-Foundation (2001–04). Recent publications in English are: *The New Migration in Europe: Social Constructions and Social Realities* (co-editor with Khalid Koser), London: Macmillan, 1998, and *Women in Transit: Between Transition and Transformation* special issue of the *European Journal of Women's Studies*, 3, 2000 (co-editor with Kathy Davis).

acknowledgements

I am indebted to Lee Mitzman and Jeannette Stiller for their translation of larger parts of this article.

references

Andall, J. (1998) 'Catholic and state constructions of domestic workers. The case of Cape Verdean Women in Rome in the 1970s' in K. Koser and H. Lutz (1998) editor, *The New Migration in Europe. Social Constructions and Social Realities*, London: Macmillan Press.

Anderson, B. (2000) *Doing the Dirty Work? The Global Politics of Domestic Labour*, London: Zed Books.

Anderson, B. and Phizacklea, A. (1997) *Migrant Domestic Workers. A European Perspective. Report for the Equal Opportunities Unit*, DGV, Commission of the European Communities.

Arendt, H. (1981) (1958) *Vita Activa. Vom täglichen Leben*. München: Piper.

Bakan, A. and Stasiulis, D. (1995) 'Making the match: domestic placement agencies and the racialization of women's household work' *Signs: Journal of Women in Culture and Society*, Vol. 20, No. 2: pp.303–335.

Becker-Schmidt, R. (1992) 'Geschlechterverhältnisse und Herrschaftszusammenhänge' in C. Kuhlke, H.K. Degetoff and U. Ramming (1992) editors, *Wider das Schlichte Vergessen*, Orlanda: Campani (1993) editor Sigma, pp.216–236.

Bock, G. and Duden, B. (1977) 'Arbeit aus Liebe - Liebe als Arbeit' in Gruppe Berliner Dozentinnen (1997) editors, *Frauen und Wissenschaft Beiträge zur Berliner Sommeruniversität für Frauen 1976*, Berlin: Courage Verlag, pp.118–199.

Campani, G. (1993) 'Labour Markets and Family Networks: Filipino Women in Italy' in H. Rudolph and M. Morokvsic (1993) editors, *Bridging States and Markets*. Berlin, pp.191–208.

Castells, M. (1996) The Rise of the Network Society. The Information Age: Economy, *Society and Culture*, Vol. 1, Oxford: Oxford University Press.

Chin, C. (1999) *In Service and Servitude. Foreign Domestic Workers and the Malaysian ''Modernity Project''*, Columbia: Columbia University Press.

Friese, M. (1991) *Frauenarbeit und Soziale Reproduktion*. Universität Bremen. Forschungsschwerpunkt Arbeit und Bildung no.20.

Friese, M. (1995) 'Modernisierungsfallen im historischen Prozess. Zur Entwicklung von Frauenerwerbsarbeit in einem gewandelten Europa' *Berliner Journal für Soziologie*, Vol. 4, No. 5, pp.149–162.

Friese, M. and Thiessen, B. (1997) *Modellprojekt 'Mobiler Haushaltsservice - ein innovatives Konzept für die Ausbildung und Beschäftigung von Hauswirtschafterinnen*, Universität Bremen.

Gregson, N. and Lowe, M. (1994) Servicing the Middle Classes: Class, Gender and Waged Domestic Labour in *Contemporary Britain*, London: Routledge.

Henkes, B. (1998) *Heimat in Holland. Deutsche Dienstmädchen 1920–1950*. Straelen: Straelener Manuskripte.

Henkes, B. (1999) 'Van inwonende dienstbode naar au-pair. Werk in de huishouding: kansen en beletsels voor vrouwen in de 20ste eeuw' in R. Holtmaat (1999) editor, *Eeuwige kwesties. 100 jaar vrouwen en recht in Nederland*, Jubileumuitgave van Nemesis, Deventer: Tjeenk Willink, pp.40–64.

Hess, S. (2000) 'Au Pairs. Die modernen Dienstmädchen' *Diskus* Vol. 2, pp.18–23.

Hillmann, F. (1996) *Jenseits der Kontinente. Migrationsstrategien von Frauen Nach Europa*, Pfaffenweiler: Centaurus.

Hochschild, A.R. (2000) 'Global care chains and emotional surplus value' in W. Hutton and A. Giddens (2000) editors, *On the Edge. Living with Global Capitalism*, London: Jonathan Cape, pp.130–146.

Irek, M. (1998) *Der Schmugglerzug. Warschau-Berlin-Warschau*, Berlin: Das Arabische Buch.

Koser, K. and Lutz, H. (1998) 'The New Migration in Europe: Contexts, Constructions and Realities' in K. Koser, H. Lutz (1998) editors, *The New Migration in Europe. Social Constructions and Social Realities*, London and Basingstoke: Macmillan, pp.1–20.

Künzler, J. (1995) 'Geschlechtsspezifische Arbeitsteilung. Die Beteiligung von Männern im Haushalt im internationalen Vergleich' *Zeitschrift für Frauenforschung*, Vol. 13, Nos. 1 and 2, pp.115–132.

Kurz-Scherf, I. (1995) 'Vom guten Leben. Feministische Perspektiven diesseits und jenseits der Arbeitsgesellschaft' in W. Beelitz (1995) editor, *Wege aus der Arbeitslosigkeit*, Reinbeck: Roro, pp.181–206.

Lippe, Tanja van der (1993) *Arbeidsverdeling tussen mannen en vrouwen*, Amsterdam: Thesis publishers.

Mendel, A. (1994) *Zwangsarbeit im Kinderzimmer. ''Ostarbeiterinnen'' in deutschen Familien von 1939 bis 1945. Gespräche mit Polinnen und Deutschen*, Frankfurt a.M.: Dipa.

Morokvasic, M. (1991) 'Fortress Europe and migrant women' *feminist review*, Vol. 39, No. 4: pp.69–84.

Morokvasic, M. (1993) ''In and out' of the labour market: Immigrant and minority women in Europe', *New Community*, Vol. 19, No. 3, pp.459–484.

Nyberg, S.N. (1999) 'Mobile Lebensführung zwischen der Dominikanischen Republik, New York und Madrid' *Migrationen. Lateinamerika, Analysen und Bericht 23*, Bad Honnef: Horlemann, pp.16–38.

Odierna, S. (2000) *Die heimliche Rückkehr der Dienstmädchen*, Opladen: Leske und Budrich.

Özyegin, G. (1996) 'Verwandtschaftsnetzwerke, Patronage und Klassenschuld. Das Verhältnis von Hausangestellten und ihren Arbeitgeberinnen in der Türkei', *Frauen in der Einen Welt* Vol. 7, No. 2, pp.9–27.

Parrenas, R.S. (2001) *Servants of Globalization: Women, Migration and Domestic Work*, Palo Alto: Stanford University Press.

Phizacklea, A. (1998) 'Migration and globalization: a feminist perspective' in K. Koser and H. Lutz (1998) editors, *The New Migration in Europe. Social Constructions and Social Realities*, London and Basingstoke: Macmillan, pp.21–33.

Puckhaber, A. (2000) ''*Big Sister*' or domestic servant? Au pairs as a neglected category in studies on domestic work.' Unpublished research paper written for the project: 'At your service, madam.', International Women's University, Hannover.

Ratzinger, A.C., Lutz, H. and Pablo, M. (1996) 'Das DH-Phänomen' *Frauen in der Einen Welt*, Vol. 96, No. 2, pp.101–109.

Rerrich, M. (1993) 'Auf dem Wege zu einer neuen internationalen Arbeitsteilung der Frauen in Europa? Beharrungs-und Veränderungstendenzen in der Verteilung der Reproduktionsarbeit' in B. Schäfers (1993) editor, *Lebensverhältnisse und soziale Konflikte im neuen Europa*. Frankfurt a.M./New York, pp.93–102.

Rerrich, M. (1997) *Frauenarbeit in der Familie zwischen Lohn und Liebe – Überlegungen zur Repolitisierung des Privaten*, Vortrag anlässlich der Verleihung des Helge-Pross-Preises der Universität GH Siegen, 3.12.1997.

Wichterich, C. (1998) *Die globalisierte Frau. Berichte aus der Zukunft der Ungleicheit*, Reinbeck: Roro.

Young, B. (1998) 'Globalisierung und Gender' *PROKLA*, Vol. 111, pp.168–174.

Judi Bari and 'the feminization of Earth First!': the convergence of class, gender and radical environmentalism

Jeffrey Shantz

abstract

This paper addresses feminist materialism as political practice through a case study of IWW-Earth First! Local 1, the late Judi Bari's organization of a radical ecology/ timber workers' union in the ancient redwood forests of Northern California. Rejecting the Earth First! mythology of timber workers as 'enemies' of nature, Bari sought to unite workers and environmentalists in pursuit of sustainable forestry practices against the devastating approaches favoured by multinational logging corporations. In so doing, she brought a working-class feminist perspective to the radical ecology of Earth First! Bari's work provided a significant instance of community organizing in opposition to the masculinist, exclusionary practices and misanthropic posturing of Earth First!'s self-proclaimed 'eco-warriors' and 'rednecks for nature'. What is perhaps most interesting about the development of Local 1 is the articulation of feminist, environmentalist and labour discourses through a series of political actions.

keywords

ecofeminism; anarchism; syndicalism; Earth First!; industrial workers of the world; deep ecology

(105–122) © 2002 Feminist Review. 0141-7789/02 $15 www.feminist-review.com

introduction

The aggressive character of capitalist expansion, that is what is inadequately termed 'globalization', challenges contemporary social movements to build unity among the diversity of those threatened by the social and environmental dislocations wrought by global capital. R.B.J. Walker (1994) stresses the crucial need for social movements to develop what he calls a 'politics of connexion'. Social movement analysis must avoid tendencies to speak of movements as singular without giving serious attention to the difficulties encountered by attempts to form alliances or broaden participation.

> Whatever the rhetorical and tactical appeal of a woman's movement, or an environmental movement in the singular, it is an appeal that cannot disguise the differences and even intolerances among such movements.
>
> (Walker, 1994: 699).

Certainly, the class locations and consciousness of participants within recent social movements (especially students and radical youth) and the issues raised by those movements (e.g. environmentalism, lesbian and gay rights, feminism) have posed compelling challenges to class analyses. New categories and experiences of subordination have emerged as points for mobilization and an awareness of these categories and the practices that sustain them has played an important part in overcoming the economism of much of Marxist theory. Class must be contextualized as it is lived and the lived experiences of class include problems of race, gender, sexuality and environment.

As several authors (Adam, 1992; Darnovsky, 1995; Starn, 1997; Tarrow, 1997) stress, social movements are resistant to unicausal explanations. As Starn suggests, the decision to mobilize 'underscores the need to insist on social analyses that avoid the extremes of an ungrounded culturalism or a deterministic economism to examine the inseparable intertwining of cultural meaning and political economy in human experience' (Starn, 1997: 235). Even movements that are viewed, and indeed view themselves, as being expressive of 'new values', such as environmentalism, have interesting intersections with class movements that are largely downplayed or overlooked in much of new movement discussion. For example, Adam (1993) raises the significant and sustained efforts of union health and safety committees to control industrial impacts upon nature. To separate these efforts from 'environmentalism' proper is purely arbitrary, especially if one considers that environmental contaminants and their consequences are concentrated and most severely felt in working-class communities.

Amidst the decay of Marxian analyses has arisen a series of theories by and about the 'new social movements', which seek to address some of the fundamental issues of social theory, such as the nature of historical agency, the role of identity in politics, and the prospects for the radicalization and extension of democracy. Discourses around nature, gender and labour suffer many of the problems of reductionism, essentialism, and unrealized syncretism, which are symptomatic of a certain disarray in 'post-Marxian' social theory. While some versions of postmodernism would affirm this disarray in a Voltairean retreat to cultivate one's own particular theoretical backyard, I prefer to attend to questions regarding the difficult construction of counter-hegemonies in advanced capitalist societies. This paper takes up the challenge by investigating the ways in which movements involving labour and ecology are rendered commensurable, both as theory and as historical practice. Particular attention is given here to the work of the late Judi Bari and the radical labour-ecology union of IWW/Earth First! Local 1 as a 'real world' project to build an alliance between timber workers and radical environmentalists.

wilderness fundamentalism and the 'rednecks for nature'

Emerging from the threatened landscape of the US Southwest in 1980, Earth First! (EF!) almost immediately established itself as the extreme edge of North American environmentalism. Arriving during a low ebb in the cycle of environmental activism, Earth First! provided an important voice for wilderness preservation against prevailing views, which reduced nature to 'our resources and private property' (Idaho Farm Bureau Federation, quoted in Short, 1991: 181). Their position of 'No Compromise in Defense of Mother Earth' quickly made them the bane of land developers, cattle ranchers, logging companies, the US National Park Service, the US Forest Service and even other environmentalists (Lange, 1990; Short, 1991).

The group's founders, most notably Dave Foreman, viewed confrontation and agitation as the only means to awaken an increasingly lethargic environmental movement, which was clearly failing to protect wilderness ecosystems (Short, 1991). Earth First! vigorously attacked mainstream environmentalists for being too close to the political establishment and too ready to make compromises that were not in the best interests of wilderness ecosystems.

In place of a 'granola-crunching' pacifist image of environmentalists, which they were quick to deride, Earth First!'s founders identified themselves as 'rednecks and cowboys for wilderness' (Lange, 1990; Short, 1991). Throughout the 1980s and early 1990s Earth First!, with its extreme rhetoric and public commitment to direct action and 'monkeywrenching',[1] served as a striking symbol of a renewed radicalism in environmental politics. Armed with a broad sense of humour they transformed the character of environmental protests by engaging in lively guerilla theatre, blockades, 'tree—sitting' and threats of sabotage[2] (Lange, 1990, Short, 1991, 1993). The group signalled a potentially important and necessary radicalization of environmentalism, both through its ecological sensibility and in the tactics deployed to realize that sensibility.

1 Edward Abbey's novel *The Monkey Wrench Gang* served as political manifesto and spiritual guide for the group's early efforts (Short, 1991). The 1975 novel presents vivid portrayals of various

Inspiring EF! practice was an underlying philosophy of 'deep ecology' or 'wilderness fundamentalism', which provided an integral part of EF!'s political agenda (Short, 1991). According to Adkin, wilderness fundamentalism 'refers to various forms of essentialism (claims about the sensual, spiritual, aesthetic, and developmental needs of humans as a species, and about the rights of other species) that are present (implicitly or explicitly) in different discourses', (Adkin, 1992a: 144). For eco-fundamentalism, commodification of life (both human and non-human) is linked to alienation from the body, from nature and from 'authentic' human needs. Themes of ethics and identity predominate in fundamentalist discourses, which are directed primarily towards the transformation of values within individuals (Adkin, 1992a,b).

However, it soon became clear that there was another, more ominous side to wilderness fundamentalism. List suggests that EF!'s wilderness fundamentalism took on a 'purist' fervour that held that 'the core of social and political life should be reoriented towards wilderness preservation and restoration, instead of to other social issues' List (1993a: 6). This biocentric orientation placed a commitment to wilderness ahead of other socio-political concerns such as struggles against racism, poverty, unemployment and patriarchy. The fundamentalists implied that 'real change in our behaviour toward wild nature could occur without revolutionizing capitalist economic systems and social structures' (List 1993b: 7). The essentialist narratives of fundamentalist ecology (Devall, 1988; Manes, 1990) tended to construct 'humanity' as a bloc, undifferentiated by power, in which a universalistic human species itself was held responsible for biospheric destruction, dangerously discounting politically constructed differences of race, gender and class.

Indeed, there emerged a harsh neo-Malthusianism fundamentalist ecology.[3] For some Earth First!ers (Manes, 1990) the most desirable or necessary transformation became 'drastically depopulating the Earth as if human numbers were all that mattered and the various kinds of society that people can create are of little or no relevance to the ecological question' (Chase, 1991). While Dave Foreman was suggesting that nature should have been allowed to take its course in the Ethiopian famine, Paul Watson[4] mused that 'to a vastly reduced population wood could be made available without killing trees' (Watson, 1994: 128). No word from Watson regarding who among the population might be subject to reduction, although he did provide some insight into the calculus which might be involved: 'To me, all of the human beings in California are not worth the extinction of one of the mighty and revered ancient forest dwellers we have chosen to call redwoods' (Watson, 1994: 128). In a notorious Earth First! article a writer using the pseudonym Miss Ann Thropy[5] 'welcomed the AIDS epidemic as 'a necessary solution' to the 'population problem' (generously including 'war, famine, humiliating poverty' along with AIDS)' (Bookchin quoted in Bookchin and Foreman, 1991: 123). Perhaps not satisfied that the message had been understood, Miss Ann Thropy

acts of sabotage in subversion of wilderness development projects.

2 Favoured acts of sabotage in defence of ecology, or 'ecotage', during the early years of Earth First! included pulling survey stakes and disabling heavy equipment.

3 A popular Earth First! bumper sticker proclaimed: 'Malthus was Right'.

4 Paul Watson is the founder of the Sea Shepherd Conservation Society, a marine ecology group whose members identify themselves as the Earth First! navy.

5 The article was written by Chris Manes, author of *Green Rage*.

continued: 'To paraphrase Voltaire: if the AIDS epidemic did not exist, radical environmentalists would have to invent one' (Miss Ann Thropy 1987: 32). While insisting that they were unconcerned with political or social issues the fundamentalists developed what were first and foremost political narratives, albeit of a reactionary nature.

Unfortunately, it is this version of Earth First! which came to represent the movement in the popular imagination. Yet, the story is much more complex. For there emerged within Earth First! itself a counter-movement of activists who attempted to bring socio-political analysis to their biocentric acts. By the late 1980s a grassroots opposition to the social and political short-sightedness of the 'rednecks for nature' was beginning to take shape in the Redwood regions of Northern California. The Northern California Earth First!ers (including Judi Bari, Daryl Cherney, Mike Rosselle[6] and Pam Davis) rejected the misanthropy, machismo, patriotism and anti-labour biases of the old guard, condemning their comments on Ethiopia, immigration and AIDS. Their actions, to reform Earth First! while fighting to preserve old growth ecosystems, would come to be among the most important examples of eco-defence in North America.

local 1 and the timber wars

The environmental struggle over the Redwoods of Northern California continues to be among the most heated in North America.[7] At the time of Judi Bari's work the fevered pitch of these conflicts had earned them the nickname 'timber wars'. Environmentalists were routinely subjected to violence, with loggers driving through picket lines and felling trees into demonstrations. Hanging in the balance was the survival of one of the few remaining old growth ecosystems in the US.

The context for the pitched battles raging in Northern California was one of rapid job loss and eroding communities. Industry spokespersons denied responsibility for the decline in logging jobs, preferring to place the blame on environmentalists. Yet the timber companies (Louisiana-Pacific, Georgia Pacific and Maxxam) removed trees at an incredible rate. Practising 'infinity logging',[8,9] the logging firms were determined to take out every tree as quickly as possible.

As a long-time union activist and labour organizer, Judi Bari was well aware that the destinies of the forests and the forest workers were inextricably linked. In her view, blaming environmentalists or endangered species like the spotted owl for the loss of logging jobs was nothing but a cynical tactic on the part of logging industry spokespersons. She identified instead the rapid industrialization of logging during the past two decades as heavy machinery and mechanized practices such as clearcutting came to replace labour-intensive and selective forms of logging. Additionally, processing jobs had disappeared as mill work was moved elsewhere and the companies pursued less expensive labour.[10] Smaller trees and fewer

6 Mike Roselle was the only Earth First! co-founder to identify himself as a political leftist.

7 In September 1998, Earth First! activist David 'Gypsy' Chain was killed when a timber worker felled a tree onto his campsite.

8 According to Scarce (1990), the environmentalist Green Ribbon Coalition reported that 13,000 loggers were laid off in the Pacific Northwest between 1982 and 1988.

9 This charming notion comes from Louisiana-Pacific President Harry Merlo: 'We log to infinity. It's out there, it's ours, and we want it all. Now'

forests, of course, also required fewer hands. The only way to save both the forests and timber jobs was to change over to sustained yield logging practices, as many environmentalists were advocating (Bari, 1994).

Unfortunately, most timber workers were being successfully mobilized by logging companies against such practices. Management initiated a jingoistic 'Yellow Ribbon Campaign', encouraging local families and businesses to display yellow ribbons to show their solidarity with the companies in the face of the environmentalist 'menace'. In some communities simply choosing not to fly a ribbon was dangerous (Bari, 1994; Heider, 1994; Purchase, 1994).

The success with which management mobilized workers against environmentalists continued to be the immediate obstacle that confronted environmentalists' attempts to change logging practices and end the slaughter of the redwoods. What was behind the success? Workers' fears over the imminent collapse of the forest ecosystems and concomitant loss of jobs, communities and ways of life were easy enough to see, even if few environmentalists took these fears seriously. Judi Bari identified something else:

> That is the utter lack of class consciousness by virtually all of the environmental groups. I have even had an international Earth First! spokesman tell me that there is no difference between the loggers and the logging companies.
> I have heard various environmentalists say that working in the woods and mills is not an 'honourable' profession, as if the workers have any more control over the corporations' policies (or are gaining any more from them) than we do. As long as people on our side hold these views, it will be easy pickins for the bosses to turn their employees against us.
>
> (Bari, 1994: 14)

Bari knew that only the interests of the timber bosses would be served if environmentalists and workers continued to view each other as the enemy.[11] She was determined to do something to end this standoff which had for too long impeded ecological defence. A possible solution gradually crystallized in Bari's mind: a radical timber workers' union organized along with Earth First!ers to save both jobs and ecosystems. The idea was soon realized as IWW-Earth First! Local 1 which brought together under one roof radical environmentalism and revolutionary syndicalism,[12] forming an improbable 'green syndicalism'. Bari immediately set out as a field organizer, against all odds signing up the Earth First! old guard's hated enemies, timber workers.

Bari recognized that workplaces offered promising bases of support. With this as her starting point, she found it surprisingly easy to make contact with workers who did not accept the companies' views on the situation in the woods. Indeed over the course of two years, between 1988 and 1990, relations with timber workers gradually improved (Scarce, 1990). A local union comprising of timber workers and environmentalists was formed in Fort Bragg, California. Bari officially represented five millworkers, victims of a PCB spill at work, to the Occupational Safety and

(quoted in Bari, 1994: 12).

10 The automation of logging was specifically aimed at reducing labour costs.

11 Watson has stated famously that 'the logger is a nothing, an insignificance, a virus, a rot, a disease and an aberration against nature, and I for one will not weep a single tear at his demise' (Watson 1994: 129). Elsewhere, Watson describes resource workers as 'just pathetic foot-soldiers for the corporate generals of the logging industry' (Watson 1994: 127). Referring to 'antiquated rights of workers' he makes it clear that such rights might be

12 Revolutionary
unionism, or
syndicalism, sought
the replacement of
capitalism through
working class
solidarity and
control of
production. The main
proponents of
revolutionary
unionism in North
America, the
Industrial Workers of
the World (I.W.W.),
had a rich history in
the forests of the
West Coast during
the first decades of
the 20th Century,
organizing timber
camps from
California to British
Columbia. Unlike
mainstream unions,
the Wobblies
organized all workers
regardless of race,
ethnic background,
gender or language.
They faced violent
repression, including
the arrests and
killings of
organizers. They
were eventually
broken in the 1920s.

Health Administration (OSHA) (Purchase, 1994). Newsletters countering management perspectives 'spontaneously' appeared at two of the local mills. The industry publication 'Timber Line' was greeted with 'Timber Lyin'. Written from the viewpoint of workers and addressing such issues as health and safety problems and job loss resulting from clearcutting, the paper called on workers to organize for the survival of their communities (Scarce, 1990; Bari, 1994). Workers also began to provide information that helped environmentalists organize effective tree-sits and blockades. After Louisiana-Pacific closed the nearby Potter Valley sawmill which had employed 136 people, Darryl Cherney's song 'Potter Valley Mill', which included two references to sabotage, became the most requested song on the local country music station. Millworkers even sold tapes of the song in Potter Valley.

An unanticipated turning point for the young labour—environment alliance emerged at an annual environmental law conference in Oregon in March 1990. Appearing on a panel with Judi Bari, timber worker Gene Lawhorn bluntly told the audience that Bari's timber worker—radical environmentalist alliance was doomed if Earth First! continued to advocate tree-spiking. This controversial tactic, in which environmentalists drove large spikes into trees to deter cutting, was perceived by loggers and millworkers as a very real threat to their lives because of the unpredictable breaking of saw blades. For Earth First!ers, however, spiking was almost an article of faith. With the audience anxiously awaiting her response, Bari spoke the words that would send shock waves through EF! circles: 'I hereby renounce tree-spiking'. Surprisingly, the Earth First!ers in attendance supported her. After discussing her decision, several Northwest groups agreed to formally denounce spiking (Scarce, 1990). In mid-April a statement was issued citing the growing timber worker—radical ecology alliance as the reason for the break with EF! orthodoxy. Significantly, monkeywrenching itself was not renounced. The formal statement encouraged sabotage *by timber workers* as a means to disrupt the labour process and slow the cutting of trees. Workers were no longer viewed as necessary targets of sabotage, they were viewed as potential eco-saboteurs.

In his book *Ecodefense: A Field Guide to Monkeywrenching*, Dave Foreman had argued that ecotage must be unorganized and the act of individuals alone. Local 1 countered that in order for eco-defence to be successful it must be based in the community. Individual acts of adventure cannot halt environmental destruction. Isolated from community support, individual adventurist acts further reinforce the divisions between environmentalists and local workers.

> I have nothing against individual acts of daring. But the flaw in this strategy is the failure
> to engage in long-term community-based organizing. There is no way that a few isolated
> individuals, no matter how brave, can bring about the massive social change necessary to
> save the planet. So we began to organize with local people, planning our logging blockades
> around issues that had local community support. We also began to build alliances with

progressive timber workers based on our common interests against big corporations. As our successes grew, more women and more people with families and roots in the community began calling themselves Earth First!ers in our area.

(Bari, 1994: 221)

Of course, timber workers were not the only workers in Mendocino County. Local Earth First!ers included students, carpenters, childcare workers, recycling centre operators and office workers (Bari, 1994). Many lived off the land as fishers or homesteaders. One even owned a small sawmill. Bari emphasized organizing tactics that mobilized people in their local communities. She knew that many were already active in local watershed associations and did regular unpaid stream restoration work. They were approached in view of the interconnection between destruction of forests through clearcuts and the damage done to local waterways.

redwood summer and the feminization of Earth First!

Still, despite the best efforts of Local 1, the trees continued to fall. It quickly became apparent that the small group of activists, isolated in the woods and beyond the media spotlight, could not save the forests on their own.

So drawing on the lessons of the Civil Rights movement, we put out a nationwide call for Freedom Riders for the Forest to come to Northern California and engage in non-violent mass actions to stop the slaughter of the redwoods.

(Bari, 1994: 222)

Through this action, nicknamed 'Redwood Summer' the activists hoped to bring international pressure to bear upon the destructive practices of the timber companies in Northern California.[13] As the organizing enjoyed cumulative successes, taking on a scale unimagined by activists and receiving support across borders, violence against organizers escalated. Bari received increasingly graphic death threats.

While driving to Santa Cruz to prepare for a benefit concert for Redwood Summer, Judi Bari was almost killed when a pipe bomb exploded beneath her seat. The blast tore through the car injuring Local 1 organizer Darryl Cherney and leaving Bari with extensive soft tissue damage and a shattered pelvis (Scarce, 1990).

Activists had long feared that timber supporters might actually make an attempt on the life of an organizer. 'Bari, especially, was too dangerous, her wood worker—environmentalist union talk a chilling proposition for companies that operated effective monopolies over their workers' lives, secluded as they are from other sources of information and employment' (Scarce, 1990: 85). Violence against anyone suspected of opposing the timber industry was readily deployed in the isolated timber-dependent communities (Stentz, 1993).

13 So powerful was the image of Earth First! hostility to loggers that one of the few mainstream accounts of the planning for Redwood Summer came with the headline: 'Eco-activist summer: Earth First! vs. the loggers in California' (Barol, 1990: 60).

There were also early indications that the bombing was motivated by explicitly misogynist sentiments. Bari reports that one of the death threats she received described the organizers of Redwood Summer as 'whores, lesbians and members of N.O.W' (Bari, 1994: 223). As an outspoken defender of abortion rights Bari received numerous death threats and hate letters from religious fundamentalists[14] (Purchase, 1994). Bari was convinced that the extreme forms of violence and hatred to which she was subjected related not simply to what she was saying but that a woman was saying it.

Unfortunately, authorities chose not to follow these leads, preferring to focus on friends of the organizers. The FBI and Oakland police almost immediately announced that the main suspects were Bari and Cherney themselves. Incredibly, they accused the two pacifists of transporting the bomb for use in a terrorist act. The only evidence offered was that the bomb was in the back seat where it would have been seen by the activists. (Never mind that the epicentre of the blast actually showed that the bomb was under Bari's seat, out of view.) Under this pretext, the FBI raided the homes of other activists and investigated supporters (Heider, 1994).

Within three weeks the district attorney decided that no charges would be filed. Not surprisingly, there was no evidence against Bari or Cherney. 'Tried and convicted in the press, Bari and Cherney were set free' (Scarce, 1990: 85).

The cynical efforts of the FBI, Oakland police and local authorities greatly interfered with organizing for Redwood Summer, already hindered by the loss of the most experienced organizers. In addition, local law enforcement agencies actively worked to suppress the unionization effort (Purchase, 1994). Activists faced continued incidents of harassment, intimidation, death threats and violence.

Redwood Summer was not defeated, however. Unlike anything previously, the bombing and the incredible response of the FBI and Oakland police galvanized the environmentalist communities. New members, from around the country, were drawn into the movement, significantly from backgrounds quite different than those of the 'mountain men'/'wilderness boys' and with new visions of ecological resistance (see Pickett, 1993). The changes in EF! worldview and strategy initiated within Local 1 contributed to the growing prominence of women in Earth First! during Redwood Summer. After the bombing, more than 20 people came forward to take on key organizing roles in Bari's absence, three-quarters of whom were women (Bari, 1994; Purchase, 1994). This was, in Bari's view, the feminization of Earth First![15] As she noted at the time: 'Redwood Summer is an almost entirely women-led action. There are women holding the base camp together, there are women holding the actions together, even the attorney team is women' (Bari, 1994: 43).

Overall, approximately 3000 people took part in Redwood Summer, many from outside the US.[16] By comparison, previous Earth First! actions had drawn no more than 150 participants. The actions preserved the 2000-year-old trees of

Headwaters Forest, which had been slated for cutting. The commitment to non-violence in relations with workers gained Local 1 a new level of respect in the local communities and allowed them to further develop the movement.

the 'redneck' resistance to the feminization of Earth First!

Still, old resentments within Earth First! remained. 'Being the first women-led action, Redwood Summer has never gotten the respect it deserves from the old guard of Earth First!' (Bari, 1994: 225).

Some of Ecotopia's toughest battles were waged with the Earth First! *Journal*, the organization's newspaper. Bari's articles were edited beyond recognition and Cherney's articles were not published at all. The *Journal* editors eventually cancelled the Ecotopia EF![17] insert which was to have reported on the 'Summer '91' action campaign (Bari, 1994).

The rivalry between Ecotopia and the old guard finally produced a showdown in March, 1992, at a national conference of Earth First! activists. A few months before the conference, the *Journal* had published an article that advocated dressing up as a hunter and going into the woods to shoot hunters. While EF! had long encouraged hunt sabotage, through such practices as noise making and alerting animals to keep hunters from making any kills, this article crossed a line for Ecotopia's activists. Some Local 1 supporters hunted to supplement their meals and were drawn to environmentalism because of growing concerns over habitat and species losses. In response, Ecotopia wrote a letter denouncing the article and withdrawing themselves from the contact list until the issue was addressed (Bari, 1994).

Their letter drew a wave of predictably negative responses in typically macho language. The contact from Santa Monica EF! snarled: 'If you are not tough enough for Earth First! then I suggest you join the Sierra Club or the Audubon Society. If that is too radical, try the Green Party. Have a nice day!' (quoted in Bari, 1994: 196). The Sugarloaf EF! contact chose to resurrect the misanthropic line, dismissing Ecotopia's concerns as 'humanist nonsense! Of course a few humans are endangered. So what! Plenty of damn humans here. The death of a few activists is not important in the evolution of Gaia. Are you warriors or whiners? I'd trade a hundred of you for one spiker' (quoted in Bari, 1994: 196–197). The contact from Sugarloaf thus managed to bring together the old EF! standards of overpopulation, the brave warrior and the worship of spiking.[18]

Bari's article against the group's lingering misanthropy, 'Why I am Not a Misanthrope', drew numerous responses. The *Journal* chose not to print thoughtful responses from Chris Manes and Murray Bookchin, instead printing Ken Shelton's

The worst was from the Sahara Club, an anti-environmental group that wrote in its newsletter: 'BOMB THAT CROTCH! Judi Bari, the Earth First bat slug who blew herself halfway to hell and back while transporting a bomb in her Subaru, held a press conference in San Francisco. Bari, who had her crotch blown off, will never be able to reproduce again. We're just trying to figure out what would volunteer to inseminate her if she had all her parts. The last we heard, Judi and her friends were pouting and licking their wounds' (Bari, 1994: 224).

15 Bari offers her insights into the feminization of Earth First! in an article by that title which appeared in *Ms Magazine* (and which is reprinted in *Timber Wars*).

What is surprising is that I, a feminist, single mother and blue-collar worker, would end up in Earth First!, a 'no compromise' direct action group with the reputation of being macho, beer-drinking eco-dudes (Bari, 1994: 219).

From the beginning Bari sought to overcome the typical gendered division of labour that existed in Earth First!

But Earth First!

angry misogynist attack, which referred to Bari's article as 'an excrementious piece of eco-femme idiocy'. The author's conclusion gave voice to the old guard's sexism, going so far as to blame women for the destruction of nature:

> Give us a break, Bari. Behind every aggressive white male stands a pampered female, wheedling, whining, and conniving, clamoring for more comforts and commodities. If you take any group of civilized people and set them down in the jungle with instructions to live like the Guatemalan Quiche, the women will set up such a din of bithching and caterwauling that the men will be forced to pave over the jungle and invent refrigerators and automobiles just to shut them up!
>
> (quoted in Bari, 1994: 205–206)

Dave Foreman further tried to discredit the efforts of the Northern California activists. He characterized Local 1 as 'anarchists and class-struggle social justice leftists' who had 'infiltrated' Earth First! and led it away from its true purpose. Foreman spoke publicly against the organizers during Redwood Summer, thus providing timber executives with the opportunity to claim that the activists were such extreme radicals that even their 'leader' disavowed their actions (Bari, 1994). Proclaiming his respect for private property, Foreman (1991) maintained that there was never any intention for Earth First! to engage in anti-corporate activism. Rather, in his view, Earth First! was founded to deal with public land use issues.[19]

Bari rightly recognized this as contradictory to biocentrism. The assertion that nature does not exist to serve humans, who are simply one part of nature, cannot be reconciled with the notion that the Earth can be owned. Similarly, defence of biodiversity should not be deterred by the presence of a 'private property' sign. Responding to Foreman's protests, Bari, playing on the Earth First! slogan, asked: 'Should our slogan be No compromise in Defense of Mother Earth on Public Land Only, And Only If We Don't Have to Confront the Corporate Power Structure?' (Bari, 1994: 105). Her answer, given through the work of Local 1, still resonates a resolute 'No'.

syndicalism, ecology and feminism

According to Judi Bari, a truly biocentric perspective must further challenge the system of industrial capitalism, which is founded upon the 'ownership' of the earth. In her view, industrial capitalism cannot be reformed since it is founded upon the destruction of nature, the profit drive of capitalism, which insists that more be taken out than is put back (be it labour or land). Bari extends the Marxist discussion of surplus value to include the elements of nature. She argues that a portion of the profit derived from any capitalist product results from the unilateral (under)valuing, by capital, of resources extracted from nature.

Because of her analysis of the rootedness of ecological destruction in capitalist relations Bari turned her attention to the everyday activities of working people, as

---

was founded by five men, and its principle spokespeople have all been male. As in all such groups, there have always been competent women doing the real work behind the scenes. But they have been virtually invisible behind the public persona of 'big man goes into big wilderness to save big trees'. I certainly objected to this (Bari, 1994: 220).

Redwood Summer saw a transformation in the activities undertaken by women within Earth First!

16 Bari's only public appearance during Redwood Summer came during a women's rally at the FBI building in San Francisco. Two hundred women took part in that demonstration alone. After the bombing, Judi Bari, along with Darryl Cherney, sued the FBI and the Oakland police for violating their civil rights. As of this writing the court case is still underway. Much of the support work has been done by the Redwood Summer Justice Project. They can be contact at P.O. Box 14720, Santa Rosa, CA, 95402 or by internet at www.judibari.org.

17 The Northern California activists adopted the name Ecotopia for their EF! local.

18 Some members even debated

noted above. Workers would be a potentially crucial ally of environmentalists, she realized, but such an alliance could only come about if environmentalists were willing to educate themselves about workplace concerns. Bari held no naive notions of workers as privileged historical agents. She simply stressed her belief that for ecology to confront capitalist relations effectively and in a non-authoritarian manner the active participation of workers is required. Likewise, if workers were to assist environmentalists it was reasonable to accept some mutual aid in return from ecology activists.

To critics, this emphasis on the concerns of workers and the need to overcome capitalist social relations signified a turn towards workerist analysis which, in their view, undermined her ecology. Criticisms of workers and 'leftist ecology' have come not only from deep ecologists, as discussed above, but from social ecologists, such as Murray Bookchin and Janet Biehl, who otherwise oppose deep ecology. Social ecology guru Bookchin has been especially hostile to any idea of the workplace as an important site of social and political activity or of workers as significant radical actors. Bookchin repeats recent talk about the disappearance of the working class (Bookchin, 1997), although he is confused about whether the working class is 'numerically diminishing' or just 'being integrated'. Bookchin sees the 'counterculture' (roughly the new social movements like ecology) as a new privileged social actor and in place of workers turns to a populist 'the people' and the ascendancy of community. Underlying Bookchin's critique of labour organizing, however, is a low opinion of workers who he views contemptuously as 'mere objects' without any active presence within communities[20] (Bookchin, 1980).

Lack of class analysis likewise leads Biehl (1991) to turn to a vague 'community life' when seeking the way out of ecological destruction. Unfortunately, communities are themselves intersected with myriad cross-cutting and conflictual class interests which, as Bari showed, cannot be dismissed or wished away. Notions of community are often the very weapon wielded by timber companies against environmentalist 'outsiders'.

Biehl recognizes the ecological necessity of eliminating capitalism but her work writes workers out of this process. This is directly expressed in her strategy for confronting capital: 'Fighting large economic entities that operate even on the international level requires large numbers of municipalities to work together' (Biehl, 1991: 152). Not specific social actors or workers with specific contributions to make, but statist political apparatuses municipalities. To confront 'macrosocial forces like capitalism... [Biehl proposes]... political communities' (Biehl, 1991: 152). All of this is rather strange coming from someone who professes to be an anarchist.

Biehl even states that the 'one arena that can seriously challenge' current hierarchies is 'participatory democratic politics' (Biehl, 1991: 151) but makes no reference to the specificity of the workplace in this regard. Yet, within capitalist

whether or not it was consistent with deep ecology principles to advocate shooting humans. Bari could not help but wonder if this implied that the attempt on her life, if successful, would have been considered an ecological act by other Earth First!ers.

19 Dissatisfied with the direction Earth First! was taking and the declining significance of the 'Rednecks for Wilderness', Foreman left Earth First! in August 1990 ironically enough to take up a position with the reformist Sierra Club.

20 Bookchin (1997) goes so far as to claim that the 'authentic locus' of anarchism is 'the municipality'. This is a rather self-serving claim given that Bookchin has staked much of his reuptation on building a 'libertarian municipalist' tendency within anarchism. It also runs counter to almost all of anarchist history.

relations, the workplace is one of the crucial realms requiring the extension of just such politics. And that extension is not likely to occur without the active participation of people in their specific roles as workers. Bari, concerned with encouraging this participation, did not have the luxury of overlooking the everyday concerns of workers.

As a longtime feminist and unionist Judi Bari was well aware of tendencies within the labour movement, and the left generally, to treat concerns of gender or environment as subordinate to the larger movement or, worse, as distractions. Bari was no vulgar materialist given to economistic analyses, however, and she rejected Dave Foreman's characterization of Local 1 as simply 'leftists' or a 'class struggle group'. She too remained sharply critical of Marxist socialism and what she saw as its acceptance of the domination of nature.

> We are not trying to overthrow capitalism for the benefit of the proletariat. In fact, the society we envision is not spoken to in any leftist theory that I've ever heard of. Those theories deal only with how to redistribute the spoils of exploiting the Earth to benefit a different class of humans. We need to build a society that is not based on the exploitation of Earth at all — a society whose goal is to achieve a stable state with nature for the benefit of all species.
>
> (Bari, 1994: 57)

For inspiration, Bari turned to non-authoritarian traditions of socialism, which she viewed as 'beyond leftism'. Specifically, her materialism took the form of syndicalism revolutionary libertarian unionism.[21] Bari developed her green syndicalist approach as an attempt to think through the forms of organization by which workers could address ecological concerns in practice and in ways which broke down the multiple hierarchies of mainstream trade unionism. She recognized in syndicalist structures and practices certain instructive similarities with the contemporary movements for ecology and radical feminism.

Historically, anarcho-syndicalists and revolutionary unionists fought for the abolition of divisions between workers based upon, for example, gender, race, nationality, skill employment status and workplace. Revolutionary unions, such as the IWW, in fighting for 'One Big Union' of all working people (whether or not they were actually employed) argued for the equality of workers and the recognition of their unity as workers while realizing that workers' different experiences of exploitation made such organization difficult.

Like radical feminists, anarcho-syndicalists have argued for the consistency of means and ends. Thus, syndicalists organize in non-hierarchical, decentralized and federated structures that are vastly different from the bureaucratic structures of mainstream trades unions that have been largely resistant to participation by women. The alternative organizations of anarcho-syndicalism are built upon participation, mutual aid and cooperation. Anarcho-syndicalism combines the syndicalist fight against capitalist structures and practices of exploitation with

21 For a detailed discussion of green syndicalist theory see Shantz (1999).

the anarchist attack on power and awareness that all forms of oppression must be overcome in any struggle for liberty. The IWW fought for the recognition of women as 'fellow workers' deserving economic and physical independence (i.e., self-determination) and access to social roles based upon interests and preferences.[22]

Regarding the affinity between anarcho-syndicalist organization and 'second wave' feminist practice, Kornegger has commented: 'The structure of women's groups bore a striking resemblance to that of anarchist affinity groups within anarchosyndicalist unions in Spain, France, and many other countries' (Kornegger, 1996: 161). Kornegger laments that feminists did not more fully explore the syndicalist traditions for activist insights.

Besides, as Purchase argues, industrial unions 'are composed of people feminists, peace activists and ecologists included and are simply a means by which people can come to organize their trade or industry in a spirit of equality, peace and co-operation' (Purchase, 1997: 28). As Barry Adam (1993) argues, the exclusion of workers from new social movements discussions is both arbitrary and inaccurate.

> Exactly what sense we are to make of such sweeping dismissals of centuries of sustained resistance to the encroachments of capital and state by ordinary working people is quite unclear.... Besides, in the absence of state-supported industrial [or green] capitalism trades unions and workers' co-operatives – be they bakers, grocers, coach builders, postal workers or tram drivers would seem to be a quite natural, indeed logical and rational way of enabling ordinary working people to co-ordinate the economic and industrial life of *their* city, for the benefit of themselves rather than for the state or a handful of capitalist barons and it is simply dishonest of Bookchin to claim that anarchism has emphasised the historical destiny of the industrial proletariat at the expense of community and free city life.
>
> (Purchase, 1997: 28)

The concerns raised by Foreman, Bookchin and Biehl are well taken. Indeed, much Old Left thinking, of various stripes, did fail to appreciate the causes or consequences of ecological damage. However, as Purchase (1997) has pointed out, the reasons for this are largely historical and practical rather than necessarily theoretical. The ecological insights of social ecologists like Bookchin (e.g. ecological regionalism, and green technologies) are not incompatible with syndicalist concerns with organizing workers.

conclusion

Judi Bari maintained that Earth First! was primarily a direct action group and viewed its theories and policies as the result of practice, valuable for informing and revising strategies and tactics. The crucial matter was the development of radical ecofeminist praxis. One necessity facing Earth First! was to broaden the

22 As Purchase awkwardly overstates:

> Moreover the IWW... was the first union to call for equal pay and conditions for women and actively sought to set up unions for prostitutes and in doing so achieved far more for the feminist cause than any amount of theorising about the evolution of patriarchy could ever hope to have done. (Purchase, 1997: 32)

group's focus. Bari (1990) viewed the early 1980s identity of the movement as concerned only with wilderness as self-defeating. As she argued, it is impossible to address seriously the destruction of wilderness without addressing the social relations responsible for the destruction. The time had come for the Earth First! movement to stop viewing itself as separate from social justice struggles. In Bari's view, the ecology movement is but one strand in a multiply woven fabric of resistance.

In her view the power that manifests itself as resource extraction in the countryside manifests itself as racism and exploitation in the city. An effective radical ecology movement (one that could begin to be considered revolutionary) must be organized among the poor and working people. Only through workers' control of production and distribution can the machinery of ecological destruction be shut down.

Ecological crises become possible only within the context of social relations that engender a weakening of people's capacities to fight an organized defence of the planet's ecological communities. Bari (1994) understood that the restriction of participation in decision-making processes within ordered hierarchies, a prerequisite to accumulation, has been a crucial impediment to ecological organizing. This convinced her that radical ecology must now include demands for workers' control and a decentralization of industries in ways that are harmonious with nature. It also meant rejecting ecological moralizing and developing some sensitivity to workers' anxieties and concerns.

> And it seems to me that people's complicity should be measured more by the amount of control they have over the conditions of their lives than by how dirty they get at work. One compromise made by a white-collar Sierra Club professional can destroy more trees than a logger can cut in a lifetime.
>
> (Bari, 1994: 105)

Bari asked how it could be that there were neighbourhood movements targeting the disposal of toxic wastes but no workers' movement to stop the production of toxins. She argued that only when workers are in a position to refuse to engage in destructive practices or produce destructive goods could any realistic hope for lasting ecological change emerge. The only way to bring the system to a standstill is through mass-scale non-cooperation, what an earlier generation of syndicalists knew as the 'General Strike'. Bari's vision for Earth First! combined a radicalization of the group's initial ideas of biocentrism and an extension of the decentralized, non-hierarchical, federative organization, the nascent syndicalist structure of EF!, into communities and workplaces.

While agreeing with the old guard that efforts should be made to preserve or re-establish wilderness areas, Bari saw that piecemeal set-asides were not sufficient. The only way to preserve wilderness was to transform social relations. This meant that Earth First! had to be transformed from a conservation movement to a social movement. Earth First! needed to encourage and support alternative lifestyles. To speak of wilderness decontextualized the destruction of nature.

Where Dave Foreman sought to keep the movement small to maintain its 'purity', Bari (1990) recognized that the profound social transformations necessary to preserve nature would require large-scale participation. She was convinced that the participation of large numbers of women in the radical ecology movement led to increased openness to Earth First! in logging communities (Purchase, 1994). Isolated and individualistic forest actions that separated environmentalist from sympathetic loggers had been a huge tactical mistake on the part of Earth First!.

Rather than 'watering down' the movement, as Foreman charged, 'Redwood Summer' brought new people into the movement and gave them experiences in direct action. It also provided a vital example of community-based coalition building under extremely disagreeable circumstances. Local 1 provided a new approach, which encouraged many environmentalists to rethink strategies for building a sustainable green future.

author biography

Jeffrey Shantz is an active member of the Ontario Coalition Against Poverty (OCAP) in Toronto, Canada. He is co-host of OCAP Radio on community station CHRY 105.5 FM. He also works with the General Defence Committee which supports political and class struggle prisoners. He has long been active in environmental and anarchist movements.

acknowledgements

An earlier version of this paper was presented at the 1998 Canadian Women's Studies Association Conference during the Congress of Social Sciences and Humanities held at the University of Ottawa. I would like to thank Angela Miles, Linda Muzzin and Sarita Srivastava for their comments and suggestions. I would also like to thank the two anonymous reviewers who commented on an earlier draft of the paper.

references

Abbey, E. (1976) The *Monkey Wrench Gang*, New York: Avon Books.

Adkin, L.E. (1992a) 'Counter-hegemony and environmental politics in Canada' in W.K. Carroll (1992) editor, *Organizing Dissent*, Toronto: Garamond.

Adkin, L.E. (1992b) 'ecology and labour: towards a new societal paradigm' in C. Leys and M. Mendell (1992) editors, *Culture and Social Change*, Montreal: Black Rose Books.

Bari, J. (1990) 'expand Earth First!' *Earth First!*, September, No. 22, p.5.

Bari, J. (1994) *Timber Wars,* Monroe: Common Courage Press.

Barker-Benfield, B. (1973) 'The spermatic economy: a nineteenth century view of sexuality' in M. Gordon (1973) editor, *The American Family in Socio-Historical Perspective,* New York: St. Martin's Press.

Barol, B. (1990) 'Eco-activist summer: Earth First! vs. the loggers in California' *Newsweek,* July, No. 2, p.60.

Biehl, J. (1989) 'Ecofeminism and deep ecology: unresolvable conflict?' in D.I. Roussopoulos (1989) editor, *The Anarchist Papers 2,* Montreal: Black Rose Books.

Biehl, J. (1991) *Finding Our Way: Rethinking Ecofeminist Politics,* Montreal: Black Rose Books.

Bookchin, M. (1990) *The Philosophy of Social Ecology,* Montreal: Black Rose Books.

Bookchin, M. (1991) *The Ecology of Freedom,* Montreal: Black Rose Books.

Bookchin, M. and Foreman, D. (1991) *Defending the Earth,* Boston: South End Press.

Chase, S. (1991) 'Whither the radical ecology movement' in M. Bookchin and D. Foreman (1991) editors, *Defending the Earth,* Biston: South End Press.

Devall, B. (1988) *Simple in Means, Rich in Ends: Practicing Deep Ecology,* Salt Lake City: Peregrine Smith Books.

Dubofsky, M. (1969) *We Shall Be All: A History of the IWW,* Chicago: Quadrangle Books.

Foreman, D. (1989) *Ecodefense: A Field Guide to Monkeywrenching,* Tucson: Ned Ludd Books.

Foreman, D. (1991) *Confessions of an Eco-Warrior,* New York: Harmony Books.

Gray, E.D. (1993) 'We must re-myth genesis' in P.C. List (1993) editor, *Radical Environmentalism: Philosophy and Tactics,* Belmont: Wadsworth.

Gusfield, J.R. (1992) 'Nature's body and the metaphor of food' in M. Lamont and M. Fournier (1992) editors, *Cultivating Differences: Symbolic Boundaries and the Making of Inequality,* Chicago: University of Chicago Press.

Heider, U. (1994) *Anarchism: Left, Right and Green,* San Francisco: City Lights.

Kornblugh, J.L. (1964) *Rebel Voices: An IWW Anthology,* Ann Arbor: U of M Press.

Kornegger, P. (1996) 'Anarchism: the feminist connection' in H.J. Ehrlich (1996) editor, *Ranventing Anarchy, Again,* Edinburgh: AK Press.

Kropotkin, P. (1955) *Mutual Aid,* Boston: Extending Horizons Books.

Kropotkin, P. (1994) *Fields, Factories and Workshops,* Montreal: Black Rose Books.

Lange, J.I. (1990) 'Refusal to compromise: the case of Earth First!' *Western Journal of Speech Communication,* Vol. 54, pp.473–494.

List, P.C. (1993a) *Radical Environmentalism: Philosophy and Tactics,* Belmont: Wadsworth.

List, P.C. (1993b) 'Introduction' in P.C. List (1993a) editor, *Radical Environmentalism: Philosophy and Tactics,* Belmont: Wadsworth.

Manes, C. (1990) *Green Rage: Radical Environmentalism and the Unmaking of Civilization,* Boston: Little Brown and Company.

Merchant, C. (1993) 'Ecofeminism and feminist theory' in P.C. List (1993) editor, *Radical Environmentalism: Philosophy and Tactics,* Belmont: Wadsworth.

Miss Ann Thropy (1987) 'Population and AIDS' *Earth First!,* May, No. 1, p.32.

Pickett, K. (1993) 'Redwood Summer retrospective' in P.C. List (1993) editor, *Radical Environmentalism: Philosophy and Tactics,* Belmont: Wadsworth.

Purchase, G. (1994) *Anarchism and Environmental Survival,* Tucson: See Sharp Press.

Purchase, G. (1997) 'Social ecology, anarchism and trades unionism' in Freedom Press (1997) editors, *Deep Ecology and Anarchism: A Polemic,* London: Freedom Press.

Scarce, R. (1990) *Eco-Warriors,* Chicago: The Noble Press.

Shantz, J. (1999) 'Beyond productivism: syndicalism and ecology' *Anarcho-Syndicalist Review,* Vol. 25, pp.20–23.

Short, B. (1991) 'Earth First! and the rhetoric of moral confrontation' *Communication Studies,* Vol. 42, No. 2, pp.172–188.

Stentz, Z. (1993) 'Osprey Grove Falls' in P.C. List (1993) editor, *Radical Environmentalism: Philosophy and Tactics,* Belmont: Wadsworth.

Watson, C.P. (1994) 'In defense of tree-spiking' in J. Zinovich (1994) editor, *Canadas,* New York/ Peter borough: Semio text (e)/Marginal Editions.

70 | interview with Carole Pateman: *The Sexual Contract*, women in politics, globalization and citizenship

Nirmal Puwar

the sexual contract

Nirmal: Could you say something about the emergence of the ideas you developed in your most famous text *The Sexual Contract*?

Carole: I will not get into the issue of whether *Participation and Democratic Theory* is better known than *The Sexual Contract*! My ideas were developed after I had written another book, on political obligation, that is also about theories of an original contract. I began to think seriously about how feminist arguments were related to the classic theories, to questions about contract and consent, and how actual contracts, such as the marriage or employment contract, fitted in. When I started re reading the famous texts from a feminist perspective I realised that a whole dimension of the story of an original contract was there in the books, but missing from accounts of the social contract.

The social contract, a claim about the legitimacy of government in the state, is only one aspect of the original contract. The other aspect, the sexual contract, is a claim about the legitimacy of men's power over women. My argument is about these very peculiar contracts about property in the person and the relationship constituted through these contracts. And by the time I had worked out enough of this to start getting it into a book, contract theory had become big academic business in the wake of Rawls. But in the light of my re reading of the famous texts, my assessment of major institutions such as marriage or employment, and the contracts through which they are created, is obviously very different from that of Rawls and his followers.

Nirmal: How would you position yourself in the debates on patriarchy and gender regimes?

Carole: I have not thought about patriarchy for a while. One of the criticisms of patriarchy was that it was ahistorical and timeless, so I tried to show in *The Sexual Contract* that actually it had a history. I distinguished traditional very broad views of patriarchy which literally took the family as the model and

(123–133) © 2002 Feminist Review. 0141-7789/02 $15 www.feminist-review.com

generalised to politics, from the classic form of patriarchy which flowered in the 17th century, which theorists of the original contract treated as their adversary. And then we have my notion of modern patriarchy which is curious because it is contractual. The conventional view in political theory is that contract won out and defeated the classic type of patriarchy. I argue that classic patriarchy was transformed into the modern type. The reason I was keen on the term patriarchy was because we do need a word to talk about the questions feminists are interested in, notably the power of men over women. If that is not named, it all too easily gets swept under the carpet. I have not thought through how it would fit in with different types of gender regimes. But insofar as these regimes involve any kind of power of men over women, whatever form it takes, and obviously the forms can be various, I cannot see why different senses of patriarchy cannot capture that. Has anyone got a better concept? That is the question — what is an alternative concept to patriarchy?

Nirmal: I suppose some people say fraternities.

Carole: Yes, I had a whole argument about that as well. I think fraternity is a much more specific concept than patriarchy.

Nirmal: There has been a move to make it specific instead of having patriarchy as a universal concept.

Carole: I was not meaning patriarchy as a universal concept. When I wrote the book I explicitly said that I was talking about Anglo-American societies. But I have been interested to find that some scholars from other parts of the world, from, for example, Middle Eastern countries, have been using my work. In Asia, a Korean translation was recently published, and has been chosen by the Ministry of Culture and Tourism as the best translation of 2001 and will be placed in many libraries, so clearly the general idea of a sexual contract, if not the specific character it has taken in countries like Britain or the USA, is relevant very widely. So, although I did not make any claims for it being universal, scholars and readers from a number of very different cultures are finding my argument useful.

Nirmal: I was really referring to how patriarchy can be universal whereas the concept of multiple masculinities and gender regimes allows for a flexible understanding of different institutional sites, which then allows class and race to enter the equation as well.

Carole: The reason I picked up the term patriarchy when I wrote the book is that it is very difficult to find a term that captures the power of men over women, in whatever form it comes. Because that form of power has not been treated as a political issue for so long, we have not had analogous terms to those developed for other types of power. But you do not have to do any extensive amount of research to see how race, gender, class and ethnicities are clearly connected in the new global order.

Nirmal: How important has the sex act been to the contract you discuss in relation to prostitution?

Carole: I was defining prostitution fairly narrowly. I was not including every thing that is involved in the sex industry, though I included hand relief, and even have a joke about it. The sex act is interesting because traditionally, although you had said the words 'I do', the marriage contract was not a valid contract unless you performed another act as well. Unless the marriage was consummated it could be treated as null and void, which, I think, is interesting and a rather significant feature. Obviously, views on and law about marriage have changed, but traditionally the sex act was central, and I suspect remains so today. Obviously, the sex act has been central to prostitution. Obviously, too, that is what men are paying for.

Nirmal: But are they also paying for their position of dominance?

Carole: Yes, but then it is a question of what that means, and why they demand that this be available as a commodity in the market. Men seem to be demanding to have paid access to women's bodies in even larger numbers than when I wrote the book. There has been a rapid expansion of the global sex industry. Today, with the collapse of so many economies around the world, and ones that have not collapsed being structurally adjusted, so many women have been pushed into poverty and on to the margins of existence. And anyone interested in feminism and human rights has to be very much interested in these issues. These are clearly human rights issues because human beings, in this case mostly women and girls, are treated merely as a commodity that can be bought, sold, kidnapped, shipped across frontiers, sent around the world purely as objects to be used, often in extraordinarily bad conditions.

Nirmal: *The Sexual Contract* has been influential to feminist thought within a wide range of areas including politics, women and work as well as a whole range of other disciplines. If you were writing it now what else would you want to include, or, how would you reconfigure it?

Carole: I must say that I have been very pleased with the widespread reception of the text not only in politics departments but also especially in history departments and literature departments and law schools.

On the whole, I do not tamper with the things I have already written. I just prefer to do something new. Of course, since I was concerned with relations between the sexes, I did not focus on the relationships and institutions that Charles Mills has now discussed in his book *The Racial Contract*. We have recently decided that we shall write something together on the two contracts, though this is still at an early stage.

Let me stress, though, that the slave contract runs all the way through *The Sexual Contract*, although people do not seem to discuss it. Well, the reviewers at least do not tend to talk about that very much. Towards the end of the book I said I had exaggerated in arguing that there was this missing half of the contract. That is an exaggeration, because there is also another contract there, which Mills has called the racial contract. And clearly, if you look at both of our books together, which people are now doing, if you look at the famous texts, and the political developments of empires and the world-wide system of states, you can see that the original contract has at least three interrelated dimensions: (1) the social contract, which of course is the standard one that everyone is taught, (2) the sexual contract, and (3) the racial contract.

Nirmal: Whilst I appreciate that the racial contract was present in your book *The Sexual Contract*, do you think that we need to spend more time on doing it altogether, that is class, gender and race?

Carole: Well, the difficult thing is that it is very hard to do it altogether because each part is so complicated. Even though the contracts are historically entwined together, it is difficult to find a way to do justice to all of the complexity involved. It remains to be seen how well Charles and I will succeed in this!

Nirmal: Could it be that the slavery part of the book, in other words the racial aspect alongside the imperialist history of social and political thought, may not have been taken up because of the nature of feminism itself, especially within the area of political science, although it is of course changing?

Carole: The whole feminist battle is such a big one. That is a part of the problem. You are always fighting the same things over and over again. But black feminists and Chicano feminists have made a big impact. So things that are written now do not look like the things that were written 25 years ago.

Nirmal: But have they managed to significantly dent the political science academy?

Carole: I was thinking about feminist work. The political science academy is another thing. There is a feminist presence in political science, but it is still rather minor. Although things have changed enormously since I was first involved, it was pretty lonely at the beginning. When I first went to an American Political Science Association meeting in the early 70s for instance, there were very few women. And as a young academic I rapidly discovered how threatened men were by women who trespassed onto their turf, and encountered quite a bit of hostility and discrimination. It has been a hard road. But now there are lots of women and panels on gender and feminist theory at APSA conferences, and gender is big publishing business. But there is still a long way to go.

Although feminism has had an impact on political science, the hopes of the pioneers in the 70s and early 80s that political science would be transformed have not been realised. The feminist critique of central assumptions of political science is very powerful. But in a discipline that is now highly professionalized and that accommodates many different approaches, feminism can be accorded a place, but normal political science can also continue on its way, and take no notice of the challenge that feminism poses.

thinking of the criticisms

Nirmal: Conceptions of power have been quite central to feminist theory. How do you position yourself within Nancy Fraser's critique of your notion of power?

Carole: Let me say that I hope one day to reply to some of the criticisms in a systematic way. For a variety of reasons I have not been able to do this yet. Let me also add that my book is about relations of subordination, that is, it is about power and freedom. I must say that Fraser fundamentally misunderstood my book, if you are thinking of her piece in *Social Text*, where she says I had a dyadic model of power. In *The Sexual Contract* I actually took a lot of trouble to emphasise that I am looking at the structure of the *institutions* of marriage, employment, or prostitution, not individual couples. Fraser seems not to have seen the importance of a point that John Stuart Mill made in *The Subjection of Women* that I refer to in my book. He said that you can find many examples of good husbands who do not use the powers that they have, legal powers in his day, but that is not the point. Couples are not being added up. The point is that the powers are structurally there in the institutions, so, as Mill was so well aware, when you make the change from 'man' to 'husband' you acquire the powers, which you can use or not. But the point is that you have the powers by virtue of the contract that has been entered into and the structure of the institution of which you are now a part.

Nirmal: Along with that critique, Fraser talked about the subject/object, master/slave being in your work. Do you think that is another miscalculation on her part?

Carole: I talked briefly about master/slave in my discussion of Hegel. I also draw attention to the resemblance between the slave contract and other contracts, and indicated how the paradox of slavery recurs in various guises. But do not forget that I was looking at those curious contracts about the property in person. My argument is that these contracts create relations of domination and subjection, but that is not to say that it is a simple matter of subject/object dyads. As I emphasised, to enter such contracts women's freedom must be presupposed, they must be subjects, even if they become subordinates and their freedom is denied.

One of the things about the book is that I have been attacked for so many different reasons, some of which are contradictory. And I think one of the reasons for that is that the book does not fit into any standard categories of the political theory or into the misleading categorisations of liberal feminism, psychoanalytic feminism, socialist feminism and so on. I have never found these categorizations helpful. In fact, I take it that I must have done something right to be criticized from all quarters. I was also warning feminists against the allure of contract.

One of the things that was unfortunate was that the book came out at the height of essentialism hunting. A lot of people seemed to spend time leafing through the book trying to find evidence of essentialism.

Nirmal: Mouffe has criticized you for a kind of essentialism that connects motherhood with citizenship.

Carole: Motherhood is not in *The Sexual Contract* — that is about marriage and wives, not the family — but it is in some other writings of mine. What I am accused of having said is that women should be citizens as mothers. That is not what I have said. In a piece published on Equality and Difference I was pointing out the importance of motherhood as a vehicle for women's political incorporation. Women have been allotted the political task of bearing and rearing the next generation of citizens. But they have often been excluded from citizenship while performing the task. Historically, and even today, motherhood is central. There are lots of different aspects to this — feminists have of course emphasized motherhood as something of particular value that women contribute as citizens that should be recognised as such, and some have said this should form a part of citizenship. I certainly argue that women's unpaid work, much of which is to do with motherhood, should be counted as a contribution to citizenship, but that is different from saying that women should be citizens as mothers. You can see how important it still is. In America there is a bizarre preoccupation with abortion, or as I prefer, forced motherhood. There is also the population question in so many countries. There is still this question 'Are *they* out-breeding *us*?' All these questions, of population, nation-building, and race and ethnicity — mass rape in conflict is partly about 'diluting' another ethnicity — are related to motherhood, although the word itself is not used.

women in positions of political leadership

Nirmal: Looking at the recent increase of women in western legislatures. In some places like the Nordic countries the increase took place well before Britain or America. While I have been watching the presence of women MPs, I was thinking about the phrase you use in your texts when you say that the political lion skin is exceedingly ill-fitting for women.

Carole: I have been observing the presence of women in Parliaments but not in a very systematic way. As a lot of people have said, obviously it is not a matter of the developed world and the less-developed world. But clearly, Nordic countries are in the lead because they have taken special measures to make this happen. In the United States, Congress still does not have a good representation of women. There are lots more women in leadership positions internationally now, as heads of state or government, or as heads of United Nations bodies, like Mary Robinson. I think it is going to be interesting over the next ten years to see what happens if the numbers go on increasing. We will see how much of a difference it will make to actual political agendas and policies. Will it change the UN at all? Because we have plenty of examples of women who have been leaders of government and have not pushed an agenda that helps women.

Nirmal: Well we cannot assume a direct connection between the two, that is women and feminist politics. In Britain, Margaret Thatcher is probably the most famous example.

Carole: We also have all those women leaders in South Asia who come from elite families. It certainly is not obvious that they have done much to help women in those countries.

Nirmal: This brings us to another longstanding debate in feminism in terms of whether women should or should not enter these traditional institutions because of what they have to become in order to exist in these incredibly male spaces.

Carole: Well, I think that they should enter them despite the problems. The institutions are there and they are powerful institutions. If you just leave them to the men to carry on as usual then the problem remains untouched. But clearly, it depends on the policies that the women pursue once they get there. There is evidence that once you get a critical mass of women it does make a bit of difference to what gets put on the agenda.

Nirmal: In the UK what we are seeing is a critical mass that is tempered by the fact that many of the women have marginal seats. Recently, breast feeding was banned in the House. The Speaker told a female MP that she could not breast feed in a committee because beverages are not allowed in committees! All of this is a sign of how, as you mention in your work, the political space is constructed at the exclusion of the private and the 'feminine'. Some ruptures are being caused by the mere presence of women in these places.

Carole: The presence of women of childbearing age in any significant public body is a very recent phenomenon. Most of the women in the past who managed to get in were past childbearing age. It is going to be interesting to see what difference it makes.

Nirmal: It has been noted that many of the women in parliament are increasingly from a middle class background and they are generally white, although not all of them. This shows that other forms of exclusion are operating with gender and how the very simplistic focus on gender does not work.

Carole: This is true in the States because (a) you need a lot of money for politics here, and (b) most people enter politics through other professions such as law, business and so forth. I suspect that, despite a few exceptions, most of the women here have come from 'good' middle class backgrounds one way or another.

Nirmal: Where would you position yourself in the mapping of feminism? Obviously, you are not a liberal feminist but at the same time you would not endorse the position that women should not participate in the state.

Carole: Well, you could make an argument that women should not participate. But those heady days of the early women's movement when the argument was stronger have gone. It is all so fragmented now. Although globally there is a great deal of activity, so many very basic battles have still to be fought. I think we have to move on all fronts if we are going to get anywhere. As I mentioned, I do not find many standard maps of feminism too helpful. I work from problems rather than a position on the map.

Nirmal: Keeping in mind the difference/sameness debates, we could say that women are entering traditional political institutions, like parliament, to be the same, or at least there is the pressure to be the same.

Carole: The pressure is always there, but part of this is the critical mass question. It is much easier for women to start achieving change, however small that may be, and not to behave completely like the men if there are more of you. If you are lonely and on your own it is much harder. And the old equality/difference debate is really a bit tired now. I do not know that anyone is really saying that everyone has got to be the same, apart from accusations from the right-wing.

Nirmal: Do you think there is enough emphasis on diversity?

Carole: If you live in Los Angeles you are engaged with diversity on a day-to-day basis, and I welcome debates on diversity. But one of the things that has tended to happen — Ann Phillips discusses this in her book *Which Equalities Matter?* — is that the emphasis on diversity can obscure another development. Over the last quarter century the gap between the rich and the poor has got wider both within countries and between the North and the South. And we should not forget that. There is, after all, a correlation between some of the 'differences' and those at the bottom of the economic ladder.

Nirmal: This brings us to the whole question of globalization.

globalization, citizenship and employment

Carole: I have been thinking about globalization, to some extent it is forced upon you. I am greatley struck by this in democratic theory, because until very recently every one who wrote about democratic theory took the borders of the nation state for granted. Now of course you cannot do that. If you are going to write something that is relevant to the 21st century, then you have got to start thinking about how globalization and democratic theory are connected. This is crucial for a lot of the questions I am interested in about citizenship.

Nirmal: You have been addressing some of these issues in your current work.

Carole: I am writing a series of essays on various aspects of democratization and rights and citizenship, some of which are historical and others contemporary. I have an essay on T.H. Marshall for example. I am writing about the policy of basic income for citizens. I have re-visited the concept of property in person in connection with a critical look at some of the discussions of self-ownership. I am still interested in some of the questions I started off with in the 60s, although I am now approaching them from a different perspective. But one of the things I am particularly interested in and have written some pieces about, is that employment has always been central to the construction of citizenship and now it is becoming more and more central. Globalization, in part, is about the global construction of labour markets. The assumption seems to be, especially in countries like Britain and the US, that every able-bodied adult must be in the labour force. There is this assumption that you are not really contributing unless you are in employment. To question this is a somewhat quixotic thing to be doing now that globalization is spreading employment to more places than ever before, and so many people have the notion that democratization means the introduction of markets, especially labour markets. I want to try and present a different view on this.

Nirmal: You are de-coupling citizenship and employment

Carole: Yes. One of the things I am trying to think about is what counts as a contribution by citizens. At the moment, increasingly, employment is seen as the thing that counts. This is true even for mothers with small children, which is a big historic departure. So I want to ask some questions about what does and should count as a contribution. And then ask another question, which is much less often asked: which is, should democratic citizenship be contingent upon a contribution at all? In other words, should the rights and benefits of democratic citizenship be contingent? I want to answer, 'no' they should not, to that question. That is where my interest in the basic income comes in.

Nirmal: Yes, you are pushing against notions of a welfare state found amongst existing conceptions of rights and duties in mainstream politics. Unfortunately, I cannot see the politicians buying your ideas, but I suppose they never have.

Carole: No, and I do not suppose that most of them have read my books anyway, though I have met one or two who have.

Nirmal: When you are questioning what counts as a contribution, are you connecting in with the questions you raised in your earlier works in the public and private?

Carole: Oh yes, very much so. There are all kinds of people doing all kinds of work, particularly of course women in the household, which is not seen as a contribution. I want to stress that, if we are to take democracy seriously, then we should think very hard about why citizenship and rights should be contingent upon a contribution.

Nirmal: People's contribution is judged differently anyway.

Carole: Oh yes. In terms of remuneration it has reached grotesque proportions where people who are running companies are getting enormous, vast sums of money. There are other people doing important jobs – the obvious ones are nurses and so forth – who are not paid properly, and there are huge numbers of 'working poor'. So I am arguing for some kind of reasonable distribution, and a guarantee of a basic, modest but decent standard of life for everyone, if we are serious about democracy, citizenship and rights.

Nirmal: In some of the debates on globalization and politics there has been a positive take by several theorists on cosmopolitanism. Do you have any thoughts on this?

Carole: I have not thought about cosmopolitanism as such. But from thinking abut human rights, and I have done some work on early modern feminists and rights, and teaching a graduate course on multiculturalism, I have come to the view that, although there is plenty of room for local interpretation and implementation, there is also a bottom line. If human rights are to be meaningful there are limits to interpretation, especially where women are concerned, who are central to this issue, since they are often regarded as symbols of tradition. Human rights are now an enormously important organising concept for women around the world in all kinds of situations. And human rights, in principle at least, cut across state borders, so they are central to globalization and democracy.

Another area in which I am interested is how to strengthen the conditions under which democratization can flourish, in the face of structural adjustment and privatization, which cut off channels of accountability, and the enormous power of transnational corporations. Democratic theorists have tended to neglect corporations, but now the most powerful have 'GDPs' bigger than most countries. How corporations, the WTO, the IMF, and the World Bank, can be made more democratic, more accountable, and more responsive to the needs of the South and marginal populations is a very hard question. All the old democratic questions of whose voices are listened to and taken into account, how agendas are constructed, and how resources are owned and distributed are more relevant than ever.

Two areas of globalization I find very disturbing are the rapid growth in the sex industry, which I have mentioned already, and the small arms trade. A number of countries have been devastated and destroyed by armed conflicts in recent years, and this would be more difficult if arms were not so cheap and readily available, and if so many countries and firms were not engaged in the trade. Millions of people are now displaced or refugees. Women have a particularly hard time in these conflicts and in the refugee camps. And, of course, refugees are increasingly unwelcome in rich countries, especially if they are from the South. And then there are the millions of land mines which make reconstruction even harder.

Nirmal: Do you see these as positive times in terms of change and resistance?

Carole: I think it is to some extent positive at present, but also depressing given the scale of poverty, conflict, the rise of fundamentalism in the world's major religions, and, for instance, the dreadful spectacle of the world watching as millions were slaughtered in Rwanda. On the positive side, there have been improvements in literacy levels, and 'human development' more generally, though unevenly distributed. Many people are now thinking about issues that were hard to hear about a decade ago, including the sex trade and the arms trade. There are global movements around these issues, and other matters such as what goes on behind the closed doors of the WTO, genetically engineered foodstuffs and 'bio-piracy', the policies of pharmaceutical companies who ignore diseases that kill and debilitate millions, and concentrate on the very profitable diseases of the affluent world. I have read that eight new drugs are being developed for impotence, which never killed a single man. Not only are these questions discussed but there are demonstrations and other forms of political activity around the world. And interest is reviving in questions that I was concerned with years ago, such as participatory democracy, that for a time were, to say the least, extremely unfashionable. Here in Los Angeles there was a big campaign for Justice for Janitors, and some improvements were won for the janitorial workers. There is a movement among young people in the US on university campuses against sweatshops that produce clothes with university logos. All of this is an encouraging sign. Times of rapid change always open up opportunities for democratization, but what the outcome of globalization will be in another decade it is very hard to tell at this point. But I am impressed by the extent to which women's movements have taken root around the world and now form a global network, and although there is a very long way to go, that is a cause for optimism.

acknowledgement

The members of The Pateman Reading Group (Leicester University, 1999) were intrinsic to the making of this interview, most especially Laura Brace.

70 | reclaiming democracy? the anti-globalization movement in South Asia

Shoba S. Rajgopal

abstract

This article studies anti-globalization activities in South Asia, and specifically the Indian subcontinent, and discovers that the common people have begun a new form of civil disobedience in the country, to counter the machinations of multinational corporations. Many of the eminent writers and activists at the forefront of the movement are Indian women, a fact that may come as a surprise to some, but is part and parcel of the movement's basis in sustainable development and resistance to patriarchal hegemony.

keywords

multinational corporations; genetically modified plants; sustainable development

This article is dedicated to my beloved younger sister, Padma Rajgopal, who passed away suddenly in August 2001. She was an activist, organic farmer, wife and mother, and was a great inspiration to me and many others in India. If you would like to find out how you can be involved in the work that she started, please look up her website: www.passionfruitcoaching.com started by friends and well-wishers from the UK.

Globalization is increasingly seen by some as a synonym for postcolonialism. For the two terms share the same idea of cosmopolitan centres in changing relations with rural areas in the Third World. The most visible actors in this sphere are those abstract entities known as multinational corporations (MNCs). Indeed, the 'McWorldization' of the world, as Benjamin Barber (1995) would have it, seems imminent. However activists and concerned scholars around the world have begun to look askance at the phenomenon of globalization as it reveals profound asymmetries between centre and periphery. In Third World countries like India, governments are increasingly seen as agents not of change but of neocolonialism, functioning as the vassals of vested interests (read the business elite), and working against the interests of vast numbers of the marginalized groups. In the words of eminent Indian

(134–137) © 2002 Feminist Review. 0141-7789/02 $15 www.feminist-review.com

newspaper columnist, George, writing in that doughty old national newspaper, the *Indian Express*, 'We have ministers and bureaucrats and scientists ready to sell the country for 30 pieces of silver (negotiable). India's worst enemies are Indians with power' (2001: 10).

With the collapse of the controls of the Nehruvian era, and the liberalization of the Indian economy, the privatization of the public sphere as well as of the entire state seems imminent. While much of the urban elite welcome this transfer of power from public to private hands, the voices of a few concerned citizens have started being heard. As writer/activist Arundhati Roy elucidates, in a country like India, 70% of the population lives in rural areas. That is 700 million people. Their lives depend directly on access to natural resources. To snatch these away and sell them as stock to private companies is a process of barbaric dispossession that has no parallel in history (Roy, 2000). However, the fallout of globalization in India does not stop with power production by MNCs like Enron. Chemical giants like the American MNC, Monsanto, have marched into the country to stake their claims, using genetic engineering and patents, even on life forms. This move has been stringently opposed by activist groups like the Karnataka Rajya Raita Sangha (KRRS), a militant farmers' association in the southern state of Karnataka.

KRRS had first come into the limelight in 1995 with their protests against transnational food chains like Kentucky Fried Chicken, which had just opened the first of its planned 30 outlets in the country in the southern metropolis of Bangalore. The activists argued that the large-scale livestock farming necessary to feed the fast food industry would lead to similar problems as those faced in the West, including soil erosion of already degraded lands as well as the rise in cancer effected through overindulgence in junk food, among other things. On 28 November 1998, KRRS, led by its fiery leader, Professor Nanjundaswamy, embarked on Operation 'Cremation Monsanto', a campaign of civil disobedience which has over the last three years been spreading to farmers in neighbouring states as well. This entails the uprooting and burning of genetically modified cotton plants being grown under the aegis of the American chemical giant, Monsanto, in experimental farms all over the state. The farmers stated in their defence that terminator technology was being tried on unsuspecting Third World farmers by the multinational seed company, and claimed that they could not respect a government that was colluding with these interests.

Ecofeminist and physicist-environmentalist Dr. Vandana Shiva puts it succinctly in her recent book, *Stolen Harvest: The Hijacking of the Global Food Supply*:

> What we are seeing today is the emergence of food totalitarianism, in which a handful of corporations control the entire food chain and destroy alternatives. The notion of rights has been turned on its head under globalisation and free trade. The right to food, the right to safety, the right to culture, are all being treated as trade barriers that need to be dismantled (Shiva 2000; 17–18).

More than a decade ago, Shiva started a movement known as 'Navdanya' or 'Nine Seeds,' wherein the farmers involved started shifting to organic agriculture and now it has expanded to thousands of villages in which farmers have basically created what they call 'Freedom Zones' free of chemicals, free of corporate inputs, free of hybrid seeds, and free of genetically engineered crops. Following this process, which had been set in motion long before globalization grew into the behemoth it now is, India today is at the forefront of a mass movement of resistance against globalization.

Be it in mega-dam projects like the Narmada Dam in northern India, or power projects like Enron in Maharashtra, in western India, or genetically modified crops via Monsanto in the southern states, the common people have begun to mobilize en masse against what they perceive as the downside of globalization. In northern and central India, for more than a decade, the people's movement of civil disobedience called the Narmada Bachao Andolan (NBA) has made great strides in raising the awareness of the country regarding the marginalization of thousands of indigenous people through the construction of a dam that they claim will ultimately benefit only the urban elite while rendering vast numbers of marginalized groups landless and destitute. This movement of resistance against globalization has evoked international attention, winning the NBA the alternative Nobel award not too long ago for its non-violent struggle against the hegemony of government totalitarianism funded by the World Bank.

The cause of the activists has been furthered through the involvement of eminent writers such as Arundhati Roy. Unlike the situation in the First World, here even mainstream publications such as *Outlook* magazine have made their lead stories major articles against globalization penned by Roy. The fact that she has been vilified by the government as a Westernized 'anti-national' writer is beside the point. At least she has been permitted to represent in print the interests of the otherwise marginalized indigenous people who have managed to eke out a living for the past so many centuries on the banks of a river that is now threatened by the vested interests of elite groups. Can one imagine a similar situation, with *Time* magazine or *Newsweek* permitting a leading activist to pen their cover story? But if there is no space for dissent, how can the public sphere be truly democratic and function as the forum of the people? As Roy (2000) puts it 'the only thing in the world worth globalizing is dissent'.

Another noteworthy point is that many of the well-known activists against globalization in India have been women. From Vandana Shiva to Medha Patkar and Arundhati Roy, they have all catapulted Indian women to the forefront of the movement against globalization. But this cannot be dismissed as a mere result of the modernization of the country, for one of the earliest mass movements against environmental degradation in the Himalayas, the 'Chipko' movement, was started by illiterate village women who embraced the trees to prevent people from felling them. Indeed, since its birth over two decades ago, Chipko has grown into a women-based movement against environmental degradation and has spread to other parts of the country as well, signs of the growing militancy amongst poor rural women. American activist in the Sierra Nevada, Julia Butterfly Hill's giant redwood project 'Luna' can in this sense be seen to have a worthy forerunner in the dedicated village women of the Himalayas. Feminist activists and scholars see the involvement of women in all these struggles as the direct connection of women with sustainable living and development and a definite stand against the iniquities of a patriarchal world order.

author biography

The author is a doctoral candidate in the Media Studies Program at the University of Colorado's School of Journalism and Mass Communication. She has worked as a broadcast journalist and writer in India, prior to her arrival in the US, focusing on the struggles of women and indigenous peoples in the postcolonial nation-state. She is currently working as an instructor in the Dept of Ethnic Studies at the University of Colorado, where she teaches a course in Asian-American Studies.

references

Barber, B. (1995) *Jihad vs McWorld*, New York: Times Books.

George, T.J.S. (2001) 'Opinion' *The Indian Express*, June 23, p. 10.

Roy, A. (2000) 'The reincarnation of rumpelstilskin,' *Outlook* magazine, November 27.

Shiva, V. (2000) *Stolen Harvest: The Hijacking of the Global Food Supply*, Cambridge, MA: South End Press.

70 | 'globalization' and the 'third way': a feminist response

Lizzie Ward

Two recent contributions to *Feminist Review* have considered the question of what a socialist feminist response to New Labour and the 'third way' entails. Both Angela McRobbie ('Feminism and the Third Way', *Feminist Review* 64) and Jane Franklin ('What's Wrong with New Labour Politics?', *Feminist Review* 66) raise the difficulty in assessing an agenda which, possibly for the first time, addresses issues long advocated by feminists, with policies aimed at improving childcare provision and encouraging women into the labour market. Angela McRobbie regards this agenda as at least opening up possibilities for socialist feminist gains, but highlights how New Labour's mission to transform the welfare state will severely limit such gains. In contrast, Jane Franklin argues that the nature of feminist politics is to demand change and that this is irreconcilable with the... third way's communitarianism: for the 'third way' supports a status quo with deeply rooted gender, class and race inequalities, favouring consensus over conflict and leading to a *politics for women without feminism*. Here I argue that any assessment of what the 'third way' might offer socialist feminism must also take into account New Labour's commitment to free market economics. The key issue here is New Labour's monolithic view about the nature of globalization which underpins a number of the 'feminist' sounding policies and determines their contradictory features. Only by addressing this question is it possible to outline a socialist feminist response to New Labour.

what distinguishes the 'third way'?

In the early 1990s, the challenge facing the architects of New Labour was to convince the electorate and the 'business community' that a Labour government could be trusted with the economy and could address the social disintegration created by the individualism promoted by almost 20 years of Conservative government. As Jane Franklin points out, the 'third way', as a synthesis of communitarian ideas and neo-liberal economics was designed to meet that challenge. The New Labour modernizers discarded Labour's historical commitment to public ownership in favour of a more pragmatic approach to the free market. How did Blair justify the discovery that, contrary to the experience of the previous 150 years of the labour movement, business and the

(138–143) © 2002 Feminist Review. 0141-7789/02 $15 www.feminist-review.com

free market were no longer the problem but the solution? Blair had to persuade us, like Thatcher, that there really was no alternative. It is here that 'globalization' comes into play. In the globalized economy, national governments are apparently powerless to intervene in their domestic economies. As Blair himself put it 'The driving force of economic change today is globalization. Technology and capital are mobile. Industry is becoming fiercely competitive across national boundaries.... (A) country has to dismantle barriers to competition and accept the disciplines of the international economy.' (Blair, 1996: 118).

The implication here is that the economic framework will determine the parameters of the social policy agenda. According to New Labour, social justice equals economic efficiency (Blair, 1996: preface). What this means in policy terms is that supply side measures are introduced which focus on providing educational and training opportunities, assistance and – in some cases, compulsion – to enter the labour market of the 'new economy' through welfare-to-work programmes. Business, as a result, is provided with a skilled flexible workforce – what's good for the people it turns out, is good for business. But the equation is double-edged. On the one hand, it persuades business interests that social policy intervention is economically justifiable. On the other, it ensures that social policy will be designed with economic priorities in mind.

how does this affect women?

Broad economic changes, notably in production processes and de-industrialization, are associated with 'the feminization of the workforce,' that is, the decline in male employment in manufacturing, traditionally more organized and unionized, and the increase in the service sector dominated by female employment, generally part-time and not organized. It is apparent that women are central to the compliant, low-paid workforce essential for contemporary capital accumulation. (Stean, 2000). Moreover, as Jill Stean argues, this is evident at a global level as structural adjustment programmes imposed on developing countries by the IMF (such as the Export Production Zones where factories are set up to produce goods for export on the global market and women make up 85% of the workforce) depend on women as the cheapest form of labour. (Stean, 2000).

This is the context in which New Labour's 'women-friendly' social polices need to be considered, especially those aimed at increasing women's participation in the labour market. Whilst policies like the New Deal for Lone Parents and tax breaks for those on low pay are presented in 'feminist' tones of enabling greater financial independence and fulfilling individual potential, in reality, the choice may be between surviving on minimal welfare benefits or surviving, albeit slightly financially better off, in the type of low-paid, insecure job typical of the 'new economy'. In the New Deal, New Labour appears to have overcome the Conservative dilemma of how to remove state support from lone mothers. The Major government looked to absent fathers to replace welfare support through the Child Support Agency, as encouraging mothers to work outside the home lies beyond the orbit of Conservative thinking on the family. New Labour, in tune with the needs of the market, has the solution. Under New Labour, a woman's place is both in the home and in the workplace, as the following quotation from former Minister for Women, Baroness Jay, makes clear:

> It is our job to make sure that women can have successful jobs but also be successful mums, grandmas, carers and homemakers. Strong families, after all, are the key to a healthy society and women are the heart of the family.

(Jay, 1999)

Thus, 'family-friendly' employment policies and 'flexible working' intended to 'help' juggle these responsibilities turn out to be little more than an intensification of the double burden of paid and unpaid work. Or as Sylvia Walby observed over a decade ago, reflecting on the emerging 'flexible' labour market, 'patriarchal and capitalist interests have found a new accommodation. In women's part-time waged work men do not lose their individual domestic labourers, while employers gain cheap labour. Whose flexibility?' (Walby, 1987: 14).

the great globalization debate

But is Blair right that 'globalization' is a fact of life that just has to be accepted — the inevitable and unstoppable outcome of the evolution of capitalist development. Contrary to the New Labour portrayal, 'globalization' is not an uncontested concept. Rather, it is a subject of considerable debate which includes a range of positions — from those sceptical of its actual existence, who regard it as a façade that masks the still substantial power of a few Western governments (principally the US) within the international economy, as well as those who view it as a multi-dimensional, complex process of profound change.[1] As Bourdieu and Wacquant point out, invoking 'globalization' as an uncontested notion of universal common sense, as Blair and 'third way' advocates do, justifies 'their voluntary surrender to the financial markets and their conversion to a fiduciary conception of the firm'. Furthermore, increasing inequality and cutbacks in welfare expenditure come to be regarded as the inevitable result in the growth of foreign trade rather than 'the result of *domestic political decisions* that reflect the tipping of the balance of class forces in favour of the owners of capital'. (Bourdieu & Wacquant, 2001: 4)

[1] See Held and McGrew for an extensive account of the debate The Global Transformations Reader, Cambridge: Polity Press, 2000.

the 'third way' as the promoter of 'globalization'

The acceptance of globalization as given is a central feature of 'third way' politics. Furthermore, the 'third way' is not just a British phenomena. It has captured the imagination of many political leaders and various manifestations have appeared both among European social democrats and beyond, finding strong support from the Clinton administration (Callinicos, 2001). Certainly, the promise of a 'third way' to transcend the failures of both the Left and Right and renew social democracy has proved irresistible to many. But there remains serious doubt as to how far it transcends the neo-liberal hegemony that dominates the world's financial institutions, in particular the IMF. During his first term of office, Blair demonstrated his intention to maintain the 'Washington Consensus' of deregulation, privatisation, monetary and fiscal stability and removal of barriers to free trade, all of which were initiated by Reagan and Thatcher during the 1980s and facilitated greater global economic integration (Callinicos, 2001). Indeed, many argue that Blair's welfare reforms and 'partnerships' with the private sector demonstrate a willingness to go further than his Conservative predecessors dared.

As New Labour's second term gets under way, the public sector has become the target for further privatization. Disguised in the language of investment and concern for providing the best service is the belief that who delivers that service is not important and there is nothing intrinsically wrong or contradictory in this role being carried out by private enterprise. This assumption opens the door for corporate interests to extend their reach into the public arena with the primary aim of doing exactly what business does — make profits. Women are closely associated with the public sector, both as workers — 75% of health care workers are women (Pascall, 1997) and as users who rely on public services. They are likely to be disproportionately affected as they see provision pitted against the drive to maximise profit. This agenda, far from being the only possible option as a result of 'globalization' as New Labour claim, is actually enhancing the processes of 'globalization', allowing globalized capital to penetrate new markets.

alternatives for feminism ?

As Jane Franklin rightly argues, Blair's communitarianism alters the framework in which 'women's issues' are addressed, shifting the emphasis from 'rights' typical of a liberal feminist approach to 'responsibility'. Arguably, the feminist modernizing presence has achieved 'gains' by persuading the Millbank elite that popularity with women voters remains essential to staying in power.[2] However, improved maternity rights and family-friendly policies, the feminist gains by 'stealth' which Angela McRobbie refers to, cannot significantly alter structural inequalities. The winners are likely to be the better off, professional career women, who can take advantage of greater availability of childcare and unpaid carer's leave, while the losers are

2 See Harriet Harman and Deborah Mattinson Winning for Women, London: Fabian Society, 2000.

more probably women already experiencing poverty, either in low paid, insecure work or on the minimal benefits that Blair is committed to under the reformed welfare system.

As Jane Franklin shows, feminism has little chance of getting anywhere with the 'third way' because of its communitarianism. Of equal significance though, is the fact that feminist advances under New Labour will be severely constrained by its commitment to neo-liberal economics, justified by acceptance of 'globalization'. This highlights the danger that feminist 'gains', paraded by New Labour as 'what all women want' will obscure the increasing marginalization and inequality that adherence to the free market will bring. Only by taking into account the connection between New Labour and globalization, can we begin to see what feminism is up against in terms of defining an appropriate response. Such a response clearly has to address the complex links between globalization, welfare restructuring and 'women-friendly' policy.

As we enter the second term, it is time for us to see the Blair government in its true communitarian and neo-liberal colours and find alternative avenues to articulate feminist arguments. The anti-capitalist movement may provide one way to do this. While it is not yet clear as to where the 'movement' is heading, incorporating elements arguing for the restoration of power to nation-states to moderate the worst effects of the market and others seeking more revolutionary solutions,[3] it does at the very least open up the debate.

Peoples' Global Action (PGA) — the coordinating alliance of the anti-capitalist protests at WTO meetings — are one of the few voices in the debate who explicitly connect 'globalization' to gender oppression, contrasting with the absence of gender perspectives within so many academic discourses. PGA's manifesto unequivocally states: 'Globalization and neo-liberal policies build on and increase existing inequalities, including gender inequality. The gendered system of power in the globalized economy, like most traditional systems, encourages the exploitation of women workers, as maintainers of family and as sexual objects.' (Peoples' Global Action, 1998 http://www.nadir.org/nadir/initiativ/agp/en/PGAInfos/manifest.htm)

Whilst the significance and development of the anti-capitalist movement may not yet be clear, the (re-)emergence of grass roots activism that recognises gender oppression may present the opportunity for closing the gap between academic feminism and feminist activism and in developing a feminist critique of New Labour. We need to be asking how at this particular moment in the history of capitalist development, the globalized relation between capitalism and patriarchy is operating and how this structures the policies of New Labour and other 'third way' governments.

3 See Benedict Seymour, 'Nationalize this! What next for the anti-globalization protests?'. Radical Philosophy 107, May/June 2001:2–5, for discussion on how this position may amount to demands that globalization should be 'fairer' and 'assumes that neo-liberalism is merely a policy mistake that may, with pressure, be rectified, rather than a structural response to capitalist crisis'.

author biography

Lizzie Ward is undertaking a Ph.D. on lone mother's experiences of the New Deal and would welcome comments: School of the Environment, University of Brighton, Lewes Road, Brighton, UK.: e.ward@bton.ac.uk

acknowledgements

Many thanks to Gill Scott, Andrew Church and Bob Brecher for their useful comments.

References

Blair, T. (1996) Speech to the Keidanren, Tokyo, 5 January 1996 in *New Britain: My Vision of a Young Country*, London: Fourth Estate.

Bourdieu, P. and Wacquant, L. (2001) 'New liberal speak: notes on the new planetary vulgate' *Radical Philosophy*, vol. 105 2–5.

Callinicos, A. (2001) *Against the Third Way*, Cambridge: Polity Press.

Jay, M. (1999) Speech to Labour Party Conference, 27 September.

Pascall, G. (1997) *Social Policy: A New Feminist Analysis*, London: Routledge.

Peoples' Global Action (1998) Peoples' Global Action Manifesto, http://www.nadir.org/nadir/ initiativ/agp/en/PGAInfos/manifest.htm.

Stean, J. (2000) 'The gender dimension', in D. Held and A. McGrew editors, *The Global Transformations Reader*, Cambridge: Polity Press.

Walby, S. (1987) *Flexibility and the Changing Sexual Division of Labour*, Lancaster: Lancaster Regionalism Group Working Paper 36.

70 | expanding the spaces of deliberation

Kay Ferres and Barbara Misztal

The liberal character of Australian political institutions and public culture has been tested by the demands of an increasingly multiethnic society. Talk of rights, equality and inclusiveness resonated with notions of tolerance in the 1960s and 1970s, but has since been displaced by a new emphasis on obligation and self-reliance. Public spaces have contracted, and public intellectuals have struggled to find ways to define a common ground. 'Globalization' has produced new divisions in Australian society.

At the 1967 referendum, indigenous people became citizens of the Commonwealth, as well as of the states, as a consequence of overwhelming popular assent to federal government's taking responsibility for Aboriginal affairs. In the 1970s, multiculturalism replaced the discredited 'White Australia' policy, and was promoted by both the Whitlam (Labour) and Fraser (Liberal) governments. Women assumed a new visibility on public life and their activism saw the passage of equal opportunity and sex discrimination legislation. Their participation also made a distinctive impression on the political culture. Although the number of women elected to state and federal parliaments increased slowly until 1996, when a new generation of Labour women made their appearance and a record number of Liberal women were successful in marginal seats, women made effective use of lobby groups to influence policy makers in the bureacracy as well as in the parliaments. This history has produced a capacity for negotiating the informal processes around policy formation.

The establishment of policy branches, state agencies and other institutions underwrote the positive recognition of the diversity and heterogeneity of an immigrant nation and of expanding social and economic citizenship. The Special Broadcasting Service was set up to provide multilingual television programming, though its reach was limited to capital cities. Women's interests were advanced by the establishment of offices of the Status of Women, the Sex Discrimination Commission within the Human Rights and Equal Opportunity Commission and the Affirmative Action Agency. Although the then federal government was slow to respond to the 1967 referendum, setting up an inactive office for Aboriginal Affairs, the land rights campaign of the 1970s forced changes. Land rights legislation required a formal system of representation of indigenous groups' interests. Land councils and later the Aboriginal and Torres Strait Islanders Commission were set up.

(144–148) © 2002 Feminist Review. 0141-7789/02 $15 www.feminist-review.com

The 1980s saw a critical shift in the nature of Australian citizenship and changes in established institutions. Since the 1980s in Australia, successive governments have pursued 'economic rationalism' and political institutions have been reformed. These shifts have altered the nature of the Australian citizenship forged in the Federation settlements. When the colonies came together to form the Commonwealth in 1901, industrial citizenship was secured through the establishment of the Arbitration Court, the enactment of restricted immigration policies and tariff protection. Australian traditions of citizenship, while weak on nationalism, have supported social and economic rights. The 'basic' wage delivered by the Harvester judgment in 1907 secured the right of a male worker to support his family in 'frugal comfort'. At Federation, the Australian citizen was a (male) worker, a subject of empire, and the political arrangements that secured his rights were liberal, not republican, in character (Beilharz, 1993). Child endowment payments directed to mothers, and more recently family allowances, have underwritten maternal citizenship (Lake, 1999). This tradition continues to assert itself: in the recent federal election campaign, the centrepiece of the Liberal policy launch was the introduction of a 'baby bonus' in the form of a tax rebate calculated on the woman's income in the previous year. This benefit, it is claimed, will enable first-time mothers to 'choose' to stay at home with their infant children.

Empire citizenship was slowly unravelled over almost a century. In 1948, the Nationality and Citizenship Act meant that Australians were no longer 'British' citizens. By the 1980s, the Australia Acts had removed the possibility of appeals to the Privy Council, so that finally the Australian legal system had stand-alone status. The last vestiges of empire citizenship have still to be shrugged off, however. The Australian republic, generally reckoned to be 'inevitable', is still to be proclaimed. The republican debate exposed differences among liberals and radical democrats within the republican movement. The 'minimalist' liberals, disparaged as urban elites, favour indirect democracy while 'real' republicans want to transform political institutions and encourage civic virtue. There is an emerging agreement that an inclusive, deliberative process, perhaps borrowing something from the federation process, will play a critical role in securing the change (Ferres and Meredyth, 2001).

The attenuated debate about the republic called forth a deeper disillusionment with political elites. This disillusionment has fastened on to the effects of globalization, and initially focussed on the figure of Pauline Hanson. Hanson has been a magnet for disaffected constituencies, and her inarticulateness has enabled their rage to register. Although the real 'bush' has benefitted from the low Australian dollar and increased exports, the decline in provincial centres seems irreversible. Globalization's losers turned away from the major parties, threatening the survival of the National party in rural areas.

The economic and technological dimensions of globalization have exposed the porousness of national boundaries. Footloose capital and the borderlessness of the Internet are notions that underpin the emphasis on government as economic managers and the shrinking realm of politics. The mobility of people and information at the high end of the population is countered by the placelessness of increasing numbers of refugees and the poor.

Australia's response to the arrival of 'illegal immigrants' (as asylum seekers have been styled) had become an election issue even before the events of September 11 in the United States focussed attention on issues of 'homeland security'. The 'dry' liberal tendency to limited government and its withdrawal from the 'private' spheres of life is now being rebranded as prioritising national security in uncertain times. The symbolism of leadership is being redeployed as anxieties are refocussed on the terrorist threat. The sentiments of a constituency disaffected by globalisation has profoundly influenced that response. John Howard was elected for a third term because he won back the constituency that had drifted to One Nation. State sovereignty and border protection were electorally critical issues, displacing domestic concerns. Campaign rhetoric emphasised the state's right to regulate entry. The nature of Australia's obligations as a signatory to the UN Convention and its relationship with newly democratic Indonesia, the largest Muslim nation and Australia's nearest neighbour were not debated. Only the Greens opposed the government's position, and their vote increased markedly.

In the 1980s and 1990s, governance has devolved increasingly to local communities. Non-profit community organisations are taking responsibility for the delivery of services such as health (which includes mental health and sexual assault services). Church-based organizations and the Salvation Army have been contracted to provide employment services, especially to the long-term unemployed who are not attractive clients for commercial operators. In the past, these organizations had provided 'alternative' services, and had played a political role as activists and lobbyists. Now they have a new relation to government departments, as 'suppliers' of services.

Liberals on the right represent the shift to voluntarism as encouraging individual initiative and responsibility and decreasing welfare dependency. Liberals on the left, such as the feminist Eva Cox, federal Labour parliamentarian Mark Latham and indigenous leader Noel Pearson, argue that devolution of decision making allows local communities to be self-determining and develops social capital.

We are undertaking a project to explore these new relationships among citizens and the state and to investigate whether new forms of governance produce new forms of active citizenship. At the same time, it will map those relationships against the changing patterns of Australia's domestic politics and international affiliations (the UN, APEC, CHOGM, ANZUS). Its focus is on forms of public reasoning and the expansion (and contraction) of sites of public debate, particularly with the opportunities provided by new media. Its starting point is the tensions created by liberal indifference to pluralism, the state's professed neutrality among different communities' versions of the good life, and the Australian tradition of political settlements to secure the 'common good'. The policies of the 1970s allowed new voices to speak, but public spaces where those voices encounter difference, disagreement and opposition and participate in the exchange of reasons have apparently diminished. There has been a lively debate about differences within Australian (and other) feminisms. Our intention is to turn these perspectives onto 'emergent publics' (Lara, 1998) and the political institutions that sustain them.

This project starts from the local level and with the informal interactions as well as the formal processes which produce 'communities' with common objectives. The new prominence of intermediary institutions — voluntary associations, charitable organisations and so on — reintroduces the question of gendered citizenship. Women's civic participation has been concentrated in local government and the voluntary sector, whether as experts, advocates or representatives. Their skills and capacities as mediators and networkers have been reproduced in the protocols of community consultation.

In Queensland, the state government has established an Office of Community Engagement within the Premier's department, and has begun to develop new protocols and procedures for enhancing citizen participation. In part, this is an experiment in producing a 'republican' political culture. At the time of the referendum's defeat, the Premier, Peter Beattie, suggested that the states, which also appoint a representative of the Queen as governor, were free to experiment with 'republican' processes, including processes that expand opportunities for participation in deliberative processes. The Queensland 'experiment' has included convening Cabinet meetings in regional centres. A further test of this initiative was to have involved the Commonwealth Heads of Government Meeting (CHOGM) in Brisbane in October 2001. Processes of consultation among protest groups and police and security agencies, mediated by community leaders, had sought to ensure that confrontations like those in Seattle, Melbourne and Genoa were not repeated. Instead, public spaces of controversy were to be opened up in the streets and parklands around the city centre where the formal meetings were to take place. CHOGM has now been postponed and relocated to a private resort for reasons of security, following the terrorist attacks in the US.

Our aim is to evaluate these strategies for building social capital by considering how they make government processes more accessible and transparent. We will look at three dimensions of participation: in deliberation about policy, in decision making, and in implementation. Participation at the local level may elicit or construct civic capacities and constitute communities around common interests, but it can also encourage protectionist sentiment. One of the important outcomes of this research might be that we distinguish some features of open, connected communities, disposed to identify their interests in both local and international contexts.

references

Beilharz, P. (1993). 'Republicanism and citizenship' In W. Hudson and D. Carter (1993) editors, *The Republicanism Debate*, Sydney: Allen & Unwin.

Ferres, K. and Meredyth, D. (2001). *An Articulate Country: Reinventing Citizenship in Australia*, St. Lucia: University of Queensland Press.

Lake, M. (1999). *Getting Equal: The History of Australian Feminism*, Sydney: Allen & Unwin.

Lara, M. P. (1998). *Moral Textures: Feminist Narratives in the Public Sphere*, Cambridge: Cambridge University Press.

70 | thinking globally, acting locally: women activists' accounts

Pam Alldred

Anti-globalization activists have been thoroughly demonized in the UK national media in the past year, receiving the kind of coverage usually reserved for 'anarchists' in the tabloid press. That is, the 'mindless thugs' caricature of young white men in black 'hoodies' intent on violence. Needless to say, this type of coverage is not often accompanied by any representation of protestors' own views. In fact, when reports of protest can focus on 'violence', actual political grievances — the issues and the need for direct action responses to them — are ignored. Even more rare is the chance to hear women's anger at the injustice of global capitalism and frustration at the broken promises of democracy. Contested though they are within the movement, at least the terms anti-globalization or anti-capitalism say something about what is being protested against.

In the lead up to May Day 2001, protesters were vilified by the mainstream media as 'evil scum', a dangerous 'terrorist' threat bringing chaos and rioting to the streets of London, justifying tens of thousands of police on duty and the 'army on stand-by'. This hype did more to publicise the idea of a May Day Monopoly (anti-privatization) game on the actual streets of London than its 'inventors' could have done, and achieved the boarding up of much of Oxford Street for a day (resulting in lost sales that were totalled up in the 'damage' reported), but made violence almost inevitable in the context of aggressive over-policing and the now familiar abuse of police powers to detain people in order to search for dangerous weapons by holding them in a police cordon for hours whilst 'intelligence' is gathered. But it is this vilification of protestors that makes possible the kind of state violence we saw in Genoa in July 2001. Protesters sleeping in a social centre could be perceived as so Other by the Italian police that they brutally beat them, threatened to rape women with batons, peed and spat on them and forced responses to their fascist rhetoric.

The big international protests that grab the media's attention represent a massive mobilization of people angry at the global economic and social order, disillusioned in the democratic process and at governments bowing to corporate pressure. But they are sometimes assumed to *be* the movement, rather than just one expression of it, and often a geographically mobile, relatively privileged segment. Many activists in the North take their inspiration

(149–163) © 2002 Feminist Review. 0141-7789/02 $15 www.feminist-review.com

from struggles and mobilizations of ordinary people in the South, and are at pains to demonstrate how issues such as the privatization of public services, the erosion of workers' rights and increasing inequality amongst people of the North, and poverty, hunger, poor health, sweatshop employment conditions, environmental contamination, the denial of land-rights and corporate claims over natural resources in the south are opposite sides of the same coin. It is essential to make these links apparent to pre-empt parochial or nationalist responses that fail to see how competition damages those on both sides.

Activism is only the tip of the ice-berg of a global movement, but across the world, opposition to injustice, ecological destruction and poverty is being criminalized. Radical dissenters in the UK have already been deemed terrorists under legislation passed in 2000. Even liberal commentators are alarmed, but this move flows with chilling logic from a communitarian urge for shared values, and Tony Blair's assertion of particular views as those the nation shares. The Terrorism Act 2000 redefines terrorism to include 'actions designed to influence a government', for the 'purpose of advancing a political, religious or ideological cause' and includes damage to property or interference with an electronic system. In self-righteous condemnation of protesters, the mainstream press then neglects to distinguish morally between damage to property and violence against a person. A current campaign by a UK socialist lawyers organisation asks: 'How can fax blockades, uprooting of GM crops, protest against refugee detention centres, protest against globalization, debt and oppressive regimes, a movement to make possible 'another world' all be terrorists'. In early 2001, an action against the Act, by London Reclaim the Streets (RTS) adorned London statues of Nelson Mandela and Emmeline Pankhurst with a plaque labelling them 'Terrorist' and asked who were the real terrorists: governments complicit in the threat to us all, who put the profits of the oil industry before the reality of climate change and the interests of the biotech industry before environmental safety, or those who uproot GM crops to remove the risk?

Several women activists who were unable to contribute to this piece in the end were going to describe women activists' imprisonment for criminal damage to fighter planes and other tools of genocide, to highlight the moral bankruptcy of a system that fails to distinguish the 'criminality' of disabling a machine from the criminality of bombing raids, of allowing agribusiness to hold hostage the environment by releasing GM crops before they are proven safe, or the 'terrorism' of political protest using NVDA from the abuse of state power to assert ideological meanings, yet deem 'terrorist' attempts to counter these meanings. Another was going to contrast Western leaders' laws to protect the free movement of capital across the globe in search of greater profits, with the increasing criminalization of people's migration as a result of poverty exacerbated by international trading laws that protect the interest of rich nations, wars caused by imperialist foreign interventions, or displacement by environmental disasters resulting from unregulated industrialization. But these concerns are now horrifyingly centre-stage, confirming what we already knew: that you can't be a terrorist if you've got an air-force.

As George W Bush and Tony Blair justify a war on Afghanistan in the name of defending a glorified Western democracy against the terrorist threat, we see the horrifying consequences of the imperialist belief in the superiority of Western culture that Berlusconi expressed, and people so Other to and threatening of 'our civilization' that 'we' cannot hear their complaints. In the self-righteous conviction of George Bush, his rhetorical use of 'democracy' and 'freedom' ring hollow, not least given the insult to democracy that his own election was and his privileging of oil industry interests (now, at Kyoto, and in Alaska). As Tony Blair defends his actions on the international stage, he presumes to speak for the British people and of the unassailable values of 'civilization'. But there is not a consensus in the UK about the values of 'civilization'. This is the 'democracy' that passes the Terrorism Act, and promotes a similar EC ruling defining terrorism as 'urban violence' by people with the aim of 'seriously altering the political, economic or social structures'. Nor is there contentment about how democracy operates — this is why there is a direct action movement. And how 'civilized' did the Italian police behave in Genoa? Neither is there a consensus about the war here (nor even is there in the US). The reporting of the war and of opposition to it says even more about the corporate media than did the accounts of May Day: where organizers estimate 100 000 people joined the London march to express their opposition to the war, the media counts 15 000, and when on 13 October 2001, people in 100 different countries demonstrated against the war on Afghanistan, there was barely a whisper in the UK national press.

The international protests and big demonstrations are just one media friendly expression of anger at the injustice of the global economic order, and even for activists who go on them, they are often just one expression of their politics (and many activists do prefer more targeted interventions or focus more on sustaining a counter-culture and developing positive alternatives). Against the weight of the media hype only a few critical voices get heard (and many prefer not to engage with the mainstream press anyway) which leaves 'media tarts' sounding like figureheads of the movement. So here are the voices of a few women whose activism I respect greatly. Their accounts don't represent all of their politics or activities, but in contrast to popular images give some first person perspectives on current activism, and the political and personal perspectives that can inform it.

The invitation to contribute framed them as anti-globalization activists, and for some the distinction between anti-capitalism and anti-globalization is significant, although in general, they chose to focus less on theoretical distinctions and identifications, and more on what they do. Perhaps the desire to make theoretical links and distinctions stems from an academic agenda, rather than an activist one. As friends and co-activists linked through aspects of a London-based activist scene, we share some social characteristics, are full time activists, some work and some have paid campaign work part time. All are based in the UK, though not all are British, first-language English or white. Some chose pseudonyms.

Six accounts cannot convey the range of perspectives among activists in this small corner of the movement, let alone women's resistance more broadly. But they do offer some illustrations of the connections that individual women draw between the politics that inform their activism and their everyday lives and local environments. They demonstrate how material practices and symbolic acts are sometimes linked in cultures of resistance. The first two accounts highlight the immediacy of activism for women, both in terms of its urgency and its connection to everyday lives through food and emotional well-being. The first contrasts the global reach of the biotech industry with resistance rooted in the local and respecting the particular. The second emphasises the importance of emotional support and self-care as values too easily trampled in the rat-race, and as essential for making activism itself sustainable. Both describe the pleasure of developing non-hierarchical ways of working with other women.

Joyce

They say that the revolution must start in the kitchen, and for me, it did. I was a waitress, and then a cook for about 16 years. I love everything about food — colours, smells, flavours, textures, preparing, eating and sharing it — I love its histories, myths, etiquettes, cultures — alimentary alchemy. It is the very stuff of life, a globally common experience and the basis for our relationships as social beings. At least it should be.

In the autumn of 1997, the first shipment of genetically engineered soy from the US was imported into Britain. I clearly remember reading an article in a newspaper magazine about genetic engineering, and thinking after the first paragraph how exciting it sounded. Half way through the article, there was a knot in my stomach and I felt sick, because this didn't just threaten the ingredients I loved, it threatened life on earth.

I realised that no matter how wonderful any 'famous' NGO was, it was no longer acceptable for me to let them save the world on my behalf. So from passive to active... I've been working on the genetics issue ever since, and it's been a steep learning curve. I work with a brilliant bunch of people, in an office that supports grassroots campaigners. We all work under the banner of the Genetic Engineering Network, which is an amazing and diverse collection of individuals and groups all over the UK, and increasingly, all around the world, resisting the imposition of genetic engineering, and ultimately of corporate control over our lives and the world we live in.

I find it no coincidence, that not only has the campaign been one of the most inspiring and truly common causes in the environmental movement, but it also has the best gender balance. There are so many ordinary women doing amazing things. The diversity of the campaign, the willingness to listen, share, and to decide things by consensus owe a lot to the way that women work best. The woman in Dorset, England, who has tirelessly written letters and produced leaflets for as long as I have known her, the grandmother in Kenya, who feeds 13 of her family on two acres of land with local seed, after having rejected the chemical cocktail promoted by the multinationals, the mother in Andra Pradesh, India, who grows 85 distinct local varieties of crops on her five acres, to share with neighbouring farmers, the woman that physically stopped a tractor sowing GE seed in Scotland, with her daughter on her shoulders, the cartoonist, the bannermaker, the women that pull up GE crops. None of them would thank me for telling you their names, none of them are (thankfully) the only ones doing what they do, but all of them gloriously unique. That's not to say there aren't amazing men working with us too, there are, but the key phrase is 'with us'.

Undoubtedly, the state of the world has become so polarized, and so desperate, that the movements resisting the dominant paradigm of trade, and the suffocating concentration of power in the hands of a few are drawing more people into them. For some, this means replacing one system with another, a 'blueprint for change', and as the corporate media insists on lumping us all into convenient boxes, we are increasingly being represented by the learned opinions of 'authorities', which really means other political parties with an axe to grind, authors whose publishers want to sell more books, or 'stars' from the cult of the media. But there is no one solution, no 'onesizefitsall', no rigid recipe or cure all – that's the whole point. This alternative evangelism stems from the same arrogance as the system that controls us now – it may look simple on paper, but authoritarian hierarchies will no more lead us to our future vision than trade liberalization will see women paid wages for housework. I rarely feel emboldened or empowered by experts, I usually feel inadequate. I get my inspiration from the dynamism and energy, the creativity, compassion and resilience of ordinary people. Change comes from listening, adapting ideas, seeking understanding and common ground, recognising and reconciling our differences and diversity.

There is a wind of change blowing, and it's coming from the South. The South is the disenfranchised, the unheard, the poor. A vast majority of the people who could be thus described are women, wherever they live.

In any war, throughout history, attacking the food supply of the enemy has been an obvious target. In 2001, Palestinian olive groves are being cut down, and fields trashed by the Israeli army. Campesinos in Colombia are having their plots indiscriminately sprayed by aeroplanes loaded with pesticides, their crops are dying and their children exposed to chemical burns – there is no particular reason for choosing these examples; there are many more. It is the nature of overt war, and control. Yet there is an implicit war being waged, that has been going on for the last 50+ years. It is the preemptive strike, to ensure there will be no choice, no alternative, no resistance. Women, especially in the North, hardly noticed when common land was disappeared into private hands, when choices at the shops became restricted to four types of fizzy drinks and two types of tomatoes, in one of four or five supermarket chains. Food autonomy was replaced by convenience, and farmers were 'persuaded' by market forces to stop saving seed, and were instructed by agro-experts to grow food to feed processing factories not people. The chemical facilities that manufactured bombs and weapons of war were converted to produce fertilisers and pesticides. Genetic engineering is the latest instalment in this catalogue of control. This is still largely to happen in the global South, the last market for expansionism. 80% of the world's seed is still farm saved, and 60% of the world's agriculturists are women.

Meanwhile, the assault continues. Transnational corporations have quietly acquired patents on the genes responsible for breast cancer, common food staples, traditional medicines. Legal mechanisms designed to protect industrial invention have been applied to the natural world, our global commons, the living earth is being poisoned and women stand and weep as they watch their children fall ill, of cancers and other diseases of industrialization.

I know that these are things that will consume the rest of my life, on a daily basis — yet I don't want to spend my life just fighting. There can be no environmental justice without social equity, and yet at least 50% of the world's finest minds and bravest spirits have never been invited to contribute towards the solutions. That's you and me, girlfriend, it's what gets me out of bed every morning... so let's go out and plant some seeds (of resistance).

To find out more about the genetic engineering network, visit www.geneticsaction.org.uk

Since the international protest against IMF–World Bank meeting in Prague in September 2000, the strategy of tactical frivolity has been visible at UK and international events in the shape of a group of women (and usually a few men) dancing at police lines wearing flamboyant, home-made carnivalesque costumes, colour-coordinated for an event, often pink and silver. It displays defiance, deep irreverence and throws aggressive policing into sharp relief.

a woman who runs with the wolves

I started my life in NVDA living in trees and defending them during evictions, lying in the road to stop the live export of young animals or generally the rape and decimation of the beautiful English countryside. My activism was all local, but archetypal. The image of a diverse group of people surrounding a grand old sweet chestnut tree on a town common, resisting strongly, defiantly, yet peacefully, spoke powerfully to me of the many ordinary people who are slowly coming to terms with the limitations of our governments. NVDA is basically like grabbing a small child away from the path of a speeding lorry.

Recently my activism has been about finding creativeness and beauty in resistance. I went to the international action in Prague with 30 other women dressed in huge 'showgirl' fantails. We danced with a samba band – cheeky and mischievous, but not aggressive. At one point we were singing to the cops and I waved a pink feather duster at one of them, which he proceeded to smash out of my hand with his baton! Many women understand this image without analysis. Surrealism is important as a critique of the lack of sanity apparent in, for instance, public transport policies, or the irony of police anti-gun campaigns while guns remain legal because of a few violent hunting enthusiasts and are used in the repression of protestors. There are many ways of using art in the struggle: adding printed 'government health warnings' to car adverts is a favourite. I helped put on a month-long art exhibition in a squatted venue at which we celebrated offering people free, interactive entertainment, breaking down the artist/consumer roles that are the death of the spirit of creation.

I resent the way they call us anarchists. I am an ordinary young woman who wants to lead a useful life. I'm a former waitress who became a worker with the homeless. I loved my job. I was good at it because I care about people. I've been forced into activism as the point of no return for the natural world draws near. I don't particularly relate to the term anti-globalization. To me, it's obviously just another, particularly damaging, arm of capitalism. In these big protests, I find it perplexing to march alongside CAFOD calling for an end to Third World debt. These people's leader bans contraception, and condones the devastating actions of missionaries! [...] The phrase 'anti-capitalist protester' is useful as it's direct and contains a simple truth. But what the media fails to represent is the depth of love for the natural world and the humanity that drives many of us; the sense of needless suffering, in a country that could offer so much, the comprehension of the dreadful mistakes being made by people who have far more power than they can handle, sometimes I think politicians, town planners, marketing execs, fashion designers, factory farmers... could be genuinely ignorant of the misery and destruction they are helping produce.

You don't need to be poor for long to feel the effects of globalized business. Contrast the Italian café, where you chat and eat in a relaxed, authentic setting amongst people who know you, with the multinational fast food experience of false smiles in a sterile, characterless environment where you're just another shifted unit. I've had a dramatic change in my quality of life since I became proud to be poor – a relief from the struggle to appear 'wealthy'. I now have endless discussions with friends about personal development and how to have more loving relationships, instead of how much we weigh and what to wear.

I believe all my politics relate to feminism as, to be a woman who refuses the victim role is an action 24/7. I have had amazing experiences doing women-only NVDA. Twenty of us stopped a London bus and painted it bright pink in protest at the owner of the large bus/coach company funding a homophobic pro-'Section 28' campaign. ['Section 28' is UK legislation introduced by the Conservatives to stop local authorities 'promoting' homosexuality as a 'pretended family relationship' which New Labour unsuccessfully attempted to repeal in 2000.] I've been to women activist weekends where we talk at length about feelings and emotions. I believe emotional health, honesty and sustainability go hand in hand. It is vital that women have the chance to gather together exclusively sometimes for many reasons, some of which words can't describe. I know that a lot of healing has taken place in these meetings. All political people MUST leave a space in their lives for emotional validation.

The following two contributors prefer the term 'anti-capitalist' to 'anti-globalization' despite writing from different ideological perspectives, and both highlight international meetings as ways of linking activists of the South and North. However, they describe different forms of organising: working either through formal structures of union and party, or through a network of non-hierarchical organisations. Issues of process, particularly the feasibility of consensus decision making, often differentiate anarchists and those on the left, but both women are critical of the emergence of (unelected) figureheads for the movement.

Sue

I've always been an anti-capitalist, because I've been a revolutionary socialist for many years. I'm a member of the group Workers Power and do various kinds of political campaign work, including anti-sweatshop protests organised by a local network, and going on some of the international demonstrations. One aspect is working in trade unions and winning support for workers such as the Dudley hospital workers who fought privatization, as well as workers overseas in sweatshops. Last year I spoke at my union conference and won support for the international demonstration in Prague. That was the first national union support in Britain. This year many more unions gave support to the anti-capitalist protests, because rank and file workers like those in Dudley have seen the connections and pushed for union involvement.

The demonstrations culminating in Genoa show that there is huge opposition to the way the world works currently, but we're up against determined and well-armed opposition. If the movement is to make headway, it has to clarify its ideas and root itself in the struggles of the majority, of workers world-wide. In Europe the anti-capitalist movement has grown up rather separated from the traditional trade union movement and we have to overcome this split, changing the trade unions in the process and challenging the old bureaucracy. Young people, especially young women, will be in the front of the movement in making these changes. That's why some of my time as an activist is spent giving back-up to the youth group 'Revolution', for instance helping with fund-raising.

The movement against globalization (which is really against the consequences of globalization) is extremely diverse. But I don't believe this means that that all the traditions are equally 'valid'. We must debate out our differences if we are to take the movement forward. For instance, many of the movement's influential figures think that capitalism can be rendered less harmful, either by local grass roots solutions or through the intervention of local or national states. People like George Monbiot or Naomi Klein argue for reforms to provide some kind of protection against the overarching ambitions of global capital. The problem with this reform perspective is that while the profit system survives it will insist on driving everything else. An increasing number of activists conclude that we need wholesale change in which all the major corporations, banks, services, etc. are taken over and run by those who work and use them. That means revolution.

We can be sure that those in control will not let themselves be reformed out of existence. Police brutality against protestors in Genoa was just a taste of what the system will do when challenged. Peaceful protest has its limits. Capitalists and their state will use violence as they did against the democratically elected socialist Allende government in Chile in 1973. We need to be prepared to defend our demonstrations, our picket lines, our occupations.

The truly international breadth of the anti-capitalist movement is a huge gain. The bosses' exploitation respects no boundaries, our opposition must do the same. There's an increasing number of international trade union meetings and conferences but these tend to be run by top officials. There are though rank and file car worker activists arguing for solidarity action across boundaries and against 'national' answers which pit one set of workers against another. The anti-capitalist movement is giving a boost to the internationalist approach.

We must continue to debate the 'party question'. Many participants in the movement are suspicious or downright hostile to 'parties'. Those of us who think that democratic revolutionary parties (and an International) are vital must work hard to convince others, but work alongside those in the movement who organise in different ways. One aspect of this debate is decision making. I've found that consensus methods of anti-capitalist networks can work for clarifying ideas and agreeing on a limited range of actions. But this method has many weaknesses. There are times when a majority just has to take a decision. If I proposed the consensus method in my trade union at work, then it would seriously weaken our ability to fight back against employers' attacks. The minority who didn't want to take action — say to defend a sacked colleague — could stop or seriously delay a strike to save their job. In such a situation we have to take a majority decision quickly and everyone then has to stick to it.

In a political party this democratic process should happen at all levels – fast or slow according to the question. What we have to ensure is that people who speak or act on behalf of everyone in the organisation are democratically elected and recallable, and that every member's views can be heard and treated with respect, even where there are fierce disagreements. This is a world away from the bureaucratic style of the old Stalinist parties and it is also different from the way that 'leaders' appear in the existing anti-capitalist movement by virtue of their academic or journalistic standing.

Finally (but crucially), our movement must continue theoretical debate, trying to understand the nature of 'globalization'. In Workers Power, we see 'globalization' as a particular phase of imperialism. The world at the start of the 21st century is still dominated by international capital, by banks, huge companies and a handful of states running the world for the benefit of a tiny number of capitalists. But new developments have produced the 'globalization' phenomenon: communication is transformed by new technologies, production shifts constantly in search of the cheapest labour, knowledge is increasingly commodified. Bosses are putting the whole world up for sale because the giant corporations are engaged in a vicious scrap for profit making opportunities. We needn't be against globalization, but against their form of globalization. International and local democratic planning could ensure we use sustainable resources. Workers are pitted against each other to drive down production costs when instead, massive reductions in production costs resulting from new technology could ensure that everyone in the globe has a life free from want [...]

June

I'm involved with Reclaim the Streets (RTS), or rather, at the moment, the People's Global Action (PGA) working group within London RTS. The PGA's origins lies with two Encuentros in Mexico and Spain, where grassroots activists from all over the world came together to talk about their fight for freedom, against all forms of exploitation and specifically neo-liberal policies which are so detriment to the lives of the majority of the world's population. Out of these Encuentros grew the idea of a more permanent grassroots network and February 1998 saw the first PGA conference in Geneva. The groups involved range from, in the North, the Italian group Ya Basta!, London Reclaim the Streets, the Russian Rainbow Keepers and the Canadian Postal Workers, to – in the South – New Zealand Maoris, Bangladeshi Garment Workers, Indian KRRS (radical farmers union), the Brasillian Momenta Sem Terra (organised landless peasants movement) and the Nigerian Ogoni people, to mention just a few. The network is a structure for communication and coordination of action, and a source of great inspiration in the day-to-day struggle. A PGA conference is organised on a rotational basis every two years, the first one in Geneva, the second one in Bangalore, India, and the third one, in September 2001, in Cochabamba, Bolivia (with an all-women team from the UK!). Between the conferences are smaller international meetings and regional gatherings.

In March 2000, we organised the first European PGA conference in Milan with Ya Basta!, attended by 300–400 people from all over Europe. In the chaos of hundreds of people trying to have fruitful discussions across cultures and languages, real links were made within what is known as the 'anti-capitalist' movement in Europe. While most groups use some form of direct action, the tactics differ from street parties to White Overalls, from black bloc to GMO crop destruction, from IndyMedia to feminist activism. The underlying politics that unite these different groups includes being anti-systemic, anti-authoritarian and having a deep respect for the democracy in/of a diversity of approaches. There is also a shared understanding that political work needs to be locally based, while globally networked because there are global political–economic processes at the root of the world's social and ecological problems.

Political commentators, academics and the media often use the global character of the anti-capitalist movement as some sort of proof of a contradiction in our politics, that we're the products of the phenomenon we're fighting against. They miss the point that many groups wouldn't describe their politics as 'anti-globalization'. Firstly, the term is largely a media construction. Secondly, it's used to describe reformist demands such as a return to a stronger nation-state and to a 'nicer', more local, form of capitalism. Thirdly, it's a term that the far right uses to justify nationalistic, racist politics. So I wouldn't describe the politics I'm involved with as part of the anti-globalization movement, but rather as a day-to-day project of liberation from capitalism, which, at this particular historical moment encapsulates all systems of oppression and exploitation, both of people and the planet.

There's no separation between my political activism and feminist activism/ perspective. Being a woman gives me a particular, gendered experience which feeds an urgency and anger in my activism, because oppression is a daily bodily experience. Meeting women activists from around the world is particularly inspiring, and I work towards having gender issues at the top of the agenda of the political work I'm involved with.

IndyMedia is an international network of DIY media activists getting independent reporting of local and global actions onto the web: http://www.indymedia.org.uk/ Whilst none of the laws on terrorism manage to make this illegal, the FBI have raided a Seattle Indymedia office and used the courts to censor reporting.

The following two contributions are from women who are involved in campaigning on economic issues of pay for women's work, against military expenditure and on 'third world debt' through international networks linking women around the globe.

Sara argues that the anti-globalization movement fails to recognise women's work or the gendered dimension of debt repayment, and offers a radical critique of the reformist demands to drop the debt or reduce debt payments. Again, both show how global analyses link with local conditions and both work to develop links between women of the North and of the South.

Cari

Women do two-thirds of the world's work — we feed the world, from breastfeeding to subsistence farming, and do most of the caring work. But two-thirds of our work is unvalued and uncounted; worst of all, it is unwaged. This lack of economic and social recognition for the backbreaking and life-enhancing work that most women do, in the face of discrimination, exploitation, war, dictatorship, displacement and often grinding poverty, is a fundamental sexist injustice, devaluing all women and everything women do. It ensures that women and children remain the majority of the poor. As a single mother who has raised three children through years surviving on diminishing Income Support and typically low wages, I've seen many friends forced to work in the sex industry to feed themselves and their families.

The Global Women's Strike is called by the International Wages for Housework Campaign, and will see women and girls in over 60 countries marking International Women's Day by striking. The call to invest in caring not killing, and to pay women, not the military, is increasingly a matter of life or death. I'm outraged at the squandering of over $880bn a year on world military budgets, when $80bn would provide everyone's basic needs. We need a total change of priorities, so investment goes into the enrichment of every life rather than the few.

The Strike demands make visible some of the ways women everywhere are opposing globalization: wages for all caring work, pay equity, paid maternity leave and breastfeeding breaks, abolition of Third World debt, clean water, non-polluting energy and technology, protection from all violence and persecution, and freedom of movement. These demands ensure that women's and girls' struggle to survive is not hidden behind the few women who've made it to boardrooms, legislatures, universities and international agencies. Such women show little or no interest in what we suffer, and those in parliament backed Tony Blair when cuts to single mothers' benefits was his first act in government.

Highlights of Strike 2001 included a 'sit-down' by 500 rural and urban women co-ordinated by Kaabong Women's group, Uganda; in Chiapas, Mexico women calling for recognition of women's work, supported by men; in India, a march of 4000, organised by Chhattisgarh Women's Organisation; in Peru, various activities coordinated by The Women's Domestic Workers' Centre, and a radio broadcast by Indigenous Aymara and Quechua women; and in London, a lively crowd, including pensioners, young anarchists, refugees, 'Dykes on Strike', and Soho sex workers marched to Parliament.

Translation has been essential to making the Strike truly global, with materials in 30 languages, and a bilingual English/Spanish website. Volunteers everywhere helped: many translators are immigrants, refugees or asylum seekers, which highlights how important immigrant communities are to our movements. A priority is women in towns and cities sharing resources with women in rural areas and villages. Among the most active and innovative in the Strike are women carrying babies on their backs, communicating by word of mouth without access to email, phones, or even transport or running water.

The Global Women's Strike calls for women everywhere to join us to 'Stop the World and Change It' on 8 March, 2002. Payday, a network of men, is coordinating men's support. To find out more or contact International Wages for Housework Campaign visit http://womenstrike8m.server101.com, or email: Womenstrike8m@server101.com or write to Crossroads Women's Centre, 230A Kentish Town Road, London NW6 5QX. UK. Tel: +44(0)207 482 2496, Fax: +44(0)207 209 4761.

Sara

I grew up in the US, the richest countries in the world, yet saw my grandmother forced to supplement her meagre income as a domestic worker by farming. Others in my family escaped poverty by joining the military. While welfare benefits were cut, mothers and grandmothers like mine struggled to raise children, only to see them used as cannon fodder for the military. Everywhere Black, Native American and immigrant women worked hard, including fighting discrimination. Later many movements began coming together, with renewed calls for reparations for slavery, but women's experience was invisible.

In the 1980s I met Black Women for Wages for Housework, a network of women of colour — African, Asian, Caribbean, Indigenous/Native American, Latina — focussing on ending women's overwork. We came together as housewives and mothers, domestic workers, rural, factory, office and hospital workers, vendors, sex workers to demand recognition and compensation. Demands like 'Pay Women Not the Military' spoke to my experience, connecting grotesque military budgets with the unpaid debt of slavery and empire. Women pay the highest price for war not least because it is our children, the product of our lifetime's work, who are slaughtered. Demanding the end of military budgets is crucial to a complete change of priorities, from killing to caring, and is increasingly urgent now that Bush is aiming to use the Middle East and others for target practice. After 11 September, US military budgets swelled by $40 billion, on top of $500 billion already committed for 'Star Wars'.

Third World women work the hardest. In societies impoverished by debt it's women's work — growing food, collecting water and fuel — that keeps people from starvation. Few have recognised this, certainly not politicians. One exception is former President of Tanzania, Julius Nyerere, who recognised that most debt repayment comes from the efforts of rural women who 'work harder than anyone else'. Women keep people from starvation, but the IMF and World Bank don't care if we work 20 hours a day, or if those we care for live or die. Awareness of women's work defending the world's population has been absent from anti-globalization and other movements. Yet everywhere women spearhead campaigns: from Bolivia, Ghana, Narmada, South Africa, Turkey, Chiapas, and Afghanistan, to 'welfare mothers' in Britain and the USA.

Most recently I've worked as part of the International Women of Colour for Wages for Caring Work (as the network's now called) with the 'IMF & World Bank Wanted For Fraud' campaign. This campaign differs from those such as Jubilee 2000 which ask for debt relief, ignoring the enormous debt owed to Third World communities, particularly women, for unpaid work and for lives lost. Why should the hardest working people in the world beg for debt relief? We owe nothing — they owe us. A women's network was launched in July 2000 to bring together women's work against debt and globalization and to plan the Global Women's Strike 2002. As Selma James, founder of the International Wages for Housework Campaign said: 'The Strike makes clear that people not profit should be the aim of every economy. If not, we face endless exploitation, and the destruction of our world. We utterly reject this as human beings and as carers of the human race'. For more information about International Women of Colour for Wages for Care Work and the IMF & World Bank is Fraud Women's Network, contact Crossroads Women's Centre at the above address or email: crossroadswomenscentre@compuserve.com

This dialogue piece began as an article that aimed to describe the range of forms women's resistance to globalization takes, emphasising diverse strategies from everyday acts, the development of practical alternative resources, organising in women's groups or trades unions, mass demonstrations and symbolic defiance. Recognising that it is the women of the South, in particular, who bear the brunt of the impact of neo-liberal 'free market' economic policies, it hoped to be sensitive to the struggles for survival that might frame the urgency of resistance amongst women of the South, and make links with some of the strategies of activist women in the more privileged North. Certainly the theme of local, international or global forms of resistance emerges in any of these women's accounts, but the difficulty of understanding the perspectives of women in the majority world when their voices were not heard directly, replicated global North–South power relations by the colonising act of representation of their 'voices' by my own and my co-author.

How do we hear the voices of women at the economic sharp end of neo-liberal economic policies and strengthen our links with them? Do international links make us a global movement, or is the idea that we are one in spite of our differences of privilege a Western construct to unify and comfort? Contributors agree the importance of making connections between people in the North and South, as well as of making the connections in the arguments about opposing privatization here and corporate leaching and sweatshop employment there, but they differ on whether they see the aim as building an international movement or a network to strengthen existing smaller forces of resistance, where multiplicity is itself a strength. It relates to whether we look to one revolution or to a myriad littler revolutions, but activists are forming coalitions to oppose the neo-liberal economic order across ideological differences — regardless of whether 'global capitalism' or 'corporate globalization' is our preferred term, and the strength of alliances might relate more to differences along the reform/revolution dimension than of ideology, certainly when the focus is on action. It might well be that the sense of a unified movement dissolves when we start to discuss/create positive alternatives, as some commentators predict, but it might also be precisely then that diversity will be a strength, as local solutions are needed within a global perspective. For activists, the priority is to get on and do something now, not to the exclusion of analysis, but even profound differences must not stop us from acting now against the things we do not like. In the face of hostile and reactionary voices that gleefully point out the significance of tools of globalization, such as the internet, in the mobilization of opposition to it, or the superficial observations of protestors wearing sweatshop brands, we must assert that we need not have all the answers before we identify the problems, as a banner at London's 2001 May Day protests said: 'Overthrow Capitalism and Replace it with Something Nicer'.

Meanwhile, what are we doing? Global forums where activists from the North do get to hear directly about struggles in the South (and no doubt simple attributions to this binary are defied) include the People's Global Action, the Global Women's Strike and International Women of Colour for Wages for Care Work networks. At the time of writing, one contributor is in Bolivia at an international PGA conference, gathering testimonies of women from around the globe (contactable afterwards for speaking/slide-shows via pgabolivia@yahoo.co.uk); another is travelling to a European food safety meeting to lobby for sustainable agriculture and to work in soup kitchens; and many of us are frantically emailing people we know around the globe in the hope that strengthening personal links can go some way to interrupting the construction of 'the West' against its Others, the 'civilised' world against the Islamic world.

acknowledgements

With thanks to the contributors, and the women who were part of the orginal project, including my co-author (with apologies for the severe cut). Thanks to the editorial collective.

70 | book review

Women's movements in international perspective: Latin America and beyond

Maxine Molyneux; Palgrave, Houndmills, Basingstoke, 2001, ix + 244pp, ISBN
0-333-78677-7

At a time when edited texts are dominating academic publishing, it is
eminently welcome to see the appearance of a volume in which a single author
is able to write with such skill, depth and insight across a broad spectrum of
interconnected themes, not to mention such a wide range of historical and
geographical contexts. In *Women's Movements in International Perspective*,
Maxine Molyneux has not only done this, but in such a way that is likely to
reach the hearts and minds of non-specialist and specialist readers alike. It is
a book in which a whole series of issues that have been hotly debated not only
by feminists, but also by wider communities of scholars, activists, politicians,
policy-makers and people in general over several years, are presented in a
manner which simultaneously informs, elucidates, and (re-)enlivens. While
refreshingly modest about her own role in taking feminist scholarship forward
over the last two decades, this book definitively distinguishes Molyneux as one
of the leading contemporary thinkers in the field.

The topics tackled by Molyneux under the broad rubric of the political sociology
of women's movements and gender-state relations reflect her rich experience
in researching feminist issues in a wide variety of places and historical periods.
These include anarchist feminism in 19th-century Argentina (Chapter 1), the
politics of abortion in Sandinista Nicaragua (Chapter 3), and state, gender and
institutional change in Cuba, which traces the evolution of the Federation of
Cuban Women (FMC) from its inception in the immediate aftermath of
revolution in 1960, through to the post-Soviet 'Special Period' of the 1990s
(Chapter 4). Although only one of the chapters (Chapter 6: 'Analysing Women's
Movements') first appeared in its present form as a journal article, many of
the others draw and elaborate on earlier papers that have become benchmark
readings in Gender Studies courses around the world. Perhaps the most notable
one here is Chapter 2 'Mobilization without Emancipation? Women's Interests,
the State and Revolution in Nicaragua', which originated in the early 1980s and
in which Molyneux introduced her seminal concept of 'practical' and 'strategic'
gender interests. The latter has not only become part of the established
lexicon of gender and development analyses, but has been incorporated (in
various guises) in gender planning and policy-making.

While some of Molyneux's key ideas in *Women's Movements in Latin America*
have been revisited, adapted and/or extended by the author herself, or by

(164–165) © 2002 Feminist Review. 0141-7789/02 $15 www.feminist-review.com

others, in the context of evolving theoretical, political and philosophical discussions, what is also striking is the way in which Molyneux remains faithful to the details of time, place and sources that gave birth to her original notions. This comes in part from her dedication to primary fieldwork, whether in archives or with activists, and her commitment to scholarship. Her ability to locate processes so firmly and engagingly in their historical and geographical contexts imbues a clarity to complex conceptual formulations that is often lacking in the contemporary Gender Studies literature.

While the discussions of individual country experiences in Chapters 1–4 indicate how theory can benefit from a solid grounding in case studies, Molyneux constantly reminds us of the broader significance of processes that emerge in different times and places. This approach extends into the second, and more explicitly comparative, part of the book in which Molyneux tackles the relatively understudied questions of women's emancipation under communism and the relationship between state socialism and feminism (Chapter 5), the interactions between states and women's movements (Chapter 6), and issues of gender and citizenship in Latin America (Chapter 7). There is far too much to note within these chapters — incisive discussions of rights, democracy, communitarianism, difference and pluralism, for example — to which the space limitations of a book review can do justice. Suffice it to say, however, that one would be hard-pressed to find so many 'big' questions dealt with so concisely and intelligently as they are here.

Women's Movements in International Perspective brings rich historical and geographical texture to gender and feminist theory, and builds a bridge between scholars who might normally remain confined to one element of Gender Studies and, through the general death of volumes such as these, miss something of the broader picture. In an age in which there is a great deal of ephemerality in academic writings and rather too much re-inventing of the wheel, this book will almost certainly stand the test of time. *Women's Movements in International Perspective* should be compulsory reading on all Gender Studies courses, not only because it tackles issues crucial to feminist debates in a sophisticated yet accessible manner, but because it is a book that students will be able to enjoy as well as learn from. If Palgrave does not bring out a paperback edition in the near future, it may well find itself in fierce competition with other publishers.

Sylvia Chant

70 | book review

Hybridity and its discontents: politics, science, culture

Avtar Brah and Annie E. Coombes (Eds.); Routledge, London, 2000, Hbk/ £50.00 Hbk, ISBN 0-415-19402-4, £15.99 Pbk, ISBN 0-415-19403-2

This collection of essays certainly achieves what it sets out to: using an interdisciplinary framework, historicise the concept of hybridity and acknowledge its geopolitical contexts. In four thematic sections the reader moves from miscegenation in colonial and postcolonial contexts, and its public and private manifestations, to mobilizations of hybridity within scientific discourse — perhaps most potently in the field of genetics — and to the interplay between science and culture. Part three explores the cultural implications and possibilities of hybrid forms in terms of public culture, ritual, memory and the body within the context of identity politics in South Africa and Polynesia. Part four pushes this exploration still further by analysing the hybrid possibilities produced by postcolonial/modernist theory itself in terms of (re)conceptualisations of nation, history, culture, and self and the interplay between the local, the national and the global.

The three contributors to this last section stopped short of interrogating why hybridity is a term being mobilised by intellectuals worldwide, across disciplines, as a 'framing device' to borrow Nicholas Thomas' words. As the three essays reminded us, intellectual traditions do not stand outside of the geopolitical contexts they are describing. In their analyses of scientific discourse, Haraway, Steinberg and Young emphasised how embedded and complicit intellectual culture is in the production and reproduction of certain knowledge at specific times and for specific political purposes. But what of the other disciplines? I ask this question in the light of the editors' comment that the volume would pay particular attention to the institutionalized frameworks through which hybridity circulates. Is the Academy neutral?

Clearly, this volume is a reflection of the fact that it is not. Contributors illustrate how hybridity is the product of specific contexts and policies and practices, supported by theoretical frameworks. Included here is the policing of racial frontiers, the management of colonial subjects, nationalistic impulses, social welfare or the manufacture of history and identity. But I wonder why it has become fashionable to speak of hybridity and to apply it in a critical sense to the past and present, especially since, as these essays reveal, it has a long history of its own. Despite regimes of power, people have always reacted in a multiplicity of, often expected, ways. But why are we now able to see/read this in a critical light?

The book suggests that part of the answer to this question is globalization and our postcoloniality. Indeed, the work was deeply relevant to contemporary national/international reflections on broader questions of identity, and what Stoler refers to in this collection as the tension between 'inclusionary impulses

(166–167) © 2002 Feminist Review. 0141-7789/02 $15 www.feminist-review.com

and exclusionary practices'. In terms of hybridity we might as fruitfully talk about exclusionary impulses and inclusionary practices. Clearly, these mould potential hybrid manifestations. The focus of Stoler's gaze is empire. For me, one of the real strengths of the collection was the lines of continuity between the past and the present, to what we might describe as continuing colonial impulses.

As I have suggested, the majority of essays focus on particular geopolitical contexts: colonial Southeast Asia, Franco Spain, contemporary Britain, Latin America, Islam, but they all have transnational appeal. It includes two meditative pieces, one by Amal Treacher about coming to terms with her own hybridity as a child of mixed parentage, and the other by Avtar Brah about her own experience of cross-class empathy for a white working-class woman. This led her to map processes of identification across class, race and gender. Their journies personalise and particularize the global and underscore two central themes of the work overall: 'the unexpected and contingent results of lived experience and the fact that we are not inevitably contained by that which seeks to produce us as bounded subjects'.

The interdisciplinary framework was very useful: it offered a kaleidoscopic view of both the debates and issues concerning hybridity and its historical and contemporary relevance. It is itself a 'hybrid' collection. Furthermore, the constant shift from the historical to the contemporary illustrated the long-term specificity of the term. Nevertheless, the collection also whetted the appetite for more discreet explorations of the term within disciplines — history, science, culture, politics — perhaps, also, within comparative frameworks.

As an Australian historian, I was struck by the resonances of some of the pieces, particularly Stoler and Coombes, to the situation in Australia. In the first instance, anxiety about inter-racial unions and, more particularly, the outcomes of such were as relevant to Australia as they were to colonial Southeast Asia, the manifestations of which were alluded to by the editors. On the other hand, I was struck by the links between the contestation over representations of national history/ies in South Africa, particularly from the late 1980s and similar contestations in Australia, centring on revisionist interpretations of sustained frontier conflict between the Indigenous population and the European immigrants. How, in the light of this evidence, do we re-write, if at all, Australian history and how, if at all, do we commemorate it?

Having said that, I suspect that such an exercise would reiterate what seems to be an underlying thread of the collection: the continued relevance of hybridity across disciplines and differing socio-political and historical contexts, and the constitutive and transgressive possibilities contained therein.

Alison Holland

Brazilian feminisms

Solange Ribeiro de Oliveira and Judith Still (Eds.); The University of Nottingham, Nottingham, Universidade Federal de Minas Gerais, Belo Horizonte, 1999, The University of Nottingham Monographs in the Humanities, Vol. XII, pp. 190

In her Introduction, Judith Still describes her principal objective in this book, as the production of work reflecting the results of 'The Interface of Critical and Cultural Studies', a project sponsored by the British Council and the Brazilian Research Institute, CAPES, at the Universities of Minas Gerais and Nottingham. The authors themselves work at a wide range of institutions, from the Universities of Manchester (Judith Still), Nottingham (Solange Ribeiro de Oliveira) and Cambridge (Maria Manuel Lisboa), to Indiana (Darlene Sadlier), the State University of Rio de Janeiro (Heloisa Toller Gomes), and the University of São Paulo (Maria Elisa Cevasco), among others. The unity of the book was achieved by focusing on all the Brazilian literary works and issues discussed within it from a cultural standpoint. Clarice Lispector, the most celebrated Brazilian woman author in the 20th Century, is the subject of three of its 12 chapters. Still tells the reader the book attempts to achieve a fair partnership between the Old (first) World and the New (Third) World, in all its characteristic plurality and mobility (13–14). It is important to note, however, that comparisons are not always fair when the observer is influenced by a pre-determined or stereotype-driven frame of mind, which can distort perception of the object of study and produce unbalanced judgements, especially when considering a dominating Empire and its dominated ex-colony.

Insight on the 'other's' culture is noticeably flawed in the Introduction and even more so in Darlene J. Sadlier's article, 'Theory and Pedagogy in the Brazilian Northeast', in which the writer draws general conclusions from a single teaching experience. Furthermore, Sadlier tries to explain how and why women authors or Negro women authors, in particular, are excluded from the literary canon in Brazil, using, as her only source, an article about intellectuals being interviewed on the subject of a possible literary canon that appeared in 1994 in the weekly magazine *Veja* — a venue which expressly excludes these women authors. Such a source can barely sustain itself. The point missed is not due to a conservative ideology on the part of the scholars, but rather, to the economic drawback of a Latin, Roman-Catholic, illiterate, and underdeveloped country. Non-whites or subalterns have limited access to education, and without the help of an adequate public education system, it is impossible for them to write at all. There is not the same kind of racial confrontation or competition in Brazil, as there is in the US. These racial 'minorities' do express

(168–170) © 2002 Feminist Review. 0141-7789/02 $15 www.feminist-review.com

their reaction to the system but in different ways, as through popular music, for example. It is also awkward to comment on the situation of subalterns in Brazil with reference to the situation of American slaves who coveted the more fertile valleys for agriculture when only mountainous lands were offered to them, as described by Toni Morison in her novel, Sula. In Brazil, such people would have been happy to get any piece of land, even on mountains where climatic conditions allow the cultivation of oranges, manioc, coffee, etc. The problem here is access to any land at all. And slaves were employed all over the country with the sole exception of the Amazon, not only in the Northeast.

Racial issues in Brazil received enlightening attention from Jane-Marie Collins in her article, 'Slavery, Subversion and Subalternity: Gender and Violent Resistance in Nineteenth-Century Bahia'. She writes about Colonial prosecutions against women slaves who killed their women masters, showing strategies for reacting still used today, which are culture-specific, indeed, impossible in most other cultures. Another interesting contribution is a study of a period that has not been dwelt upon sufficiently of late in Luiz Carlos Villalta's 'Eve, Mary, and Magdalene: Stereotypes of Women in Seventeenth-Century Brazil'. This study of misogyny in the Catechists' literature by Manoel da Nóbrega and José de Anchieta can barely be considered a piece of feminist writing, but it is very informative. When extended to present-day Brazilian society, however, its conclusion is strikingly awkward: 'Women who live their sexuality freely, rather than accepting virginity or sex exclusively within the context of marriage, are often... stigmatized and demonized' (30). Once again one must ask, which particular Brazil is the author talking about, when and where does it exist?

Feminism proves to be extremely productive in this book when Sandra Regina Goulart Almeida employs Kristeva and Jacqueline Rose to present madness, hysteria, insanity and depression in a positive light, for instance, as a reaction to repressive male society in 'The Madness of Lispector's Writing'. Although Almeida values a form of literature that has been traditionally criticized for being too introspective, she does shed new light on women's ability to subvert and disrupt the 'rigidity of pragmatism' (113) and, ultimately, the 'pre-established binary dichotomies' of patriarchal society (114). Also along those lines, Maria Manuel Lisboa values the female figure of 'motherhood' and 'motherland' in 'Darkness Visible: Alternative Theology in Lygia Fagundes Telles'.

One drawback in the book is that cultural analysis of literature sometimes gives an impression that the author is trying to include too much in a single text. Solange Ribeiro de Oliveira's 'The Dry and the Wet: Cultural Configurations in Clarice Lispector's Novels' is a prime example. Her book A barata e a crisálida (1984) is a major interpretation of Lispector's A paixão segundo G.H., but the 'cultural' approach encompasses so much, that it becomes weighty and difficult to grasp in a single literary object. The opposite happens in Ruth Silviano Brandão's 'Light, camera, fiction'. Her option to analyse objects in the media par excellence, such as theatre and TV, seems to relegate written texts, or fiction, to an almost expendable category. Hilary Owen, on the other hand, presents a close and very well-documented reading of a novel by a modernist, communist writer from São Paulo in the 1930s in her piece, 'Dispensable Discourses' on Patricia Galvão's '*Parque Industrial*'. Using very precise quotations from the novel, Owen is able to draw acute conclusions and then proceed to general discussions of class, politics and society.

The reader will probably derive more pleasure from the essays exclusively about literature than from those that attempt a more ideological discussion of feminism, or of racial or political problems in Brazil. In the latter, it seems as if the Old or *First* World is always used as a ruler to measure works from the New or *Worst* World. There is a deplorable notion that Brazilians are incapable of reacting to these issues in particular, predetermined ways. Clearly, Hélène Cixous's insight that one can only understand an 'other's' culture by first achieving an adequate level of identification with it and its differences should be heeded here. An outward, objective, uncompromising look — based on Cartesian binaries — can never reveal the subtler tonalities that exist in between interracial colours.

Luiza Lobo teaches Comparative Literature and Theory of Literature at Federal University of Rio de Janeiro. She is the author of *Crítica sem Juízo* (Rio de Janeiro: Francisco Alves, 1993), a book that presents Brazilian Negro authors since the 19th century, among other critical works. Her latest book of short stories is *Estranha aparicão* (Rio de Janeiro: Rocco, 2000).

Luiza Lobo

Megan Sullivan: Women in Northern Ireland: Cultural Studies and Material Conditions.

University Press of Florida, Gainesville, FL, 1999, ISBN: 0-8130-1698-3 HB

Sullivan's stated aim in this book is to provide a materialist analysis of contemporary cultural production by women from Northern Ireland. In particular, she examines films and theatre productions by women in order to illustrate the particular material concerns and conditions of women in Northern Ireland. However, the introduction quickly makes it clear that, despite the inclusive title, this book examines the experiences and cultural productions of women whose politics, or the politics of their cultural production, can be broadly classified as nationalist and/or Republican. Although there is plenty of material to justify this, no argument is presented for the exclusion of Unionist and loyalist women as a means to looking at the material concerns that are particular to women in Northern Ireland.

Sullivan's theoretical approach to the texts discussed draws on Spivak as well as local feminists such as Monica McWilliams and Eileen Evason. In the introduction (which provides the inevitable historical contextualization for readers), Sullivan emphasizes the centrality to her thesis of the specificity of women's experiences and needs, and how the war in Northern Ireland has shaped these concerns. She points to the Unionist/nationalist schism within women's politics in Northern Ireland and argues that a materialist approach is essential for understanding women's positions(s) in Northern Ireland. In particular, Sullivan singles out prison as *the* state apparatus which underscores the material conditions of women in Northern Ireland. In her consideration of the centrality of the prison, Sullivan begins by discussing the incarceration of Róisín McAliskey, privileging McAliskey's own analysis of the impact of the prison, as a state apparatus, on herself as a woman. The psychological isolation to which McAliskey was subjected is highlighted as a tool through which (deviant) women are disciplined, desexed and dehumanized by the state.

The discussion of McAliskey's incarceration in Britain serves as a backdrop to the discussion of film and theatre in the next chapters of the book. Sullivan's choice of texts is both welcome and interesting. In particular, she examines the work of the acclaimed Charabanc Theatre Company, a collective and cross-community women's theatre group, which enjoyed success in Northern Ireland in the 1990s. It was within the Charabanc group that the playwright Marie Jones, now enjoying West End success with '*Stones in their Pockets*', developed her skills. Ironically, Charabanc's aim was to produce theatre by women and for women, actors and audience alike: Jones's current play has been staged with two male actors.

(171–172) © 2002 Feminist Review. 0141-7789/02 $15 www.feminist-review.com

In addition to a close discussion of the Charabanc, Sullivan examines film productions by women directors including *Anne Devlin* and *Maeve* (Pat Murphy), *Mother Ireland* and *Hush-A-Bye-Baby* (Derry Women's Film Co-Operative), and *The Visit* (Orla Walsh). Along with the play *Give Them Stones*, by Mary Beckett, these texts are closely analyzed for their examination and presentation of the impact of the war on women and material conditions in Northern Ireland. Sullivan's critiques of her chosen texts are thorough and detailed. However, it is not always apparent that the texts chosen can bear the weight of the critical reading that Sullivan is developing from them. At times, she depends too heavily on the work of others in order to move her analysis forward, which (rightly or wrongly) suggests a lack of confidence in the author's own readings of the texts. For example, in her analysis of *Maeve*, Sullivan tentatively suggests that the doorman at the Republican club 'does not appear to be a member of the Northern Ireland security forces, but is probably a Republican' (p. 75). There really should be no doubt that a Republican club would have a Republican doorman.

Sullivan's analysis of how the texts illustrate women's position in Northern Ireland and the impact and curtailing effect of the war, and the omnipresence of the prison as a state institution, is sympathetic and engaging. It is clear that her political and feminist approach to nationalist and Republican women in Northern Ireland is heartfelt and her theoretical arguments in the opening chapters for a materialist approach to understanding nationalist and Republican women in Northern Ireland are convincing.

However, there are a number of errors in this book, which detract from the aims and focus of the book. Some of these are minor but others are more serious and suggest a lack of familiarity with Northern Irish politics and history: for example, Anne Maguire is referred to as a member of the 'Birmingham Eight' who is still 'working to prove her innocence' (p. 38).

The analysis Sullivan presents is convincing and engaging, and the texts are well chosen. However, the errors of fact will annoy the informed reader, while the level of analysis, with sometimes scanty excerpts, will make this a difficult reading for those unfamiliar with the texts. The overall impact is to detract from Sullivan's argument for the centrality of material conditions and state apparatuses, especially the prison, in understanding the position(s) of nationalist and Republican women in Northern Ireland. This is reinforced by a conclusion that examines the possible impact of recent changes to Northern Ireland's governance and economy for the material conditions of women, but which neglects the future of women's cultural production in the 'new' Northern Ireland.

Dr Sarah Morgan
Irish Studies Centre
University of North London

70 | book review

Screening culture, viewing politics: an ethnography of television, womanhood and nation in postcolonial India

Purnima Mankekar; Duke University Press, Durham and London, 1999, £13.50 (Pbk), £40.00 (Hbk), ISBN: 0-8223-2390-7

In this clearly written and always engaging ethnographic study of women and television in contemporary India, Purnima Mankekar makes an important contribution to the growing body of postcolonial feminist scholarship that reveals the crucial ways in which both representations of women and women's activities are bound up in processes of constituting national, ethnic and other community identities. For feminist thinkers seeking to work with models of women's identity that take as their starting point the simultaneity and intersectionality of gender, ethnicity, sexuality, class and community, Mankekar's grounded and specifically located study provides numerous productive insights.

Mankekar began her research in Delhi in 1990, in the context of heated protests against the Indian government's Mandal Commission Bill, which aimed to set quotas for the so-called 'backward castes' in both education and civil service employment, and of a brutal wave of Hindu right-wing violence against Muslim communities and holy sites. In both cases, notions of womanhood, community, belonging nation and culture emerged as inter-linked sites of violent contestation, and in both, women and representations of women were foregrounded (3–4). Mankekar keeps this broader social and political context in focus as she looks at both the production and reception of representations of women in the programming of Doordarshan, the state-run television network. She thus takes the time (and over 400 pages) to work simultaneously at three levels: to 'read' the representational codes and discursive systems at work in a variety of Doordarshan narratives; to explore the relationship between these discursive productions and the narratives that viewers weave of their own lives (8); and to track the articulation of both cultural production and reception with the broader structure of power and inequality (21).

Four key discursive clusters emerge from this analysis: family, community, violence, and the transnational connections through which these themes, as well as notions of the local and the national, 'tradition' and 'modernity' are being reconfigured (39). A recurrent theme across these discursive clusters is the problematic way in which women are simultaneously foregrounded as key players in producing and sustaining national, class, caste and religious identities, and constrained by the gendered hierarchies embedded in prevailing

(173–175) © 2002 Feminist Review. 0141-7789/02 $15 www.feminist-review.com

definitions of those identities. Mankekar argues that, from its earliest productions of television serials, Doordarshan promoted the configuration of its national audience as a 'viewing family'. In both the serials and the closely coordinated advertising campaigns that accompanied them, 'the family' became a prism through which themes such as national integration, development and modernity, middle-class aspiration and consumerism are elaborated. Within this, the positioning of women is key, not least as consumers, who, through their choices, are being called upon to hold together tradition and modernity and to consolidate the family's class status and aspirations through its acquisition of consumer goods. Similarly, Doordarshan's 'women-oriented' serials stress the centrality of family to discourses of Indian culture and nationhood (105). The 'New Indian Woman' at the heart of these discourses is both accommodated and subsumed within master narratives of family and nation: she participates in the nation's march to modernity and at same time, preserves all that is unique and authentic about 'Indian culture' (137). Women's agency is at once enabled and domesticated by these narratives of nation and family. Nationalism creates the horizon for women as it constitutes them as citizen-subjects, leaving little room for radical critiques of women's position within the family and nation, and importantly, also foreclosing discussion of inequalities among women along axes of religious identity, caste or class (153–154).

This theme is continued in the excellent chapter 'Television Tales, National Narratives and a Woman's Rage' (versions of which have already been anthologized) which focuses on one episode of the serialization of the ancient Indian epic, the *Mahabharata*, known as 'Draupadi's disrobing'. In Mankekar's reading of this telling of the tale, Draupadi, a woman caught in the conflict between the men of two warring families, is pressed into service as an emblem of the Nation, her ill-treatment a symbol of social decay. Draupadi's rage at her betrayal reflects the power of Woman, but this remains constrained within the interests of preserving the integrity of the family, and the unity of the nation (235). Here again, the representation of woman becomes a site for inquiry into tradition and nationhood, rather than the structural conditions that make women vulnerable (252). Nevertheless, Mankekar also identifies the ways in which some of her women viewers disrupt the producer's preferred reading, by relating Draupadi's situation to their own fears and worries about their personal vulnerability in a patriarchal society. Indeed throughout the book, Mankekar is careful to present her research subjects as complex agents, who may be constrained by their positioning along multiple axes of power, but who are, nevertheless, actively interpreting, and at times contesting, these popular cultural narratives, whose meanings are never fully stable.

Screening Culture, Viewing Politics also addresses the crucial issue of the role of Woman as symbol, and of the complicity of some women, in communal conflict. In her textual analyses of both the television version of the *Ramayan*, and of the

Hindi serial *Tamas*, which depicts the communal violence at the time of the 1947 partition of India and Pakistan, Mankekar tracks the ways in which questions of gender and sexuality are made central to constructions of right-wing Hindu communal identities, and to their othering of non-Hindu communities. The sometimes very different ways in which Hindu and non-Hindu women viewers engaged with these narratives provide an opportunity for Mankekar to address the problematic question of 'ordinary people's' (including ordinary women's) investment in communal violence. In particular, she suggests that the silence with which her Hindu viewers reacted to the scenes of partition violence in *Tamas* reflects a dangerous kind of collective forgetting of the potentially violent exclusions at the heart of some versions of community identity, from which women are not immune. On this as on many other issues, *Screening Culture* is a text that respects the complexity of both its ethnographic subjects and the theoretical issues raised by its subject matter. It is a welcome contribution to our understanding of women's positioning in postcolonial India, and to feminist thinking on women's identity more generally.

Irene Gedalof

70 | back issues

1 Women and Revolution in South Yemen, **Molyneux**. Feminist Art Practice, **Davis & Goodal**. Equal Pay and Sex Discrimination, **Snell**. Female Sexuality in Fascist Ideology, **Macciocchi**. Charlotte Bronte's *Shirley*, **Taylor**. Christine Delphy, **Barrett & McIntosh**. OUT OF PRINT.

2 Summer Reading, **O'Rourke**. Disaggregation, Campaign for Legal & Financial **Independence and Rights of Women**. The Hayward Annual 1978, **Pollock**. Women and the Cuban Revolution, **Murray**. Matriarchy Study Group Papers, **Lee**. Nurseries in the Second World War, **Riley**.

3 English as a Second Language, **Naish**. Women as a Reserve Army of Labour, **Bruegel**. Chantal Akerman's films, **Martin**. Femininity in the 1950s, **Birmingham Feminist History Group**. On Patriarchy, **Beechey**. Board School Reading Books, **Davin**.

4 Protective Legislation, **Coyle**. Legislation in Israel, **Yuval-Davis**. On 'Beyond the Fragments', **Wilson**. Queen Elizabeth I, **Heisch**. Abortion Politics: **a dossier**. Materialist Feminism, **Delphy**.

5 Feminist Sexual Politics, **Campbell**. Iranian Women, **Tabari**. Women and Power, **Stacey & Price**. Women's Novels, **Coward**. Abortion, **Himmelweit**. Gender and Education, **Nava**. Sybilla Aleramo, **Caesar**. On 'Beyond the Fragments', **Margolis**.

6 'The Tidy House', **Steedmam**. Writings on Housework, **Kaluzynska**. The Family Wage, **Land**. Sex and Skill, **Phillips & Taylor**. Fresh Horizons, **Lovell**. Cartoons, **Hay**.

7 Protective Legislation, **Humphries**. Feminists Must Face the Future, **Coultas**. Abortion in Italy, **Caldwell**. Women's Trade Union Conferences, **Breitenbach**. Women's Employment in the Third World, **Elson & Pearson**.

8 Socialist Societies Old and New, **Molyneux**. Feminism and the Italian Trade Unions, **Froggett & Torchi**. Feminist Approach to Housing in Britain, **Austerberry & Watson**. Psychoanalysis, **Wilson**. Women in the Soviet Union, **Buckley**. The Struggle within the Struggle, **Kimble**.

9 Position of Women in Family Law, **Brophy & Smart**. Slags or Drags, **Cowie & Lees**. The Ripper and Male Sexuality, **Hollway**. The Material of Male Power, **Cockburn**. Freud's *Dora*, **Moi**. Women in an Iranian Village, **Afshar**. New Office Technology and Women, **Morgall**.

10 Towards a Wages Strategy for Women, **Weir & McIntosh**. Irish Suffrage Movement, **Ward**. A Girls' Project and Some Responses to Lesbianism, **Nava**. The Case for Women's Studies, **Evans**. Equal Pay and Sex Discrimination, **Gregory**. Psychoanalysis and Personal Politics, **Sayers**.

11 **Sexuality issue**
Sexual Violence and Sexuality, **Coward**. Interview with Andrea Dworkin, **Wilson**. The Dyke, the Feminist and the Devil, **Clark**. Talking Sex, **English, Hollibaugh & Rubin**. Jealousy and Sexual Difference, **Moi**. Ideological Politics 1969–72, **O'Sullivan**. Womanslaughter in the Criminal Law, **Radford**. OUT OF PRINT.

12 ANC Women's Struggles, **Kimble & Unterhalter**. Women's Strike in Holland 1981, **de Bruijn & Henkes**. Politics of Feminist Research, **McRobbie**. Khomeini's Teachings on Women, **Afshar**. Women in the Labour Party 1906–1920, **Rowan**. Documents from the Indian Women's Movement, **Gothoskar & Patel**.

13 Feminist Perspectives on Sport, **Graydon**. Patriarchal Criticism and Henry James, **Kappeler**. The Barnard Conference on Sexuality, **Wilson**. Danger and Pleasure in Nineteenth Century Feminist Sexual Thought, **Gordon & Du Bois**. Anti-Porn: Soft Issue, Hard World, Rich. Feminist Identity and Poetic Tradition, **Montefiore**.

14 Femininity and its Discontents, **Rose**. Inside and Outside Marriage, **Gittins**. The Pro-family Left in the United States, **Epstein & Ellis**. Women's Language and Literature, **McKluskie**. The Inevitability of Theory, **Fildes**. The 150 Hours in Italy, **Caldwell**. Teaching Film, **Clayton**.

(176–184) © 2002 Feminist Review. 0141-7789/02 $15 www.feminist-review.com

15 Women's Employment, **Beechey**. Women and Trade Unions, **Charles**. Lesbianism and Women's Studies, **Adamson**. Teaching Women's Studies at Secondary School, **Kirton**. Gender, Ethnic and Class Divisions, **Anthias & Yuval-Davis**. Women Studying or Studying Women, **Kelly & Pearson**. Girls, Jobs and Glamour, **Sherratt**. Contradictions in Teaching Women's Studies, **Phillips & Hurstfield**.

16 Romance Fiction, Female Sexuality and Class, **Light**. The White Brothel, **Kappeler**. Sadomasochism and Feminism, **France**. Trade Unions and Socialist Feminism, **Cockburn**. Women's Movement and the Labour Party, **Interview with Labour Party Feminists**. Feminism and 'The Family', **Caldwell**.

17 Many voices, one chant: black feminist perspectives
Challenging Imperial Feminism, **Amos & Parmar**. Black Women, the Economic Crisis and the British State, **Mama**. Asian Women in the Making of History, **Trivedi**. Black Lesbian Discussions, **Carmen, Gail, Shaila & Pratibha**. Poetry. Black women Organizing Autonomously: a collection.

18 Cultural politics
Writing with Women. A Metaphorical Journey, **Lomax**. Karen Alexander: Video Worker, **Nava**. Poetry, by **Riley, Whiteson Davies**. Women's Films, **Montgomery**. 'Correct Distance' a photo-text, **Tabrizian**. Julia Kristeva on Femininity, **Jones**. Feminism and the Theatre, **Wandor**. Alexis Hunter, **Osborne**. Format Photographers, Dear Linda, **Kuhn**.

19 The Female Nude in the work of Suzanne Valadon, **Betterton**. Refuges for Battered Women, **Pahl**. Thin is the Feminist Issue, **Diamond**. New Portraits for Old, **Martin & Spence**.

20 Prisonhouses, **Steedman**. Ethnocentrism and Socialist Feminism, **Barrett & McIntosh**. What Do Women Want? **Rowbotham**. Women's Equality and the European Community, **Hoskyns**. Feminism and the Popular Novel of the 1890s, **Clarke**.

21 Going Private: The Implications of Privatization for Women's Work, **Coyle**. A Girl Needs to Get Street-wise: Magazines for the 1980s, **Winship**. Family Reform in Socialist States: The Hidden Agenda, **Molyneux**. Sexual Segregation in the Pottery Industry, **Sarsby**.

22 Interior Portraits: Women, Physiology and the Male Artist, **Pointon**. The Control of Women's Labour: The Case of Homeworking, **Allen & Wolkowitz**. Homeworking: Time for Change, **Cockpit Gallery & Londonwide Homeworking Group**. Feminism and Ideology: The Terms of Women's Stereotypes, **Seiter**. Feedback: Feminism and Racism, **Ramazanoglu, Kazi, Lees, Safia Mirza**.

23 Socialist-feminism: out of the blue
Feminism and Class Politics: A Round-Table Discussion, **Barrett, Campbell, Philips, Weir & Wilson**. Upsetting an Applecart: Difference, Desire and Lesbian Sadomasochism, **Ardill & O'Sullivan**. Armagh and Feminist Strategy, **Loughran**. Transforming Socialist-Feminism: The Challenge of Racism, **Bhavnani & Coulson**. Socialist-Feminists and Greenham, **Finch & Hackney Greenham Groups**. Socialist Feminism and the Labour Party: Some Experiences from Leeds, **Perrigo**. Some Political Implications of Women's Involvement in the Miners' Strike 1984–85, **Rowbotham & McCrindle**. Sisterhood: Political Solidarity Between Women, **Hooks**. European Forum of Socialist-Feminists, **Lees & McIntosh**. Report from Nairobi, **Hendessi**.

24 Women Workers in New Industries in Britain, **Glucksmann**. The Relationship of Women to Pornography, **Bower**. The Sex Discrimination Act 1975, **Atkins**. The Star Persona of Katharine Hepburn, **Thumim**.

25 Difference: A Special Third World Women Issue, **Minh-ha**. Melanie Klein, Psychoanalysis and Feminism, **Sayers**. Rethinking Feminist Attitudes Towards Mothering, **Gieve**. EEOC v. Sears, Roebuck and Company: A Personal Account, **Kessler-Harris**. Poems, **Wood**. Academic Feminism and the Process of De-radicalization, **Currie & Kazi**. A Lover's Distance: A Photoessay, **Boffin**.

26 Resisting Amnesia: Feminism, Painting and Post-Modernism, **Lee**. The Concept of Difference, **Barrett**. The Weary Sons of Freud, **Clément**. Short Story, **Cole**. Taking the Lid Off: Socialist Feminism

33 Restructuring the Women Question: *Perestroika* and Prostitution, **Waters**. Contemporary Indian Feminism, **Kumar**. 'A Bit On the Side'?: Gender Struggles in South Africa, **Beall, Hassim and Todes**. 'Young Bess': Historical Novels and Growing Up, **Light**. Madeline Pelletier (1874–1939): The Politics of Sexual Oppression, **Mitchell**.

34 Perverse politics: lesbian issues
Pat Parker: A tribute, **Brimstone**. International Lesbianism: Letter from São Paulo, **Rodrigues**; Israel, **Pittsburgh**, Italy, Fiocchetto. The De-eroticization of Women's Liberation: Social Purity Movements and the Revolutionary Feminism of Sheila Jeffreys, **Hunt**. Talking About It: Homophobia in the Black Community, **Gomez & Smith**. Lesbianism and the Labour Party, **Tobin**. Skirting the Issue: Lesbian Fashion for the 1990s, **Blackman & Perry**. Butch/Femme Obsessions, **Ardill & O'Sullivan**. Archives: The Will to Remember, **Nestle**; International Archives, **Read**. Audre Lorde: Vignettes and Mental Conversations, **Lewis**. Lesbian Tradition, **Field**. Mapping: Lesbians, AIDS and Sexuality: An interview with Cindy **Patton, O'Sullivan**. Significant Others: Lesbians and Psychoanalytic Theory, **Hamer**. The Pleasure Threshold: Looking at Lesbian Pornography on Film, **Smyth**. Cartoon, **Charlesworth**. *Voyages* of the Valkyries: Recent Lesbian Pornographic Writing, **Dunn**.

35 Campaign Against Pornography, **Norden**. The Mothers' Manifesto and Disputes over 'Mutterlichkeit', **Chamberlayne**. Multiple Mediations: Feminist Scholarship in the Age of Multi-National Reception, **Mani**. Cagney and Lacey Revisited, **Alcock & Robson**. Cutting a Dash: The Dress of Radclyffe Hall and Una Troubridge, **Rolley**. Deviant Dress, **Wilson**. The House that Jill Built: Lesbian Feminist Organizing in Toronto, 1976–1980, **Ross**. Women in Professional Engineering: the Interaction of Gendered Structures and Values, **Carter & Kirkup**. Identity Politics and the Hierarchy of Oppression, **Briskin**. Poetry: **Bufkin, Zumwalt**.

36 'The Trouble Is It's Ahistorical': The Problem of the Unconscious in Modern Feminist Theory, **Minsky**. Feminism and Pornography, **Ellis, O'Dair Tallmer**. Who Watches the Watchwomen? Feminists Against Censorship, **Rodgersson & Semple**. Pornography and Violence: What the 'Experts' Really Say, **Segal**. The Woman In My Life: Photography of Women, **Nava**. Splintered Sisterhood: Antiracism in a Young Women's Project, **Connolly**. Woman, Native, Other, **Parmar** interviews **Trinh T. Minhha**. Out But Not Down: Lesbians' Experience of Housing, **Edgerton**. Poems: **Evans, Davies, Toth, Weinbaum**. Oxford Twenty Years On: Where Are We Now?, **Gamman & O'Neill**. The Embodiment of Ugliness and the Logic of Love: The Danish Redstockings Movement, **Walter**.

37 Theme issue: Women, religion and dissent
Black Women, Sexism and Racism: Black or Antiracist Feminism?, **Tang Nain**. Nursing Histories: Reviving Life in Abandoned Selves, **McMahon**. The Quest for National Identity: Women, Islam and the State in Bangladesh, **Kabeer**. Born Again Moon: Fundamentalism in Christianity and the Feminist Spirituality Movement, **McCrickard**. Washing our Linen: One Year of Women Against Fundamentalism, **Connolly**. **Siddiqui** on *Letter to Christendom*, **Bard** on *Generations of Memories*, **Patel** on *Women Living Under Muslim Laws Dossiers 1–6*, Poem, **Kay**. More Cagney and Lacey, **Gamman**.

38 The Modernist Style of Susan Sontag, **McRobbie**. Tantalizing Glimpses of Stolen Glances: Lesbians Take Photographs, **Fraser and Boffin**. Reflections on the Women's Movement in Trinidad, **Mohammed**. Fashion, Representation and Femininity, **Evans & Thornton**. The European Women's Lobby, **Hoskyns**. **Hendessi** on *Law of Desire: Temporary Marriage in Iran*, **Kaveney** on *Mercy*.

39 Shifting territories: feminism & Europe
Between Hope and Helplessness: Women in the GDR, Dölling. Where Have All the Women Gone? Women and the Women's Movement in East Central Europe, **Einhorn**. The End of Socialism in Europe – A New Challenge For Socialist Feminism? **Haug**. The Second 'No': Women in Hungary, **Kiss**. The Citizenship Debate: Women, the State and Ethnic Processes, **Yuval-Davis**. Fortress Europe and Migrant Women, **Morokvasíc**. Racial Equality and 1992, **Dummett**. Questioning *Perestroika*: A Socialist Feminist Interrogation, **Pearson**. Postmodernism and its Discontents, **Soper**. Feminists and Socialism: After the Cold War, **Kaldor**. Socialism Out of the Common Pots, **Mitter**, 1989 and All That, **Campbell**. In Listening Mode, **Cockburn**, **Women in Action: Country by Country:** The Soviet Union; Yugoslavia; Czechoslovakia; Hungary; Poland. **Reports**: International Gay and Lesbian Association: Black Women and Europe 1992.

40 Fleurs du Mal or Second-Hand Roses?: Nathalie Barney, Romaine Brooks, and the 'Originality of the Avant-Garde', **Elliott & Wallace**. Poem, **Tyler-Bennett**. Feminism and Motherhood: An American 'Reading' **Snitow**. Qualitative Research, Appropriation of the 'Other' and Empowerment, **Opie**. Disabled Women and the Feminist Agenda, **Begum**. Postcard From the Edge: Thoughts on the 'Feminist Theory: An International Debate' Conference at Glasgow University, July 1991, **Radstone**. Review Essay, **Munt**.

41 Editorial. The Selling of HRT: Playing on the Fear Factor, **Worcester & Whatley**. The Cancer Drawings of Catherine Arthur, **Sebastyen**. Ten years of Women's Health 1982–92, **James**. AIDS Activism: Women and AIDS activism in Victoria, Australia, **Mitchell**. A Women's Subject, **Friedli**. HIV and the Invisibility of Women: Is there a Need to Redefine AIDS?, **Scharf & Toole**. Lesbians Evolving Health Care: Cancer and AIDS, **Winnow**. Now is the Time for Feminist Criticism: A Review of *Asinimali!*, **Steinberg**. Ibu or the Beast?: Gender Interests in Two Indonesian Women's Organizations, **Wieringa**. Reports on Motherlands: Symposium on African, Carribean and Asian Women's Writing, **Smart**. The European Forum of Socialist Feminists, **Bruegel**. Review Essay, **Gamman**.

42 Feminist fictions
Editorial. Angela Carter's *The Bloody Chamber* and the Decolonization of Feminine Sexuality, **Makinen**. Feminist Writing: Working with Women's Experience, **Haug**. Three Aspects of Sex in Marge Piercy's *Fly Away Home*, **Hauser**. Are They Reading Us? Feminist Teenage Fiction, **Bard**. Sexuality in Lesbian Romance Fiction, **Hermes**. A Psychoanalytic Account for Lesbianism, **Castendyk**. Mary Wollstonecraft and the Problematic of Slavery, **Ferguson**. Reviews.

43 Issues for feminism
Family, Motherhood and Zulu Nationalism: The Politics of the Inkatha Women's Brigade, **Hassim**. Postcolonial Feminism and the Veil: Thinking the Difference, **Abu Odeh**. Feminism, the Menopause and Hormone Replacement Therapy, **Lewis**. Feminism and Disability, **Morris**. 'What is Pornography?': An Analysis of the Policy Statement of the Campaign Against Pornography and Censorship, **Smith**. Reviews.

44 Nationalisms and national identities
Women, Nationalism and Islam in Contemporary Political Discourse in Iran, **Yeganeh**. Feminism, Citizenship and National Identity, **Curthoys**. Remapping and Renaming: New Cartographies of Identity, Gender and Landscape in Ireland, **Nash**. Rap Poem: Easter 1991, **Medbh**. Family Feuds: Gender, Nationalism and the Family, **McClintock**. Women as Activists; Women as Symbols: A Study of the Indian Nationalist Movement, **Thapar**. Gender, Nationalisms and National Identities: Bellagio Symposium Report, **Hall**. Culture or Citizenship? Notes from the Gender and Colonialism Conference, Galway, Ireland, May 1992, **Connolly**. Reviews.

45 Thinking through ethnicities
Audre Lorde: Reflections. Re-framing Europe: Engendered Racisms, Ethnicities and Nationalisms in Contemporary Western Europe, **Brah**. Towards a Multicultural Europe? 'Race' Nation and Identity in 1992 and Beyond, **Bhavnani**. Another View: Photo Essay, **Pollard**. Growing Up White: Feminism, Racism and the Social Geography of Childhood, **Frankenberg**. Poem, **Kay**. Looking Beyond the Violent Break-up of Yugoslavia, **Coulson**. Personal Reactions of a Bosnian Woman to the War in Bosnia, **Harper**. Serbian Nationalism: Nationalism of My Own People, **Korac**. Belgrade Feminists 1992: Separation, Guilt and Identity Crisis, **Mladjenovic** and **Litricin**. Report on a Council of Europe Minority Youth Committee Seminar on Sexism and Racism in Western Europe, **Walker**. Reviews.

46 Sexualities: challenge and change
Chips, Coke and Rock-'n-Roll: Children's Mediation of an Invitation to a First Dance Party, **Rossiter**. Power and Desire: The Embodiment of Female Sexuality, **Holland, Ramazanoglu, Sharpe, Thomson**. Two Poems, **Janzen**. A Girton Girl on the Throne: Queen Christina and Versions of Lesbianism 1906–1933. Changing Interpretations of the Sexuality of Queen Christina of Sweden, **Waters**. The Pervert's Progress: An Analysis of 'The Story of O' and The Beauty Trilogy, **Ziv**. Dis-Graceful Images: Della Grace and Lesbian Sadomasochism, **Lewis**. Reviews.

68 Women and Mental Health
Editorial. Women and Mental Health, **Bondi and Burman**. Black Women and Mental Health, **Wilson**. Growing Up Young, Asian and Female in Britain, **Bhardwaj**. Violence and Violation, **Aitken and Noble**. Mental Health Services for 'Difficult' Women, **Williams, Scott and Waterhourse**. The Role of Body Image in Women's Mental Health, **Cussins**. Disrupting Identity through Visible Therapy, **Warner**. Kiss and Tell, **Hodgson-Blackburn**. The Political is Personal, **McInnes**. Surplus Suffering, **James & Clarke**. Feminist Therapy 'Institutes' in England, **Heenan**. Threshold Women's Mental Health Initiative, **Coleman and Guildford**. Falling through the Gap, **Downie**.

69 The Realm of the Possible: Middle Eastern Women in Political and Social Spaces
Editorial. **Treacher and Shukrallah.** Women in Arab Non-governmental Organisations, **Darwiche**. Where Have All the Women (and Men) Gone? Reflections on Gender and the Second Palestinian Intifada, **Johnson and Kuttab**. Feminist Contestations of Institutional Domains in Iran, **Povey**. Women and Poverty in Morocco: The Many Faces of Social Exclusion, **Skalli**. Embodying Transition: FGC, Displacement and Gender-making for Sudanese in Cairo, **Fabos**. On Selective Consumerism: Egyptian Women and Ethnographic Representations, **Wassif**. Theorising the Politics of 'Islamic Feminism', **Mojab**.

If you would like to purchase any back issue of Feminist Review please contact the Palgrave Customer Service Department.
Telephone: +44 (0) 1256 357893
Fax: +44 (0) 1256 812358
E-mail: subscriptions@palgrave.com

New journal for 2003

Comparative European Politics

Editors:

Colin Hay, *University of Birmingham, UK,* **Ben Rosamond,** *University of Warwick, UK, and* **Martin A. Schain,** *New York University, USA*

Spanning political science, international relations and global political economy, the aim of **Comparative European Politics (CEP)** is to provide an international and interdisciplinary forum for research, theory and debate. It arises out of a unique editorial partnership linking political scientists in Europe and North America.

As the most regionally integrated political and economic space within the global system, Europe presents a particular opportunity to political scientists to explore the dynamic relationship between transnational, international and domestic processes and practices. The editors welcome original theoretical, empirical and theoretically-informed pieces which deal with these relationships.

Volume 1 of **Comparative European Politics** (ISSN: 1472-4790) will consist of 3 issues. The first issue is scheduled to appear in March 2003.

For further information and to request a FREE sample copy, please contact:

Palgrave Journals, Houndmills, Basingstoke, Hants RG21 6XS, UK

Telephone: +44 (0) 1256 357893 · Fax: +44 (0) 1256 812358 · Email: subscriptions@palgrave.com

In North America:

Palgrave Journals Subscriptions, 175 Fifth Avenue, New York, NY 10010, USA

www.palgrave-journals.com

New journal for 2002

Contemporary Political Theory

General Editor: **Gary Browning,**
Oxford Brookes University, UK.
Editors: **Kimberly Hutchings,** *University of Edinburgh, UK*
and **Raia Prokhovnik,** *Open University, UK.*

Contemporary Political Theory is a significant and distinctive addition to the top rank of international, peer-reviewed journals in political philosophy and theory. It provides a forum for contributions that make connections across theoretical approaches, that cross disciplinary boundaries and that apply theory to practice.

■ Encompassing a wide range of topics in political theory.

■ A focus on accessibility and scholarly excellence.

■ International perspectives - a rich selection of styles.

■ **CPT** is available online - **www.palgrave-journals.com/cpt**

For further information and to request a FREE sample copy, please contact:

Palgrave Journals, Houndmills, Basingstoke, Hants RG21 6XS, UK

Telephone: +44 (0) 1256 357893 • Fax: +44 (0) 1256 812358 • Email: subscriptions@palgrave.com

In North America:

Palgrave Journals Subscriptions, 175 Fifth Avenue, New York, NY 10010, USA

www.palgrave-journals.com

*f*eminist *r*eview|

www.palgrave-journals.com/fr

Feminist Review is published by Palgrave Macmillan.
Feminist Review is published three times a year.
It is edited by a Collective which is supported by
an international group of Corresponding Editors.

The Collective

Amal Treacher, Annie E. Coombes, Avtar Brah, Dot
Griffiths, Helen Crowley, Lucy Bland, Lyn Thomas,
Merl Storr, Nirmal Puwar, Pam Alldred, Rita Rupal
and Vicki Bertram.

Corresponding Editors

Ailbhe Smyth, Ann Curthoys, Deborah Kasente,
Firdous Azim, Gulsum Baydar Nalbantolglu,
Hala Shukrallah, Kamala Kempadoo, Kum-Kum
Bhavanani, Lidia Curti, Meera Kosambi,
Patricia Mohammed, Vesna Nikolic-Ristovic
and Zarina Maharaj.

Correspondence

Contributions, books for review and editorial
correspondence should be sent to:
Feminist Review, c/o Women's Studies,
University of North London, 166-220 Holloway Road,
London N7 8DB, UK. E-mail: feminist-review@unl.ac.uk

Notes for Contributors

Authors should submit their article electronically to:
feminist-review@unl.ac.uk
If e-mailing is not possible 4 hard copies can be
submitted but authors should note this may cause
some delay in the reviewing process. Submissions
must include an abstract (300 words), author(s)
biographical notes, 6 keywords, a current address
and an e-mail address.
Please note that contributions will not be submitted
to our review process until we have received all of
this information.

We assume that you will keep a copy of your work.
Submission of work to Feminist Review will be taken to
imply that it is original, unpublished work, which is
not under consideration for publication elsewhere.
All work is subject to a system of anonymous peer
review. All work is refereed by at least two external
(non-Collective) referees.

Our full Notes for Contributors can be seen at:
www.palgrave-journals.com/fr/instructions.html

Publisher

All business correspondence and enquiries should be
addressed to Feminist Review, The Journals Publisher,
Palgrave, Brunel Road, Houndmills, Basingstoke,
Hampshire RG21 6XS, UK.
Tel: +44 1256 329242. Fax: +44 1256 320109.

Feminist Review is online at:
www.palgrave-journals.com/fr
Visit the journal's home pages for details of the aims
and scope, readership, instructions to authors and
how to contact the Feminist Review Collective and
the publishing staff. Use the website to search online
tables of content and abstracts; register to receive
the tables of contents by e-mail as soon as each
issue is published; and order a subscription, reprints,
a sample copy or individual articles.

Subscriptions — 2002 subscription rates

INSTITUTIONS
Combined (online & print): EU £174, Rest of World
£174/$282; Online only: £158/$256; Print (hard copy)
only: EU £158, Rest of World £158/$256

INDIVIDUALS
Combined (online & print): EU £31, Rest of World
£31/$48; Online only: £28/$44; Print (hard copy) only:
EU £28, Rest of World £28/$44